Lecture Notes in Computer Science 6306

Commenced Publication in 1973
Founding and Former Series Editors:
Gerhard Goos, Juris Hartmanis, and Jan van Leeuwen

Rolf Nordahl   Stefania Serafin
Federico Fontana   Stephen Brewster (Eds.)

Haptic and Audio Interaction Design

5th International Workshop, HAID 2010
Copenhagen, Denmark, September 16-17, 2010
Proceedings

 Springer

Volume Editors

Rolf Nordahl
Stefania Serafin
Aalborg University Copenhagen, Medialogy
Lautrupvang 15, 2750 Ballerup, Denmark
E-mail: {rn, sts}@media.aau.dk

Federico Fontana
Università degli Studi di Udine, Dipartimento di Matematica e Informatica
via delle Scienze 206, 33100 Udine, Italy
E-mail: federico.fontana@uniud.it

Stephen Brewster
University of Glasgow, Department of Computing Science
Glasgow G12 8QQ, UK
E-mail: stephen@dcs.gla.ac.uk

Library of Congress Control Number: 2010934137

CR Subject Classification (1998): H.5.2, H.1.2, H.5, I.3, K.4, I.5

LNCS Sublibrary: SL 3 – Information Systems and Application, incl. Internet/Web and HCI

ISSN   0302-9743
ISBN-10   3-642-15840-4 Springer Berlin Heidelberg New York
ISBN-13   978-3-642-15840-7 Springer Berlin Heidelberg New York

springer.com

© Springer-Verlag Berlin Heidelberg 2010
Printed in Germany

Typesetting: Camera-ready by author, data conversion by Scientific Publishing Services, Chennai, India
Printed on acid-free paper   06/3180

Preface

The 5th International Workshop on Haptic and Audio Interaction Design (HAID) was held in September 2010 in Copenhagen, Denmark.

Technologies to enable multimodal interaction are now mature to the point that research is turning away from pure hardware development, looking towards interaction and design issues to improve usability and the user experience. Robust solutions exist to display audio and haptic feedback in many forms, for instance as speech and non speech sounds and through tactile and force feedback sensations. Furthermore, it has been demonstrated that the novel interactions supported by these modalities can provide benefits for all users. However, many questions remain concerning the appropriate use of haptics and audio in interaction design: how can we design effective haptic, audio, and multimodal interfaces? In what new application areas can we adopt these techniques? Are there design methods that are useful, or evaluation techniques that are particularly appropriate?

HAID 2010 was a direct successor to the successful workshop series inaugurated in Glasgow in 2006, then held in Seoul in 2007, in Jyväskylä in 2008, and in Dresden in 2009. The aim of HAID was to bring together researchers and practitioners who shared an interest in investigating how the haptic and audio modalities can synergize in human computer interaction. The research challenges in the area are best approached through user-centred design, empirical studies, or the development of novel theoretical frameworks. A total of 21 papers were accepted for HAID 2010, each containing novel work on these human-centric topics. Each paper was peer reviewed at least twice using an esteemed set of leading international figures, to whom we are grateful for the quality of their reviews, time, and patience. The papers were divided into five categories described below, which range from psychophysical experiments on pure stimuli to possible applications of audio-haptic interaction in different fields such as virtual reality, virtual prototyping, navigation, and design of novel musical instruments.

Multimodal Integration

The first series of articles present interesting psychophysical experiments in multimodal interaction. Merchel and Altinsoy present two experiments whose goal is to determine the point of subjective equalities for pure tones and sinusoidal whole-body vibrations. Among the results obtained, it is interesting to notice that small intra-individual and large inter-individual variations were observed. In a follow-up experiment, Altinsoy and Merchel investigated the ability of subjects to match the frequency of two different sensory modalities. Results show that the subjects are able to match the frequency of both modalities with some tolerances. Tuuri, Eerola, and Pirhonen describe a study which examines three designs for speed regulations in mobile devices, and test their ability to function across modalities. All three designs showed to communicate the intended meaning in both the auditory and the tactile domain. Altinsoy investigates spatial factors involved in the integration of auditory and tactile information. The results show that the perceived location of auditory stimuli is influenced by tactile stimulation. Yoon, Perry, and Hannaford present a study to determine thresholds of curvature discrimination in visual-haptic experiments. Results indicate that on average, the visual sense is about three times more sensitive than the haptic sense in discriminating curvature in virtual environments. Although the auditory modality is not investigated in this paper, results are nonetheless interesting and provide some novel insights in perceptual performance of the sensory modalities.

Tactile and Sonic Explorations

While the previously described papers are mostly concerned with basic psychophysical experiments, several applications of sonic and tactile interaction design have also been exploited. Audioworld by Melzer, Kindsmuller, and Herczeg is a novel game-like application for goal-oriented computer-supported learning. The game was evaluated to assess its novelty, entertainment factor and reward. Bakker, van den Hoven, and Eggen present three demonstrations that use sound to subtly convey information to users in an open office. Delle Monache, Hug, and Erkut present an exploration in the field of sonic interaction design, whose goal is to combine two areas which have been traditionally kept apart, i.e., narrative sound design and sound synthesis by physical models. Kuber, Yu, and O'Modhrain describe the design and evaluation of an extension to an existing browser, which enables blind individuals to explore web pages using tactile feedback. Gonzales, Garbaya, and Merienne present a study which investigates the effect of using audio cueing and head-related transfer functions in sound source localization.

Walking and Navigation Interfaces

Audio-haptic interaction in navigation interfaces is a topic of investigation that can be applied in areas such as sensory substitution for visually impaired users. Turchet, Serafin, Dimitrov, and Nordahl describe an experiment whose goal is to assess the ability to recognize virtually simulated surfaces when incongruent stimuli are provided via shoes enhanced with actuators to the auditory and haptic modality. Results show a dominance of the auditory modality in the recognition task. Magnusson, Rassmus-Gröhn, and Szymczak present a study whose goal is to gain a better understanding of the influence of the angle interval in which users get feedback on navigation performance, gestures, and strategies in a more realistic outdoor setting. Papetti, Fontana, Civolani, Berrezag, and Hayward describe an audio-tactile stimulation system that can be worn and that is capable of providing the sensation of walking over ground of different types. The strategy adopted to capture force data with high accuracy is also presented. Srikulwong and O'Neill compare two wearable tactile devices which aid pedestrian navigation: a back array and a waist belt. Participants performed significantly faster and more accurately with the belt than with the array.

Prototype Design and Evaluation

Zappi, Gaudina, Brogni, and Caldwell describe a multimodal musical interface made of a virtual sequencer with a low cost tactile feedback device. Some experiments which investigate the use of the interface by musicians are also presented. Another interface targeted to musical applications is the LapSlapper by Andresen, Bach, and Kristensen. The goal of the LapSlapper is to promote exploration and innovation in musical creation. Multimodal interaction shows interesting applications also in the field of virtual prototyping. Ferrise, Bordegoni, and Lizaranzu describe an application for product design review where haptic, sound, and vision channels have been used to simulate the interaction with a household appliance. Vanacken, De Boeck, and Coninx compare the performance of two relatively low-cost haptic devices: the Falcon and the Phantom.

Gestures and Emotions

Recently there has been a growing interest in the investigation of the use of haptic devices to communicate emotions. Cooper, Kryssanov, and Ogawa investigate a possible framework for communication through haptic interface devices using existing models of emotional state. Results of the experiments show that the range of possible responses depends as much on the type of interaction used as on the users understanding of emotive content. Wilhelm, Roscher, Blumendorf, and Albayrak describe an approach to multimodal interaction in smart home environments which focuses on device independent gesture recognition.

September 2010

Rolf Nordahl
Stephen Brewster
Federico Fontana
Stefania Serafin

Organization

The 5th International Workshop on Haptic and Audio Interaction Design was organized by the Medialogy Department at Aalborg University in Copenhagen.

Conference Chairs

Rolf Nordahl	Aalborg University Copenhagen, Denmark
Stephen Brewster	University of Glasgow, UK

Scientific Program Chairs

Federico Fontana	University of Udine, Italy
Stefania Serafin	Aalborg University Copenhagen, Denmark

Posters and Demos Chairs

Sofia Dahl	Aalborg University Copenhagen, Denmark
Kristina Daniliauskaite	Aalborg University Copenhagen, Denmark

Local Organizing Committee

Sofia Dahl	Aalborg University Copenhagen, Denmark
Kristina Daniliauskaite	Aalborg University Copenhagen, Denmark
Rolf Nordahl	Aalborg University Copenhagen, Denmark
Stefania Serafin	Aalborg University Copenhagen, Denmark
Bob Sturm	Aalborg University Copenhagen, Denmark

Program Committee

M. Ercan Altinsoy	Dresden University of Technology, Germany
Federico Avanzini	University of Padova, Italy
Stephen Barrass	University of Canberra, Australia
Durand R. Begault	NASA Ames Research Center, USA
Eoin Brazil	Irish Centre for High-End Computing, Ireland
Andrew Crossan	University of Glasgow, UK
Cumhur Erkut	Aalto University, Finland
Georg Essl	University of Michigan, USA
Bruno Giordano	McGill University, Canada
Vincent Hayward	Pierre and Marie Curie University, France

Charlotte Magnusson	Lund University, Sweden
Antti Pirhonen	University of Jyväskylä, Finland
Matthias Rath	Deutsche Telekom, Germany
Michal Rinott	Holon University of Technology, Israel
Davide Rocchesso	IUAV, Italy
Augusto Sarti	Politecnico di Milano, Italy
Tamara Smyth	Simon Fraser University, Canada
Bill Verplank	Stanford University, USA
Paul Vickers	Northumbria University, UK
Bruce Walker	Georgia Institute of Technology, USA

Sponsoring Projects

Natural Interactive Walking, ICT-2007.8.0 FET Open 222107
Sonic Interaction Design, EU COST Action IC601

Table of Contents

Multimodal Integration

Tactile and Sonic Explorations

Walking and Navigation Interfaces

Prototype Design and Evaluation

Gestures and Emotions

Cross-Modality Matching of Loudness and Perceived Intensity of Whole-Body Vibrations

Sebastian Merchel and M. Ercan Altinsoy

Chair of Communication Acoustics, Dresden University of Technology, Germany
sebastian.merchel@tu-dresden.de

Abstract. In this study, two experiments were conducted to determine the point of subjective intensity equality (PSE) of pure tones and sinusoidal whole-body vibrations (WBV) at various frequencies (50 Hz, 100 Hz and 200 Hz). In these experiments, sounds and vertical vibrations were simultaneously presented to subjects using circumaural headphones and a flat hard seat. In total, 10 participants were subjected to tones with a fixed loudness level (40 phon, 60 phon, 80 phon and 100 phon). The participants were asked to match the intensity of the vibration to the loudness of the tone, using the method of adjustment. In the first experiment, the participants were subjected to a vibration and tone with the same frequency. Alternatively, in the second experiment, the frequency of the vibration was maintained at 50 Hz, while that of the tone was varied.

The results revealed that a 20 phon increase in loudness level resulted in a 5-6 dB increase in matched acceleration level at loudness levels greater than 40 phon. This result was reproducible with small intra-individual variations; however, large inter-individual differences were observed.

Keywords: Cross-Modality Matching, Whole-Body Vibration, Audio-tactile Perception, Intensity.

1   Introduction

By matching different sensory percepts in a virtual environment, a coherent and immersive image can be formed. For instance, vibro-tactile perception can be integrated with other senses (e.g., vision and hearing) to form one multi-modal event.

Previous studies have shown that a synchronous presentation of vertical whole body vibrations during concert reproductions can improve the perceived quality of the concert experience [1,2]. Since sound and vibration are often coupled in real life, a vibration signal can be generated from an audio recording, for example by low-pass filtering. In the reproduction process, the amplitude of the reproduced vibration must be selected. However, the perceived vibration in a concert hall is often weak and varies with position and frequency, depending on the airborne and structure-borne transmission paths between the source of sound and vibration and the concert visitor. The preferred vibration in a reproduction setting may be different from those in a real environment; thus, a cross-modality

R. Nordahl et al. (Eds.): HAID 2010, LNCS 6306, pp. 1–9, 2010.

matching experiment can be used as a basis for amplitude selection. However, the meaning of the vibration and the user's expectation of concert reproduction cannot be neglected. A similar example is the generation of vibration for action oriented home cinema applications using the audio track [3].

A number of experimental studies have focused on the perception of synchrony between acoustical and vibrational stimuli [4,5,6,7,8]. The subjective equivalence of noise and whole-body vibrations has been investigated, and many studies have focused on the level of participant annoyance. The stimuli used in these studies varies from sinusoidal signals (1000 Hz tone matched with a 10 Hz vibration) [9] to railway noise [10]. The combined effect of noise and vibration on participant performance has also been investigated [11]. Moreover, Kaufmann et al. [12] produced narrow band white noise of vibration (center frequency 31.5 Hz) and sound (center frequency 100 Hz) at three different levels of sound pressure (70 dB, 75 dB, 80 dB). The results of these studies indicated that a 5 dB increase in sound pressure level led to a 2 dB increase in matched acceleration level.

In this study, the point of subjective equality of the intensity of sound and vibration was determined using three sinusoidal stimuli at various loudness levels.

2   Experiments

Two experiments were conducted to determine the point of subjective equality (PSE) for pure tones and sinusoidal whole-body vibrations (WBV). In the first experiment, tones and vibrations with an identical frequency were employed. Alternatively, WBVs and tones with differing frequencies were emitted in the second experiment.

2.1   Setup

Figure 1 shows the general setup used to reproduce sound and vibration. Whole-body vibrations were generated vertically using an electro-dynamic shaker, and

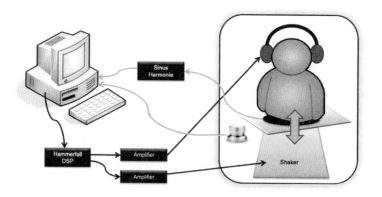

Fig. 1. Experimental setup

the subject was asked to sit on a flat hard wooden seat with both feet on the ground. The transfer characteristic of the vibrating chair is strongly dependent on the individual person [13]. This phenomenon is referred to as the body related transfer function (BRTF). The BRTF of each subject was individually monitored using a vibration pad (B&K Type 4515B) and a Sinus Harmonie quadro measuring board and compensated using inverse filters in Matlab.

The audio signals were delivered through an external Hammerfall DSP Multiface sound card, amplified by a Phone-Amp G93 and reproduced through a set of Sennheiser HDA 200 closed dynamic headphones.

The participant was able to control the amplitude of the vibration using a rotary knob that was infinitely adjustable and did not possess any indicators, such as an on or off mark (Griffin Technology, PowerMate).

2.2   Subjects

10 subjects voluntarily participated in both experiments (8 male and 2 female). Most of the participants were students between 20 and 29 years old (mean 23 years). The participants had masses between 58 and 95 kg (mean 77 kg) and indicated that they did not have any hearing or spinal damage.

2.3   Stimuli and Experimental Design

Three sinusoidal frequencies were selected for this study (50 Hz, 100 Hz and 200 Hz).Tonal and vibrational signals were simultaneously emitted for one second and were faded in and out using half a hanning window of 50 ms flanks. Tones with a fixed loudness level of 40 phon, 60 phon, 80 phon and 100 phon were used as a reference. Figure 2 shows the selected reference tones and corresponding isophones, which were based on ISO 226:2003 [14]. To compare the results to isovibrational contour plots in future studies, isophones were selected as a reference for cross-modality matches.

The task of the participant was to match the amplitude of a vibration to the loudness of a tone. The subjects were able to adaptively adjust the intensity of the vibration using a rotary control knob (with a minimum step size of 0.25 dB). The initial acceleration level of the whole-body vibration was 90±5 dB (a random offset was used for each trial). A low initial acceleration was necessary because the dynamic range of the perception of vibration is small [15], and a high level of vibration may cause discomfort. However, during the training period, subjects were encouraged to test the entire dynamic range of the reproduction system using the manual amplitude adjustment.

The test stimulus was followed by a one second break, and this sequence was repeated until the subject was satisfied with the intensity match. The subject was free to take as much time as necessary to make the proper adjustment. Each condition was repeated five times for each participant. Before the test began, a five minute training period was conducted to familiarize the participant with the stimuli and test procedure. The total duration of the experiments varied between 20 minutes and 40 minutes, depending on the individual participant.

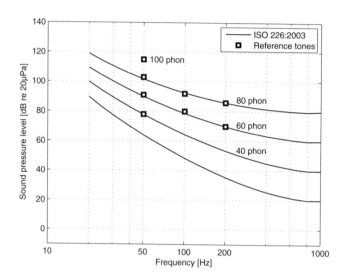

Fig. 2. The reference stimuli were selected to fit loudness contour curves based on ISO 226:2003 [14]

In the first experiment, the frequency of the tone and vibration was identical. All three frequencies (50 Hz, 100 Hz and 200 Hz) were tested at a loudness of 60 phon and 80 phon. To evaluate the effect of loudness in more detail, additional tones with a loudness of 40 phon and 100 phon, and a frequency of 50 Hz were selected.

Audible harmonics of the vibration frequency are suitable for integrating the two perceptual components [8]. To use this effect for the generation of a vibrational signal from an audio recording, the relationship of cross-modal intensity was investigated for non identical frequencies in the second experiment. In this experiment, the frequency of vibration was fixed at 50 Hz, and the frequency of the tone was varied between 50 Hz, 100 Hz and 200 Hz at a constant loudness level of 60 phon.

3   Results and Discussion

3.1   Experiment 1 - Identical Frequencies

Figure 3 shows the level of acceleration that was matched to the 60 phon (lower curve) and 80 phon (upper curve) tone (averaged over all subjects and repetitions). As expected, the amplitude of the matched vibrations was higher for the 80 phon tone than the 60 phon tone. As shown in Fig. 3, the curves parallel each other at a distance of approximately 6 dB. In addition, the 50 Hz and 100 Hz tone were matched to the same level of acceleration. However, at 200 Hz, the matched acceleration increased by approximately 10 dB. The loudness of the reference tones was equal; thus, these curves may parallel equal-vibration-intensity

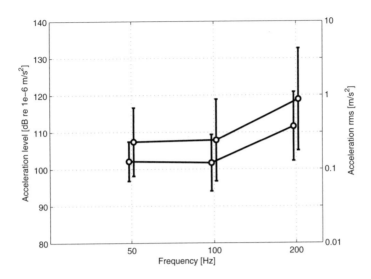

Fig. 3. Mean ± the standard deviation of the inter-individual results of cross-modality matching studies based on reference tones with a loudness of 60 phon (lower curve) and 80 phon (upper curve). To clearly illustrate the results, the frequency of each data point was shifted slightly.

contour lines. Equal-sensation contour lines are often similar to shifted thresholds. The results from this study can be compared with the threshold for vertical whole-body vibrations, which is flat between 20 Hz and 100 Hz and increases at higher frequencies (for a review see [16]). However, the reported thresholds in previous studies are highly variable, which may be due to large inter-individual deviations [17].

Also in this study, inter-individual differences were much larger than intra-individual deviations. This effect can be readily observed in the results shown in Figure 4, which displays the results of the 60 phon reference tones.

Figure 5 shows the acceleration that was matched to a 50 Hz tone with a loudness of 40 phon, 60 phon, 80 phon and 100 phon. A significant difference was not observed between the matched acceleration of a tone with a loudness of 40 phon and 60 phon. However, at higher loudness levels, the matched acceleration increased by approximately 5 to 6 dB with a 20 phon increase in loudness level. Note that, for a tone with a frequency of 50 Hz, a 20 phon increase in loudness corresponds to a 12 dB increase in sound pressure level (see Figure 2).

3.2   Experiment 2 - Different Frequencies

In the second study, different tones (50 Hz, 100 Hz and 200 Hz) of equal loudness (60 phon) were matched to a single vibration (50 Hz). As expected, the amplitude of the matched vibration was equal under all three conditions, as shown

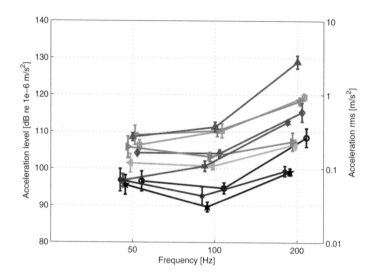

Fig. 4. Mean ± the standard deviation of intra-individual results of cross-modality matching studies based on reference tones with a loudness of 60 phon. To clearly illustrate the results, the frequency of each data point was shifted slightly.

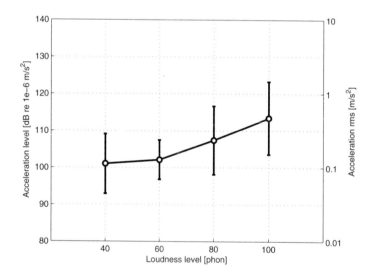

Fig. 5. Mean and standard deviation of the results of cross-modality matching with a 50 Hz vibration and a 50 Hz reference tone at a loudness level of 40 phon, 60 phon, 80 phon and 100 phon. Note that at 50 Hz, a 20 phon increase in loudness level does not correspond to 20 dB increase in acceleration level (see Figure 2).

in Figure 6. Thus, the difference between the three conditions was not significant. The absolute value of the matched acceleration was similar to previously reported results. For instance, Kaufmann et al. [12] observed a matched acceleration of approximately 107 dB using narrow band white noise (vibration: center frequency $= 31.5$ Hz; sound: center frequency $= 100$ Hz and a sound pressure level of 80 dB, which corresponded to a loudness level of approximately 60 phon). In comparison, the results from this study indicated that an acceleration level of 106 dB matched the 100 Hz reference tone.

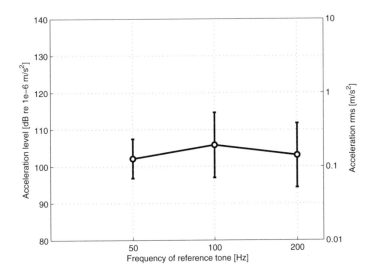

Fig. 6. Mean and standard deviations of the results of cross-modality matching studies for a 50 Hz vibration and reference tones at 50 Hz, 100 Hz and 200 Hz with a loudness level of 60 phon

The method of adjustment used in this study was fast and reliable. However, the beginning acceleration values were consistently lower than the matched values; thus, the results may slightly underestimate the PSE of intensity.

4   Summary and Outlook

In this study, points of subjective equality for the loudness of pure tones and the perceived intensity of sinusoidal whole-body vibrations were determined, and the following results were obtained:
- The matched acceleration level of a tone with a specific loudness (60 phon or 80 phon) was similar at 50 Hz and 100 Hz; however, the matched acceleration increased significantly at 200 Hz.
- A 20 phon increase in loudness level resulted in a 5-6 dB increase in matched acceleration level.

- Small intra-individual and large inter-individual variations were observed.
- For a 50 Hz whole body vibration, tones of equal loudness were matched to the same acceleration level, even if the acoustic frequencies were different from the frequency of vibration.

The results of this study will be compared with equal-vibration-sensation contour plots, which are investigated at the moment. Moreover, in a subsequent study, the frequency range or resolution could be expanded, or natural (broad band) signals could be employed.

Acknowledgements

The authors wish to thank Prof. U. Jekosch for her support and informative discussions.

References

1. Merchel, S., Altinsoy, M.E.: Vibratory and Acoustical Factors in Multimodal Reproduction of Concert DVDs. In: Altinsoy, M.E., Jekosch, U., Brewster, S. (eds.) HAID 2009. LNCS, vol. 5763, pp. 119–127. Springer, Heidelberg (2009)
2. Merchel, S., Altinsoy, M.E.: 5.1 oder 5.2 Surround - Ist Surround taktil erweiterbar? In: DAGA, Dresden, Germany (2008)
3. Walker, K., Martens, W.L.: Perception of Audio-Generated and Custom Motion Programs in Multimedia Display of Action-Oriented DVD Films. In: McGookin, D., Brewster, S. (eds.) HAID 2006. LNCS, vol. 4129, pp. 1–11. Springer, Heidelberg (2006)
4. Altinsoy, M.E., Blauert, J., Treier, C.: Intermodal effects of non-simultaneous stimulus presentation. In: Proceedings of the 7th International Congress on Acoustics, Rome, Italy (2001)
5. Daub, M., Altinsoy, M.E.: Audiotactile simultaneity of musical-produced whole-body vibrations. In: Proc. of the Joint Congress CFA/DAGA, Strasbourg, France (2004)
6. Martens, W.L., Woszczyk, W.: Perceived Synchrony in a Bimodal Display: Optimal Delay for Coordinated Auditory and Haptic Reproduction. In: ICAD, Sydney, Australia (2004)
7. Kim, S., Martens, W.L., Walker, K.: Perception of Simultaneity and Detection of Asynchrony Between Audio and Structural Vibration in Multimodal Music Reproduction. In: AES 120th Convention, Paris, France (2006)
8. Altinsoy, M.E.: Auditory-Tactile Interaction in Virtual Environments. Shaker Verlag, Aachen (2006)
9. Fleming, D.B., Griffin, M.J.: A Study of the Subjective Equivalence of Noise and Whole-Body Vibration. Journal of Sound and Vibration 42(4), 453–461 (1975)
10. Howarth, H.V.C., Griffin, M.J.: The Relative Importance of Noise and Vibration from Railways. Applied Ergonomics 21.2, 129–134 (1990)
11. Sandover, J.: Some Effects of a Combined Noise and Vibration Environment on a Mental Arithmetic Task. Journal of Sound and Vibration 95(2), 203–212 (1984)
12. Kaufmann, A., Bellmann, M., Weber, R.: "Cross-Modality-Matching" zwischen Schall- und Vibrationssignalen. In: DAGA, Stuttgart, Germany (2007)

13. Altinsoy, M.E., Merchel, S.: BRTF - Body Related Transfer Functions for Whole-Body Vibration Reproduction Systems. In: DAGA, Rotterdam, Netherlands (2009)
14. ISO 226:2003, Normal equal-loudness level contours, International Organization for Standardization, Geneve (2003)
15. Merchel, S., Altinsoy, M.E., Stamm, M.: Tactile Music Instrument Recognition for Audio Mixers. In: AES 128th Convention, London, UK (2010)
16. Morioka, M., Griffin, M.J.: Thresholds for the Perception of Fore-And-Aft, Lateral and Vertical Vibration by Seated Persons. In: Acoustics 2008, Paris, France (2008)
17. Merchel, S., Leppin, A., Altinsoy, M.E.: The Influence of Whole Body Vibrations on Loudness Perception. In: ICSV, vol. 16, Krakw, Poland (2009)

Leaping across Modalities: Speed Regulation Messages in Audio and Tactile Domains

Kai Tuuri[1], Tuomas Eerola[2], and Antti Pirhonen[1]

[1] Department of Computer Science and Information Systems
[2] Department of Music
FI-40014 University of Jyväskylä, Finland
{krtuuri,ptee,pianta}@jyu.fi

Abstract. This study examines three design bases for speed regulation messages by testing their ability to function across modalities. Two of the design bases utilise a method originally intended for sound design and the third uses a method meant for tactile feedback. According to the experimental results, all designs communicate the intended meanings similarly in audio and tactile domains. It was also found that melodic (frequency changes) and rhythmic (segmentation) features of stimuli function differently for each type of message.

Keywords: audio, tactile, crossmodal interactions, crossmodal design.

1 Introduction

When designing applications for mobile or ubiquitous contexts, the means to present information redundantly in audio and tactile domains can provide valuable flexibility. Since the actual context of use is hard to anticipate, it is important that there are options for interacting with the application. Users can also have different preferences about either hearing feedback in audio or feeling it on their skin in a more intimate manner. This is the usual rationale for *crossmodal design approach* [1].

Physical training applications, used in a varying contexts, would benefit of crossmodal design. They use the information from, e.g., heartbeat or Global Positioning System (GPS) sensors, and provide feedback for the user for controlling his or her training performance accordingly. This study focuses on messages that relate to the regulation of running speed. Sounds and vibrations, as gaze-independent presentation modes, are well suited for such an interaction.

As a starting point, this study picks up two existing methods for designing messages for the regulation of running speed: one for sounds [2], and one for vibrotactile feedback [3]. Both methods aim at intuitive interaction, so that sounds and vibrations would communicate their messages as effortlessly as possible – with a minimum requirement for learning. This study examines empirically how these design methods can be applied for crossmodal design, i.e., utilising them in creating both non-speech sounds and vibrotactile stimuli.

R. Nordahl et al. (Eds.): HAID 2010, LNCS 6306, pp. 10–19, 2010.

1.1   The Quest for Amodality

The concept of crossmodal design is based on an assumed existence of *amodal* content, which can be presented more or less interchangeably in different sensory domains. Communication of such content would then mean the articulation of certain amodal attributes in terms of the chosen presentation modality.

Traditional cognitivist view [4] has seen amodality as information processing on an abstract level, operating independently from modalities, well above sensory domains. But in the light of recent neurostudies, it seems that the thing we call amodality actually refers to close and early interconnections between widely integrated sensory-motor aspects of perception and the very roots of conceptual thinking [5]. According to the embodied perspective to human cognition [6,7], understanding and thinking indeed are modality dependent, essentially bound with the human body and all of its modalities of interaction. Even the concepts of language are thus strongly dependent on senses and bodily experiencing of the physical world, and on how these experiences are schematised [8,6,5].

We must stress that when amodal attributes are referred to in this study, we are talking about certain mental imagery relating naturally to multiple modalities rather than being modality independent (see also [9]). For example, when thinking of an amodal concept of "roughness", one can easily express the mental image with hand gestures, or describe physical attributes that relate to different sensory domains: seeing, hearing and feeling a rough surface as an action-related perception.

According to *image schema theory* [8,6], "image-like" schematic structures multimodally capture the contours of recurrent sensory-motor experiences of interacting with the environment. They simultaneously act as pre-conceptual, directly meaningful *gestalt* structures of perception, thinking and acting. Despite being called "image", such gestalts have a kinaesthetic character which integrates sensory-motor information. Therefore, in principle, they should be key points of crossmodal design, when trying to find certain sounds and vibrations that evoke similar associations as gestalt completions. Basic image schemas refer to experiences of, e.g., spatial motions or relations, forces and object interactions. In thinking, image schemas are often projected metaphorically.

1.2   Communicative Functions and Design Methods

Within the context of physical training, speed regulation feedback has three main communicative functions: to tell the runner 1) to decrease the pace (*Slow*), 2) to increase the pace (*Urge*) or 3) to keep the current pace (*Ok*). In terms of communication, Slow and Urge functions are directive, as they try to get the runner to undertake a change in speed. The Ok function, in contrast, primarily approves the current state of speed.

For these functions, a *prosody-based* (PB) method for designing non-speech sounds has been proposed [2]. This method aims to utilise "speech melodies" (i.e., intonation) of short vocal expressions which are spontaneously produced for each communicative function. It has previously been found that independently of verbal content, humans rely on intention-specific forms of intonation in communication, especially when interacting with infants [10]. Studies on prosody-based sound design [2,11] have found intonation patterns specific to Slow, Urge and Ok functions (along with an additional Reward function), which can be utilised as "musical" parameters in design.

The other design approach is a method which simply utilises the *direct analogy* (DA) between changes in frequency and the corresponding messages of "decelerate", "accelerate" and "keep it constant" [3]. It has been utilised in the design of vibrotactile stimuli, in which the vibration frequency decelerates for the Slow function, accelerates for the Urge function and keeps unchanged for the Ok function.

At the physical level of implementation, both methods basically concern simple frequency-related features along the temporal dimension. In this study, we test their crossmodal functionality by using the physical vibrations as stimuli for different sensory domains.

1.3   Research Questions

1. *How effectively do the different designs serve the intended communicative functions?* Both design methods (PB and DA) have already proven their usefulness in their original domains [12,3]. Although not being the main focus of this study, it is interesting to see how the designs based on vocal gestures of human expressions compare to the "mechanically" straightforward direct analogy designs.

2. *How does communication vary across the audio and tactile domains?* Both design methods are based on principles which suppose the attribution of certain amodal meanings to physical cues presented in a temporal continuum. In the PB method, such meanings refer to kinaesthetic imagery of projected gestural forms which reflect "bodily affect" in vocalisation [13]. In the DA method, amodal meanings also refer to kinaesthetic imagery such as "decelerating" or "falling". We hypothesise that the designs would work across the domains; i.e, stimuli would still crossmodally resonate with similar "embodied gestalts" and evoke the corresponding spatio-motor mental imagery. We are also interested to see how crossmodal attributions vary across design bases and functions.

3. *What is the role of melodic and rhythmic factors (i.e., frequency changes and segmentation) in communicating the intended functions?* We want to explore how important are the roles these features serve in communication, and whether these roles are weighed differently across functions, domains and different design bases. We especially want to see what kind of effect the melodic factors have within tactile domain, which is not commonly thought of as being in compliance with "melody".

2   Method

2.1   Apparatus

Two Engineering Acoustic C-2 vibrotactile actuators (http://www.eaiinfo.com/) were used for tactile presentation and high-quality active speakers were used for audio. As actuators are driven by audio signal (usually in sine waves), it was

Fig. 1. Experimental setting with a participant performing the tactile task

possible to use the same sound file as a source for both the audio and tactile stimulus. Optimal signal levels were set separately for both domains. To enhance tactile sensation, two actuators were used concurrently, both attached under a wristband in the backside of a left wrist (see Figure 1).

2.2   Stimuli

Three different design bases were prepared, two of them utilising the PB method. The first design base (*PB1*) consists of the same intonation contours for Slow, Urge and Ok functions that were used in the previous evaluation study [12]. These contours were "designerly" chosen from the bulk of 40 source utterances for each function. In contrast, the second design base (*PB2*) uses intonation contours chosen by a statistical classification model based on function-specific prosodic characteristics [11]. The third design base of this experiment represents the DA principle. From the previous study [3], we chose the stimuli designs of 1750 ms duration as they were highly rated and are also better in accordance with the stimuli durations of other design bases.

The stimuli of the DA base were already optimised for C-2 actuators [3], but all source contours of the PB bases were preprocessed to conform with the tactile presentation technology. Intonation contours were first centered to 250 Hz within each source utterer to remove the pitch differences caused, e.g., by the utterer's gender. This center frequency is the recommended operating frequency of C-2. A pilot testing revealed that the original pitch ranges of contours were too ample for the actuator's optimal range. Also, in terms of temporal sensitivity of touch, the contours felt too quick. Therefore the pitch ranges were scaled down by a factor of 0.75 and the contour lengths were scaled up by a factor of 1.25. Excess fluctuations in pitch were finally smoothed out. All modifications were subtle enough to retain the original characteristics of the contours for audio domain.

For each function within each design base, three different versions of stimuli were prepared: one with frequency changes and segmentation (*FC+Seg*) and other ones without any frequency changes (*NoFC*) or segmentation (*NoSeg*). All FC+Seg versions are illustrated in Figure 2. The segmentation in the PB bases is derived from the original utterances. As the DA pitch contours originally had no segmentation, it was implemented by inserting short gaps of silence to

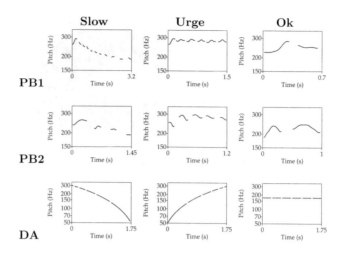

Fig. 2. Visualisations of stimuli containing frequency changes and segmentation

the FC+Seg and NoFC contours in accordance with the DA principle: for Slow function the onset time intervals of consecutive segments decelerate, for Urge they accelerate and for Ok they remain even. All NoFC versions retain the segmentation but their pitch is flattened to the mean frequency (in Hz) of the contour. Within the DA base, the NoFC versions have the same pitch level (175 Hz) for all functions, but in other cases flattened pitch levels varied across functions. For prosody based NoSeg versions, gaps in the contour were filled by using interpolation. Short rising and falling ramps of intensity envelopes were added to all segment onsets and offsets respectively, to prevent audible "pops".

All 27 stimuli (3 design bases × 3 functions × 3 versions) were finally synthesised as sine waves. Intensity levels were the same for all. Despite the optimisations for tactile domain, they all are also in a comfortable hearing range. The preparation of stimuli was made with Praat software (http://praat.org/).

2.3 Participants and Procedure

Twenty-two students of our university took part in the experiment. They were from different departments, representing many different major subjects. Of the participants, 8 were male and 14 were female. The average age in the group was 25.5 years. All participants reportedly had normal hearing and sense of touch.

Each participant performed rating tasks for both the audio domain and the tactile domain. Half of the participants did the tasks in reverse order, in order to counterbalance the learning effect. In both tasks, all stimuli were presented twice. The participants rated the amount of each of the three functions that were represented by the 54 stimuli (2 × 27). The ratings were carried out in a random order and using a five-level Likert scale (0-4). In order to block the audible sounds produced by the actuators during the tactile task, the participants wore closed earphones through which white noise was played at a comfortable level.

Before the first task, instructions were read aloud to each participant. Participants were encouraged to rely on their intuition and give ratings relatively quickly. Three novel training stimuli were presented before each task to help the participants to adapt themselves to the type of stimuli. After both tasks, they were asked to freely comment on the experiment.

3 Results

3.1 Effectiveness of Design Bases

For each rating scale (Slow, Urge, and Ok), a separate two-way within-subjects ANOVA was conducted with the within-subjects factors being function (3 levels, Slow, Urge, Ok) and design (3 design bases: PB1, PB2, DA) and the dependent variable being the ratings across the two domains, repetitions and pitch and segmentation variants. The means for all three ratings across the two variables are displayed in Figure 3. It is noticeable that within the ratings for each function, the mean ratings for correct target function were clearly the highest ones.

For the ratings of Slow, ANOVA yielded a significant effect of function, $F(2,42) = 83.05$, $p<.001$ and design, $F(2,42) = 19.44$, $p<.001$, as well as a significant interaction between the two, $F(4,84) = 14.03$, $p<.001$. The ratings of Slow for the correct function (Slow) were clearly separated from the other two functions. The design bases worked significantly differently from each other, PB1 producing the highest overall ratings, followed by the DA base.

The ratings of Urge showed a significant effect of function, $F(2,42) = 118.9$, $p<.001$, but not design, $F(2,42) = 1.13$, $p=.33$. However, a small but significant interaction between the two exists, $F(4,84) = 3.86$, $p<.01$. In other words, overall, the design bases produced equal results, but within the correct communicative function the DA base conveyed the intended meanings more effectively.

Finally, an analysis of the ratings of Ok, ANOVA indicated a significant effect of function, $F(2,42) = 81.70$, $p<.001$, and design, $F(2,42) = 12.47$, $p<.001$, as well as a significant interaction between the two, $F(4,84) = 6.99$, $p<.001$. The ratings for the correct function were distinct from the other target functions (Slow and Urge), and the direct analogy (DA) produced the highest overall ratings. The prosody-based designs were not statistically significantly different from each other.

3.2 Domain-Related Differences

To explore the effect of domain on the ratings, separate three-way ANOVAs were conducted for each rating scale. This time the within-subjects factors consisted of domain (2: audio and tactile), design (3 design bases: PB1, PB2, DA), and function (3 communicative functions). ANOVAs yielded a non-significant effect of domain, $F(1,21) = 0.07, 2.38, 0.05$, respectively for the Slow, Urge and Ok ratings (all $p>0.20$). However, there were few interactions between the domain and the other two factors, especially in the ratings of Slow. The interactions between domain and function were significant, $F(2,42) = 6.82$, $p<.01$, and the interactions between domain and design were also significant, $F(2,42)=10.98$, $p<.001$.

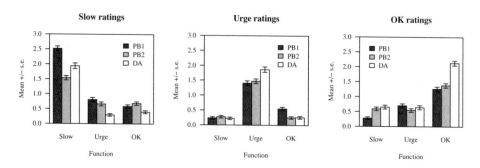

Fig. 3. Mean ratings of Slow, Urge and Ok across design bases and communicative functions

Table 1. Recognition rates across domains, functions and design bases

Domain	Audio			Tactile		
Design	PB1	PB2	DA	PB1	PB2	DA
Slow	0.82	0.64	0.75	0.82	0.64	0.55
Urge	0.47	0.50	0.68	0.46	0.52	0.55
Ok	0.64	0.61	0.81	0.47	0.60	0.80

In Urge ratings, the domain and design interaction was significant, $F(2,42) = 4.39$, $p<.05$. The sources of these interactions seem to relate to better functionality of the direct analogy (DA) for Slow and Urge within the audio domain (see Table 1). In all, differences due to the domain were surprisingly small.

To illustrate the differences between the domains and other factors, the ratings of the three communicative functions were converted into recognition rates. In this, the highest rating across the three rating scales was compared with the corrected intended function for each example. If the highest rating and the target function matched, the item received a value of 1 (correct) and mismatching items received a value 0 (incorrect). This individual classification was aggregated across participants, domains, functions and design bases, and the mean recognition accuracy is shown in Table 1. These numbers illustrate the sparsity of the domain effect in recognising the functions. The overall recognition rate was somewhat better with the audio (66%) than with the tactile stimulation (60%), and this difference was statistically significant with Kruskal-Wallis test, $\chi^2 = 8.83, p < .01$. The fact that the DA design base, in particular, seemed to work better in the audio domain was surprising.

3.3   Effects of Melodic and Rhythmic Manipulations

The roles of frequency changes and segmentation were investigated with a series of three-way ANOVAs. Frequency change factor (two levels: FC and NoFC), segmentation factor (two levels: Seg and NoSeg) and communicative function

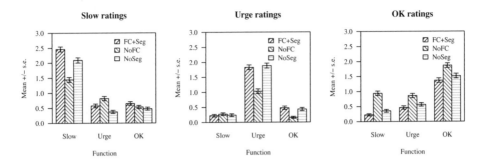

Fig. 4. Mean ratings of Slow, Urge and Ok across pitch and rhythm manipulations and communicative functions

were the within-subject factors for the three ratings given by the participants. To constrain the number of interactions, only frequency change × function and segmentation × function were tested in this analysis since the previous analyses contain most of the other possible interactions.

In Slow, both the frequency change and segmentation factors achieved statistical significance, $F(1,21) = 4.55$, and 14.44 $p<.05$ and .001, respectively. Also the interactions between the function and the frequency change and segmentation factors were statistically highly significant, $F(2,42) = 74.2$ and 47,9, both $p<.001$. These interactions are interestingly demonstrated in Figure 4: nonsegmented versions seem to convey the intended meaning of the message more effectively than the segmented version with no frequency changes. Therefore, leaving out the pitch information would harm the communicative function more than leaving out the segmentation. The best rated stimuli for Slow function, in all design bases and in both domains, were the versions that contained both features (FC+Seg).

The Urge ratings were different across frequency changes, $F(1,21) = 28.8$, $p<.001$, but not across segmentation despite the interactions between function and frequency changes, $F(2,42) = 21.7$, $p<.001$, and function and segmentation, $F(4,84) = 97.4$, $p<.001$. As can be observed in Figure 4, the frequency changes seems to be the most effective feature for the Urge function, and leaving out the segmentation does not seem to harm the communication. For the Urge function, the best rated stimuli in the DA and PB1 bases indeed were the ones with no segmentation (NoSeg), while in PB2 it contained both features (FC+Seg).

In the Ok ratings, only a significant main effect of frequency changes was observed, $F(1,21) = 21.9$, $p<.001$, although an interaction effect between function and segmentation was also observed, $F(4,84)=65.1$, $p<.001$. The interpretation, evident from the Figure 4 as well, points out that the apparently best communication of this function was without frequency changes (NoFC). The best rated stimuli for the Ok function also lacked frequency changes within all designs and in both domains. It must be noted that the DA principle for the Ok function did not permit frequency changes (FC+Seg and NoFC were identical). The lack of this feature might partly explain the superior success of the DA base for the Ok function, illustrated in Figure 3 and Table 1. Figure 4 also shows that NoFC stimuli for other functions were given relatively high ratings in the Ok scale.

With two-way ANOVAs, we finally tested if the domain factor had any interactions with either the frequency change factor or the segmentation factor. The only statistically significant interaction was found between domain and frequency changes in the ratings of Urge, $F(3,63) = 17.2$, $p<.001$. In other words, the melodic and rhythmic features generally functioned similarly for each function, regardless of domain. The tactile domain thus did not have any apparent handicap with respect to the usage of melodic features.

4   Conclusions and Discussion

All design bases performed well in terms of communicating the intended meaning, bearing in mind that the ratings were given on the basis of intuitive associations rather than any learnt or accustomed coding. Due to its straightforward nature, the DA design base generally seemed to function best. However, both PB design bases functioned effectively as well, especially PB1 which scored the best ratings in communicating the Slow function. The affect-based character of PB designs was evident in the spontaneous expressions of some of the participants, stating that certain stimuli "...just felt like someone were telling you to slow down", for example.

When compared with the previous studies concerning DA and PB1 designs [12,3], the new results accords with some earlier findings. For example, the NoSeg DA version for Urge (88% recognition) and the FC+Seg PB1 version for Slow (89% recognition) performed especially well. In the previous evaluation of the PB1 design base [12], some participants interpreted the "agitating" imagery associated with Urge samples as warning against going too fast. A similar recognition ambiguity was found in this experiment as well, weakening the ratings for the Urge function. One participant pondered this issue spontaneously: "...it felt like rushing, but it was similar to the warnings in heart-rate meters".

Although there are similarities in the function-specific features between the DA and PB designs, they also differ in many aspects. This indicates that the coupling between the features and the related attributions is not exclusionary. Thus, it should be possible to combine the features relating to the same function. For example, the ascending pitch could be applied to PB Urge designs to potentially reduce the ambiguity in interpretation. Similarly, DA designs could benefit from affect-related features of PB designs.

The most important finding of this study is that domains indeed seem to function in an interchangeable manner, thus supporting the hypothesis. This finding suggests that, regardless of the original usage of any design principle or presentation feature, it might be worth exploring their applicability across modality domains. Many of the participants expressed that "...understanding was easy to 'catch' in both domains", and that "...both domains felt comprehensive" or "...in tactile domain, I played the rhythm in my mind". The audio domain, however, was preferred by the majority of the participants.

In the experiment, the same stimuli were used directly in both domains. This might not be the optimal usage for real-life designs. Of course, we would recommend better utilisation of the domain-related strengths and restrictions: for instance, using the most suitable pitch register and timbre for audio. When audio and tactile stimuli are presented concurrently, the "fused" perception (i.e., synchresis [14]) can be something different from the sum of its "parts". Therefore we also recommend creative uses of crossmodal attributes, which would not only be justified as a modality option but also as a multimodal enrichment in supporting the contextually appropriate perception.

Acknowledgments. This work is funded by Finnish Funding Agency for Technology and Innovation, and the following partners: GE Healthcare Finland Ltd., Suunto Ltd., Sandvik Mining and Construction Ltd. and Bronto Skylift Ltd.

References

1. Hoggan, E., Brewster, S.: Designing audio and tactile crossmodal icons for mobile devices. In: Proc. of the 9th International Conference on Multimodal Interfaces, pp. 162–169. ACM, NY (2007)
2. Tuuri, K., Eerola, T.: Could function-specific prosodic cues be used as a basis for non-speech user interface sound design? In: Proc. of ICAD 2008. IRCAM, Paris (2008)
3. Lylykangas, J., Surakka, V., Rantala, J., Raisamo, J., Raisamo, R., Tuulari, E.: Vibrotactile Information for Intuitive Speed Regulation. In: Proc. of HCI 2009, pp. 112–119 (2009)
4. Fodor, J.A.: The language of thought. Harvard University Press, Cambridge (1975)
5. Gallese, V., Lakoff, G.: The brain's concepts: The role of the sensory-motor system in reason and language. Cognitive Neuropsychology 22, 455–479 (2005)
6. Johnson, M., Rohrer, T.: We are live creatures: Embodiment, American pragmatism and the cognitive organism. In: Zlatev, J., Ziemke, T., Frank, R., Dirven, R. (eds.) Body, language, and mind, vol. 1, pp. 17–54. Mouton de Gruyter, Berlin (2007)
7. Leman, M.: Embodied Music Cognition and Mediation Technology. MIT Press, Cambridge (2008)
8. Johnson, M.: The Body in the Mind: The Bodily Basis of Meaning, Imagination, and Reason. University of Chicago, Chicago (1987)
9. Pirhonen, A., Tuuri, K.: In Search for an Integrated Design Basis for Audio and Haptics. In: Pirhonen, A., Brewster, S. (eds.) HAID 2008. LNCS, vol. 5270, pp. 81–90. Springer, Heidelberg (2008)
10. Fernald, A.: Intonation and communicative intent in mothers' speech to infants: Is the melody the message? Child development, 1497–1510 (1989)
11. Tuuri, K., Eerola, T.: Identifying function-specific prosodic cues for non-speech user interface sound design. In: Proc. of the 11th International Conference on Digital Audio Effects, pp. 185–188 (2008)
12. Tuuri, K., Eerola, T., Pirhonen, A.: Design and Evaluation of Prosody Based Non-Speech Audio Feedback for Physical Training Application (Journal submission)
13. Tuuri, K.: Gestural attributions as semantics in user interface sound design. In: Kopp, S., Wachsmuth, I. (eds.) Gesture in Embodied Communication and Human-Computer Interaction. LNCS (LNAI), vol. 5934, pp. 257–268. Springer, Heidelberg (2010)
14. Chion, M.: Audio-vision: Sound on screen. Columbia University Press, NY (1990)

The Effect of Spatial Disparity on the Integration of Auditory and Tactile Information

M. Ercan Altinsoy

Chair of Communication Acoustics, Dresden University of Technology,
Helmholtzstr. 10, 01069 Dresden, Germany
ercan.altinsoy@tu-dresden.de

Abstract. Spatial origin is an important cue for humans to determine whether auditory and tactile signals originate from the same event/object or not. This paper addresses spatial factors involved in the integration of auditory and tactile information. Perceptual threshold values for auditory-tactile spatial origin disparity were measured using tactile information and sound such as those generated by touching (scraping) an abrasive paper. The results of the study show that the minimum angle subjects need to notice that the locations of the auditory and tactile events do not coincide is 5.3°. Simultaneously presented tactile stimulation enlarges the auditory localization blur in the horizontal plane. The results show that the perceived location of auditory stimuli is influenced by tactile stimulation.

Keywords: Audiotactile interaction, multimodal integration, localization blur, spatial origin.

1 Introduction

In our daily life, we perceive most of the time events through more than one sensory modality (e.g., auditory, tactile, visual). Physical signals which originate from a single source are inputs to different sensory channels and are combined in the central nervous system to produce a unified percept. Our brain can easily separate the single-origin co-occurring inputs (multimodal event) from the inputs of independent origins (multiple unimodal events).

For years or even decades each of us has learned that different physical stimuli which are received simultaneously by various sensory channels (auditory, visual, tactile etc.) are usually caused by one and the same physical event in our environment. Therefore, amongst spatial location one of the most important cues available for the multimodal integration is simultaneity (synchronous onsets). If auditory and tactile events occur at the same time, there is strong evidence that they come from the same physical event. Separation of the onsets of the auditory and tactile inputs is a powerful tool for the perceptual segregation of the concurrent information. In recent years several studies have discussed the perceived simultaneity of audiotactile stimuli and the effect of temporal asynchrony on the multimodal integration [1,2,3,4,5,6].

Another important physical property which plays a role for the multi-modal integration is the location of the event. Naturally, if auditory, tactile and visual information

R. Nordahl et al. (Eds.): HAID 2010, LNCS 6306, pp. 20–25, 2010.

have been generated by (one) same multi-modal event, the locations of the auditory, tactile and visual events should coincide. For example, when manipulating an object, the tactile, auditory, and visual information related to that object will all typically emanate from approximately the same spatial location [7]. Neurophysiological studies showed that the various receptive fields of SC (Superior Colliculus) neurons are organized into overlapping visual, auditory, and somatosensory maps, in effect creating a multisensory map of space [8], and the multisensory stimuli which are delivered in close space proximity evoke higher responses in multisensory neurons in superior colliculus [9,10]. The existence of a multisensory system that integrates acoustic and tactile inputs within near-peripersonal space around the head in humans is demonstrated in different studies [11,12]. Ladavas and Farnè claim that this spatial representation (near-peripersonal space) might be functionally distinct from that which codes auditory information in far space [13].

Recent studies show that spatial location also plays a role in audiotactile interactions. Kitagawa et al. found that people's performance in audiotactile temporal order judgment (TOJ) tasks typically deteriorates (i.e. the just noticeable difference, JND, increases) when the stimuli in the two modalities are presented from the same location rather than from different locations [3]. These results show that in some cases (sources situated close behind the head) the spatial location can even modulate the audiotactile interactions.

The purpose of our study is to determine the minimum angle between auditory and tactile events that leads the subject to perceive that the locations of the auditory and tactile events do not coincide so that the percept segregates into individual percepts in each modality (two separate events) instead of forming an integrated multi-modal event.

Localization blur ($\Delta(\varphi = 0)$min) is defined by Blauert as "the smallest change in a specific attribute or in specific attributes of a sound event or of another event correlated to an auditory event that is sufficient to produce a change in the location of the auditory event" [14]. A number of measurements were conducted to measure the localization blur for horizontal displacement of the sound source away from the forward direction (see Blauert 1997). The absolute lower limit for the localization blur is about $1°$ and the localization blur for broadband noise is $3.2°$.

In multi-modal interaction research there are several studies regarding different visual-auditory interaction effects on sound-source localization such as the ventriloquist effect (for more details, see [15]). Blauert reported an experiment in directional hearing with simultaneous visual stimulation [16]. He measured the localization blur of speech from the front with and without a simultaneous video image of the person speaking. The loudspeakers were 7m in front of the subject and they were switched on in random order. The subjects were asked to say whether their auditory event was above or below, to the left or right of the forward axis. Localization blur of the direction of the auditory event in both the horizontal and median planes proved not to depend on whether the visual image of the person speaking was shown.

To investigate the minimum angle between auditory and tactile events that leads the listener to perceive that the locations of the auditory and tactile events do not coincide, a methodology similar to that applied by Blauert was used in this study.

2 Experiments

Set-up

In this experiment, a loudspeaker array which consists of nine loudspeakers was used to present the acoustic stimulus (Fig. 1). Loudspeakers were placed 75 cm in front of the subject. The subjects were instructed not to rotate or move their head during the experiment (head-guidance was used). By representing the tactile information, electro-tactile stimulation technique was selected according to its advantages. The electro-tactile stimulation doesn't cause any noise, this makes it especially suitable for auditory-tactile virtual environment applications. (Detailed information see [17]). Self adhesive electrodes were used to excite the user's fingertip. Two electrodes were attached to the index finger of the subject's right hand.

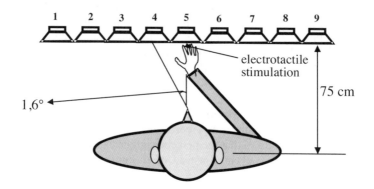

Fig. 1. Experimental setup

Subjects

Eight subjects, four males and four females, aged between 22 and 29 years, partici-pated in the experiment. The subjects were undergraduate students and paid on an hourly basis. All subjects had normal hearing and were right handed, with no known hand and heart disorders. They used their right hand for the experiment.

Stimuli and procedure

Scraping a surface with the finger tip was selected as stimulus condition. Scraping a surface with the finger tip is a very common multisensory event in our daily life so that this experimental setup close to real life experiences [18].

Touch-induced sound and tactile feedback such as caused by the scraping on an abrasive paper (sandpaper, grid number 60) were generated in the computer environment. To synthesize touch-induced scraping sounds, the subtractive synthesis method was used, because the scraping sounds have a broad-band noise character. To track the position of fingers, a data glove is used in the tactile system. The data glove is a P5 type device from the company "Essential Reality".

The loudspeakers were switched on in random order. Each condition was presented ten times. The subject's vision was blocked in each condition by an acoustically transparent curtain placed between subject and loudspeaker array. In the first part of the experiment, the localization blur of touch-induced sound was measured (Exp.1: sound only condition). While the participants made the scraping movement on the air, the touch-induced sounds were presented without a simultaneous tactile feedback. The reason for the movement on the air was to avoid any tactile feedback. In the second part of the experiment, the localization blur was measured with a simultaneous tactile feedback (Exp.2: sound & tactile condition). While the participants made the scraping movement on the air, the touch-induced sounds were presented with a simultaneous tactile feedback.

Subjects were asked whether the sound was perceived as being caused by their index finger or not (i.e. whether the position of the auditory event and the position of the tactile information coincide or not).

3 Results

The percentages of positive responses for the "sound only" condition are shown in Fig. 2.

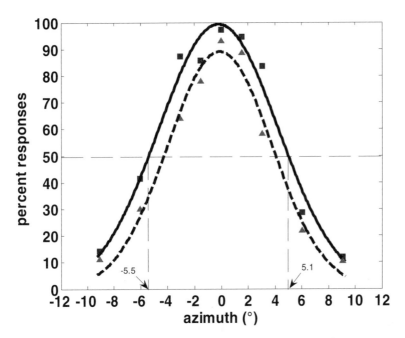

Fig. 2. The percentages of positive responses for "sound only (▲)" and "sound & tactile stimuli (■)" condition

A psychophysical model was obtained by fitting ogive results using a gaussian fit with exponential background. The goodness of the fitted curves was evaluated. The R-square value is 0.95 and the sum of squares due to error (SSE) is 0.048. The localization blur ($\Delta(\varphi = 0)$min) of a scraping sound from the front without tactile stimulation is $4° \pm 0.1°$.

The percentages of positive responses for "sound and tactile" condition are shown in Fig. 2. Again, a model was obtained by fitting the ogive results by using gaussian fit with exponential background. R-square value is 0.94 and the sum of squares due to error (SSE) is 0.054. The localization blur ($\Delta(\varphi = 0)$min) of scraping sound from the front with simultaneous tactile stimulation is $5.3° \pm 0.3°$.

4 Discussion and Conclusions

The localization blur of scraping sound from the front was measured to be 3.9°. This is in agreement with literature data, taking into account that the spectrum of the scraping sound has similarities with the broadband noise. For example, localization blur of broadband noise is 3.2° [19]. The minimum angle that allows the subjects to notice the locations of the auditory and tactile events do not coincide is 5.3°. The results show that humans are very sensitive to the spatial source differences.

Simultaneously presented electrotactile stimulation enlarges the localization blur in the horizontal plane from 3.9° to 5.3°. Dependent t-tests of the means show that both conditions differ significantly from each other (t(9)=-3.25, p < 0.05; 2-tailed). This result shows that tactile stimulation has an influence on the localization of the sound sources and it is likely that the tactile stimulation pulls the auditory source to the direction of its location.

The thresholds which were obtained in this study are based on the tactile information and sound such as those generated by touching an abrasive paper. In multimodal-interaction research there are several studies regarding the detection of synchronization thresholds. Obtained results vary, depending on the kind of stimuli. Future investigations will need to replicate and extend this work to include other conditions (for example the one of manipulating an object such as hitting it).

References

1. Adelstein, B.D., Begault, D.R., Anderson, M.R., Wenzel, E.M.: Sensitivity to haptic-audio asynchrony. In: Proc Fifth Int. Conf. Multimodal Interfaces, pp. 73–76 (2003)
2. Altinsoy, E.M.: Perceptual aspects of auditory-tactile asynchrony. In: Proc. Tenth Int. Cong. Sound and Vib., pp. 3831–3838 (2003)
3. Kitagawa, N., Zampini, M., Spence, C.: Audiotactile interactions in near and far space. Exp. Brain Res. 166, 528–537 (2005)
4. Navarra, J., Soto-Faraco, S., Spence, C.: Adaptation to audiotactile asynchrony. Neurosci. Lett. 413, 72–76 (2007)
5. Occelli, V., Spence, C., Zampini, M.: Audiotactile temporal order judgments in sighted and blind individuals. Neuropsychol. 46, 2845–2850 (2008)
6. Zampini, M., Brown, T., Shore, D.I., Maravita, A., Röder, B., Spence, C.: Audiotactile temporal order judgments. Acta Psychol. 118, 277–291 (2005)
7. Driver, J., Spence, C.: Crossmodal spatial attention: evidence from human performance. In: Spence, C., Driver, J. (eds.) Crosmodal space and crossmodal attention, pp. 170–220. Oxford University Press, New York (2004)
8. Stein, B.E., Meredith, M.A.: The merging of senses. MIT Press, Cambridge (1993)

9. King, A.J.: Development of multisensory spatial integration. In: Spence, C., Driver, J. (eds.) Crosmodal space and crossmodal attention, pp. 1–24. Oxford University Press, New York (2004)

10. Stein, B.E., Stanford, T.R., Wallace, M.T., Vaughan, J.W., Jiang, W.: Crossmodal spatial interactions in subcortical and cortical circuits. In: Spence, C., Driver, J. (eds.) Crosmodal space and crossmodal attention, pp. 25–50. Oxford University Press, New York (2004)

11. Farnè, A., Ladavas, E.: Auditory peripersonal space in humans. J. Cogn. Neurosci. 14, 1030–1043 (2002)

12. Ladavas, E., Pavani, F., Farnè, A.: Auditory peripersonal space in humans: a case of auditory–tactile extinction. Neurocase 7, 97–103 (2001)

13. Ladavas, E., Farnè, A.: Neuropsychological evidence for multimodal representations of space near specific body parts. In: Spence, C., Driver, J. (eds.) Crossmodal space and crossmodal attention, pp. 69–98. Oxford University Press, Oxford (2004)

14. Blauert, J.: Spatial hearing: the psychophysics of human sound localization, 2nd edn. MIT Press, Cambridge (1997)

15. Kohlrausch, A.G., van de Par, S.: Audio visual interaction in the context of multi-media applications. In: Blauert, J. (ed.) Communication Acoustics, pp. 109–138. Springer, Berlin (2005)

16. Blauert, J.: Ein Versuch zum Richtungshören bei gleichzeitiger optischer Stimulation. Acustica 23, 118–119 (1970)

17. Altinsoy, E.: The Effect of Auditory Cues on the Audiotactile Roughness Perception: Modulation Frequency and Sound Pressure Level. In: Pirhonen, A., Brewster, S.A. (eds.) HAID 2008. LNCS, vol. 5270, pp. 120–129. Springer, Heidelberg (2008)

18. Altinsoy, E.M.: Auditory-Tactile Interaction in Virtual Environments. Shaker Verlag, Aachen (2006)

19. Haustein, B.G., Shirmer, W.: Messeinrichtung zur Untersuchung des menschlichen Gehörs. Hochfrequenztech u Elektroakust 79, 96–101 (1970)

Parametric Study of Virtual Curvature Recognition: Discrimination Thresholds for Haptic and Visual Sensory Information

W. Jong Yoon[1], Joel C. Perry[2], and Blake Hannaford[3]

[1] Department of Mechanical and Industrial Engineering,
Qatar University, Qatar
wjyoon@qu.edu.qa
[2] Health and Quality of Life Unit,
Fatronik-Tecnalia, San Sebastian, Spain
jperry@fatronik.com
[3] Department of Electrical Engineering
University of Washington, Seattle, USA
blake@u.washington.edu

Abstract. The senses of vision and touch are vital modalities used in the discrimination of objects. In this research effort, a haptic device is used to determine thresholds of curvature discrimination in visual-haptic experiments. Discrimination thresholds are found for each sense independently as well as for combinations of these with and without the presence of conflicting information. Results indicate that on average, the visual sense is about three times more sensitive than the haptic sense in discriminating curvature in virtual environments. It is also noticed that subjects seem to rely more heavily on the sense that contains the most informative cues rather than on any one particular sense, in agreement with the sensory integration model proposed by Ernst and Banks. The authors believe that the resulting thresholds may serve as relative comparisons between perceptual performance of the sensory modalities of vision and haptics in virtual environment.

Keywords: Curvature Recognition, Discrimination Thresholds, Haptic Perception, Sensory Discrepancy.

1 Introduction

In exploring and perceiving geometric objects, our most prominent senses are sight and touch. As a result, these two senses have attracted considerable research interest over the past century. Recent advances in human-computer-interface technologies have produced a number of haptic devices for the industries of rehabilitation, information technology, entertainment, and more [1].

As haptic modalities become increasingly prevalent, the value of quantifying human perceptual thresholds also continues to grow. It is well known that discrepancy perception in the visual, auditory, and tactile senses require a minimum difference of

R. Nordahl et al. (Eds.): HAID 2010, LNCS 6306, pp. 26–36, 2010.

8 - 23 % between compared stimuli before subjects can report a noticeable change [2], [3], [4], and [5]. This value is referred to as the JND (just noticeable difference).

Several researchers have found thresholds for curvature discrimination in synthetic haptic environments using various force reflective haptic interfaces. In two studies, [6] and [7], researchers have measured thresholds for curvature discrimination using novel fingertip haptic devices without graphical feedback. One study investigated the integration of force and position cues using a thimble-like holder and a visuo-haptic workbench [8]. However, other studies utilizing virtual environments with haptic interfaces equipped with a stylus for touching the surface have not reported specific quantitative results for either visual or haptic perception of curved surface objects. Addressing this gap is one of the primary goals of the present research effort.

Although sensory dominance has been explored in numerous studies [9], [10], and [11], conclusions are diverse. According to Earnst and Banks (2002), the amount of weight given to the information from active sensory modalities is a function of the relative discrimination threshold of each sense according to the following relation [12]:

$$T_{VH}^{\ 2} = \frac{T_V^{\ 2} \cdot T_H^{\ 2}}{T_V^{\ 2} + T_H^{\ 2}} \tag{1}$$

where T_V and T_H are the discrimination thresholds of visual and haptic information, respectively, and T_{VH} is the combined discrimination threshold.

While this sensory integration model was developed using perception of flat surfaces, a second research goal of the present study is aimed at examining whether this relation is valid for perception of curved surfaces. Thus, the following work utilizes a haptic display device to determine the thresholds of curvature discrimination of the visual and haptic cues.

In addition, examining the effects of discrepant cues on both visual and haptic perceptual thresholds is the third interest of this research. Along these aims, three hypotheses were identified as follows:

- Hypothesis #1: the visual curvature discrimination threshold is lower than the haptic curvature discrimination threshold.
- Hypothesis #2: the addition of non-conflicting input from an additional sensory pathway will synergistically reduce the resulting combined curvature discrimination threshold.
- Hypothesis #3: when provided both haptic and visual stimuli that express conflicting information, subjects will rely more heavily on sensory input from sight rather than from touch.

2   Methods

2.1 Participants

Twelve subjects (eight males and four females) ranging in age from 21 to 59 (32 on average) completed a series of six visual and/or haptic experiments including one training experiment, all of which follow a forced-choice protocol using adaptive thresholds. Eleven out of twelve subjects were right handed and all subjects used their dominant hand during the experiments.

2.2 Apparatus/Software Framework

The haptic stimuli were created using a PHANTOM® Omni™ haptic force-feedback device (SensAble Technologies, MA). A picture of the experimental setup is shown in Fig. 1. The experiments were run in a normal office environment (see Fig. 1b). The software framework implementing the test set was written using OpenHaptics Toolkit (SensAble Technologies, MA) within Microsoft Visual C++ 6.0.

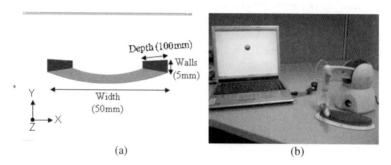

(a)   (b)

Fig. 1. (a) Screen shot of the virtual environment with the coordinates and dimensions; The curved surface is rotated 5 degrees in the positive direction around the x-axis to give a 3-dimensional perspective to the viewer (b) PHANTOM® Omni™ and virtual environment

2.3 Stimuli

During the experiments, both haptic and visual stimuli are rendered from stereo-lithogrphy (STL) CAD files. A set of thirty-nine surfaces, including one surface termed the 'standard' surface and an array of thirty-eight peripheral surfaces (nineteen on either side of the 'standard'), had been previously generated. The available surface files include fine graduations near the standard curvature and increasingly coarser around the periphery. The thirty-eight peripheral surfaces are arranged in six regions (2 x R1, 2 x R2, 2 x R3) symmetrically placed about the standard surface. The curvature of the standard surface is constant for all experiments and for all subjects. This removes potential effects of regional influences of curvature on curvature discrimination, and therefore the resulting thresholds of discrimination can be directly compared within and between subjects. Fig. 2 illustrates the distribution of surfaces around the standard (STD) surface using three step sizes of 0.02, 0.06, and 0.18 mm in regions R1, R2, and R3, respectively.

Because the standard surface is always presented with a fixed radius, it is important that the comparison stimulus be randomly presented as a surface of either higher or lower curvature as compared to the standard. Whether the comparison surface is predetermined to be higher (S_H) or lower (S_L), the perceived difference in height between the standard (S_{STD}) and comparison (S_H or S_L) should remain constant (see Equation 2).

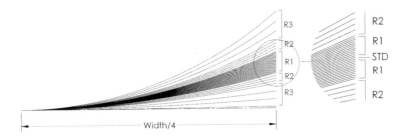

Fig. 2. The distribution of surfaces around the standard (STD) surface are spanned by three step sizes in regions R1, R2, and R3

$$S_H(x) - S_{STD}(x) = S_{STD}(x) - S_L(x) = \Delta Y \tag{2}$$

According to Equation 2, a stimulus of either higher (S_H) or lower (S_L) curvature could potentially be perceived as a stimulus of equivalent difference, relative to the standard, if the two curves $(S_H$ and $S_L)$ possess the same height offset (ΔY) from the standard (STD) at a given horizontal distance, x, from the center. A horizontal distance of ¼ the surface width was chosen as the measurement point for the curvature metric (Fig. 3). Thus, for a surface width of 50 mm, the lateral measurement location of ΔY was selected at a distance 12.5 mm horizontally from the center, midway between the minimum and maximum heights of the curve. The height of the standard surface at the measurement point was set at 1.06 mm and ΔY started from a value of 0.66 mm. Expressed in terms of radii, the standard and comparison surfaces began with radial values of 74.1 mm and 195.2 mm, respectively. It may be noted that while some studies have used change in slope rather than change in height as the defining metric for curvature, the use of height in the present study is statistically equivalent for the range of heights used near the thresholds.

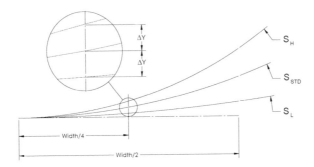

Fig. 3. Surfaces of equal difference (S_H and S_L) with respect to the standard stimulus (S_STD) are calculated based on a change in height (ΔY)

2.4 Procedures

A training video was shown to each subject prior to the experiments in order to minimize instructional error and to standardize the instruction process. Descriptions of the six experiments are listed in Table 1. For all subjects, the training experiment was presented first; data was recorded but not used in compiled results. The core five experiments were randomly ordered by a prearranged matrix to minimize learning effects in the data. A typical experiment lasted approximately 30 minutes per subject, ranging from 24 to 35 minutes.

Table 1. Experimental description of stimulus information (Constant: constant radius, Interactive: changing radius)

Experiment	Description
exp P	Training experiment (both Haptic/Visual information presented)
exp H	Only Haptic information presented (interactive)
exp V	Only Visual information presented (interactive)
exp HV	Both Haptic/Visual information presented (interactive)
exp Hv	Constant Visual information/ interactive Haptic information presented
exp Vh	Constant Haptic information/ interactive Visual information presented

Throughout the paper, the term 'presentation' will be used to describe the sequential display of a pair of stimuli to be compared. A single presentation is composed of a first surface (the standard) and then a second surface (the comparison), where each surface is displayed for three seconds. During the 3-second interval, subjects were instructed to analyze the surface either through touch or sight, or through both touch and sight, whichever was appropriate for the given experiment. After three seconds, the surface is removed, both visually and haptically.

At the end of each presentation, subjects were asked to answer a single question, displayed on the screen, regarding the curvature of the two previous stimuli. The question was presented as follows: "*Does the second stimulus have a higher or lower curvature? (1) Higher- Press button #1 (2) Lower- Press button #2.*" After pressing either button #1 or #2 on the stylus, one 'presentation' was complete. The number of presentations for a given subject varied with the sequence of correct and incorrect answers provided by the subject. The detailed structure of a test set is in Fig. 4.

The radius of the standard surface remains constant throughout the protocol at 74.1 mm and, based on subject response, an adaptive algorithm computes the successive radial values to be displayed. The adaptive algorithm checks the correctness of the current and previous answers, and then updates and stores the value of ΔY. The program also tracks the number of direction changes of ΔY, (i.e., sign changes of ΔY slope), the value of which is relevant to the uncertainty of response. Based on the previous work, [13] and [14], the method can be used to adjust ΔY according to subject responses in order to obtain convergence at the 71% accuracy level. The experiment ends after the algorithm has changed directions a total of eight times. All ΔY values during the last four reversals are collected and used for analysis.

The variety of perceptual responses from the previous pilot study on effects of discrepant cues on both visual and haptic prompted the addition of two experiments (*exp Hv* and *exp Vh*) to observe the effects of illusory cues from either visual or haptic stimuli. In the experiments *exp Hv* and *Vh* one modality was kept constant in the stimuli, whereas the alternative modality was varied depending on the subjective answers. In discrepant presentations, Fig. 5, the curvature of the visual stimulus (solid line) does not match the curvature of the haptic stimulus (dashed line), and a visual offset (ΔY^*) is applied to the cursor.

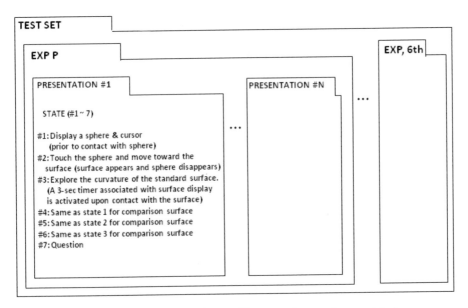

Fig. 4. "Test set" (six experiments, N presentations, and seven states)

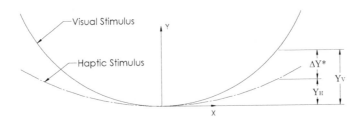

Fig. 5. Discrepancies between visual (solid) and haptic (dashed) surfaces are handled by applying a visual offset (ΔY^*) to the cursor

3 Results

3.1 Reducing Learning Effects

The initial experiment for all subjects (*exp P*), was administered for the purpose of reducing learning effects in the data as a result of unfamiliarity with the experimental setup. Erroneous responses in the early presentations were significantly diminished in *exp HV* after the initial training experiment, *exp P*. The calculated thresholds were reduced from 0.137 ± 0.110 mm in *exp P* to 0.085 ± 0.065 mm in *exp HV*.

3.2 Haptic and Visual Thresholds

Exp H presented haptic information without visual stimuli to subjects in order to determine thresholds of pure haptic discrimination of curvature. Three of the twelve subjects yielded thresholds near 0.5 mm, and one at 0.35 mm, while the remaining 8 subjects all produced threshold at or below 0.25 mm (Fig. 6a).

The visual-only experiment (*exp V*) produced visual threshold values ranging from 0.05 to 0.22 mm as shown in Fig. 6b.

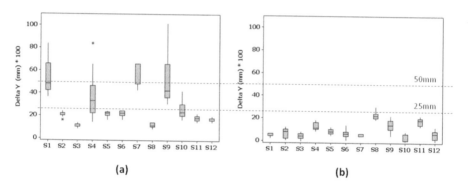

(a)   (b)

Fig. 6. Boxplots of (a) Haptic-Only experiment (exp H) and (b) Visual-Only (exp V) according to subject number (s1 – s12)

3.3 Stimuli Discrepancies

Visual discrepancy. When presented with constant visual stimuli and interactively variable haptic information, half of the subjects were unable to converge to a threshold. In these cases, the responses exceeded the allowable range and the algorithm ended the experiment (Fig. 7a). The effect of the discrepant cues on perceptual

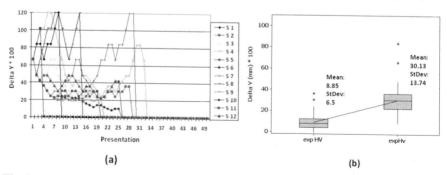

(a)   (b)

Fig. 7. Irregular increasing data profiles (a) illustrate that six of the twelve subjects in exp Hv were unable to detect haptic information with a ΔY value as high as 1.02 mm. (b) Threshold comparison between exp HV and Hv.

thresholds can be seen in Fig. 7b. Both the perceptual thresholds and standard deviation were significantly increased (ANOVA p<0.001, lower perceptual ability) in the presence of a visual discrepancy relative to the comparison *exp HV*.

Haptic discrepancy. To observe the effects of discrepant cues on visual perception, a combination of haptic and visual cues were presented in which the haptic cue was discrepantly held constant while the visual cue varied based on user responses to curvature. In this scenario, all subjects were able to complete the experiment (Fig. 8a), however, the perceptual thresholds were still increased (ANOVA p<0.001, lower perceptual ability) in the presence of a haptic discrepancy relative to the comparison *exp HV* (Fig. 8b).

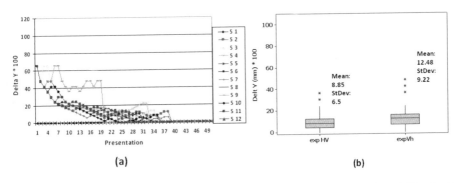

(a)   (b)

Fig. 8. Subject data profiles (a) for exp Vh with constant haptic and interactively variable visual cues. (b) Threshold comparison between exp HV and Vh

3.4 Curvature Discrimination Thresholds

Fig. 9 illustrates collectively the resulting thresholds for all five conditions across all subjects. Two notable conclusions can be drawn; first, statistically significant differences between perceptual thresholds may be noted between haptic and visual perception (p<0.001, mean: 26.73 vs. 9.35, StDev: 18.29 vs. 6.76), and second, alterations to these thresholds are seen in the presence of visual and haptic discrepancies. It could be stated that in general only two thresholds emerge, with minor experimental variations appearing from these, depending on the inclusion of stimuli and/or discrepancy.

The addition of haptic input to visual input in *exp HV* produces a slight decrease in threshold over having a visual stimulus alone (*exp V*), although not a statistically significant change (p=0.469, mean: 9.35 vs. 8.85, StDev: 6.76 vs. 6.50). Adding a visual cue to haptic input (*exp HV*) shows a statistically significant decrease in threshold (p<0.001, mean: 26.73 vs. 8.85, StDev: 18.29 vs. 6.50) over having a haptic stimulus alone (*exp H*). This experimental result (*exp HV*=8.50) also agrees with the model of sensory integration (equation 1) previously proposed by Ernst and Banks (2002) [12] within 3.7% error.

The ANOVA also reveals that the addition of a constant haptic stimulus in *exp Vh* yields a statistically significant increase in threshold (decrease in ability, p<0.001) of 0.031 mm over the visual only experiment (*exp V*), and similarly, the addition of a constant visual stimulus in *exp Hv* to the haptic only experiment (*exp H*) yields a statistically insignificant increase in threshold (p=0.119) of 0.034 mm, despite a decrease in standard deviation by 0.046 mm.

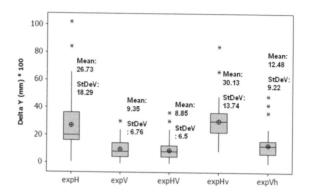

Fig. 9. Thresholds of curvature perception for haptic only (exp H), visual only (exp V), visual and haptic combined (exp HV), haptic with constant visual (exp Hv), and visual with constant haptic (exp Vh) experiments

4 Discussion

The difference in curvature between standard and comparison surfaces was based upon incremental changes in height (ΔY) of the curve at a 12.5 mm lateral distance from the center. While discrimination thresholds from literature are typically reported in terms of curvature, c, or radius, r, the range of all plots in this study are shown in terms of the absolute value ΔY. Surface magnitudes can be expressed in terms of curvature, c, using the following relation:

$$c = \frac{1}{r} = \frac{2(\Delta Y + Y_{STD})}{\Delta Y^2 + x^2 + 2 \cdot \Delta Y \cdot Y_{STD} + Y_{STD}^2} \tag{3}$$

where ΔY is computed as the difference in height between the standard and comparison surfaces, and the height of the standard surface, Y_{STD}, is 1.06 mm. x is the horizontal distance of 12.5 mm, where the measure of ΔY is taken.

Recalling the three hypotheses listed in Section 1, the results of Section 3 validate the first hypothesis. From *exp H* and *V*, it appears that the visual sense is about three times more sensitive than the haptic sense in the average sighted individual. Perhaps the dominance of vision is a direct result of this lower threshold.

The second hypothesis is found to be true only if the threshold of the sensory pathway being added is near or less than that of the pre-existing pathway. Adding a pathway that possessed a discrimination threshold three times higher than that of the existing pathway, such as the addition of a non-conflicting haptic stimulus to a visual stimulus, produced an insignificant reduction of the discrimination threshold. Perhaps improvements in perception would be found in combinations of senses whose discrimination thresholds are closer in magnitude. This finding also agrees with the model of sensory integration [12].

The third hypothesis are inconclusive at best. In both cases of sensory discrepancy, the resulting discrimination thresholds remain only a small amount (3 – 4%) higher than respective threshold for detecting the changing stimulus alone, regardless of whether the changing stimulus was visual or haptic. It is clear that subjects do rely, at least in part, on haptic information in the presence of discrepant visual information, but the degree of reliance is unclear. It seems instead that subjects rely on the sense that contains the most informative cues [12].

5 Conclusion

In this paper, the thresholds of curvature recognition for both visual and haptic surfaces have been reported. While the thresholds of curvature detection reported above are limited by the resolution of the haptic/visual display devices and several experimental factors, it is believed that the resulting thresholds may serve as relative comparisons between perceptual performance of the sensory modalities of sight and haptics in virtual environments.

References

1. Hayward, V., Astley, O.R., Cruz-Hernandez, M., Grant, D., Robles-De-La-Torre, G.: Haptic interfaces and devices. Sensor Review 24(1), 16–29 (2004)
2. Craig, J.C.: Difference threshold for intensity of tactile stimuli. Percept. Psychophys. 11, 150–152 (1972)
3. Jones, L., Hunter, I.: A Perceptual analysis of stiffness. Experimental Brain Research 79, 150–156 (1990)
4. Allin, S., Matsuoka, Y., Klatsky, R.: Measuring just noticeable differences for haptic force feedback: implications for rehabilitation. In: 10th Symposium on Haptic Interfaces for Virtual Environment and Teleoperator Systems, HAPTICS 2002 (2002)
5. Lubin, J.: A human vision model for object picture quality measurement. In: International Broadcasting Convention, (447) (1997)
6. Frisoli, A., Solazzi, M., Salsedo, F., Bergamasco, M.: A fingertip haptic display for improving curvature discrimination. Presence 17(6), 550–561 (2008)
7. Kuchenbecker, K.J., Ferguson, D., Kutzer, M., Moses, M.: and Okamura, A.M.: The touch thimble: providing fingertip contact feedback during point-force haptic interaction. In: Symposium on Haptic interfaces for virtual environment and teleoperator systems, Reno, Nevada, pp. 239–246 (2008)
8. Drewing, K., Ernst, M.O.: Integration of force and position cues for shape perception through active touch. Brain Research 1078(1), 92–100 (2006)
9. Posner, M., Nissen, M., Klein, R.: Visual dominance: An information-processing account of its origins and significance. Psychological Review 83(2), 157–171 (1976)
10. van Beers, R.J., Wolpert, D.M., Haggard, P.: When feeling is more important than seeing in sensorimotor adaptation. Current Biology 12(10), 834–837 (2002)

11. Burns, E., Whitton, M.C., Razzaque, S., McCallus, M.R., Panter, A.T., Brooks Jr., F.P.: The hand is slower than the eye: A quantitative exploration of visual dominance over proprioception. In: IEEE Virtual Reality, pp. 3–10 (2005)
12. Ernst, M.O., Banks, M.S.: Humans integrate visual and haptic information in a statistically optimal fashion. Nature 415(6870), 429–433 (2002)
13. Stevens, J.C., Foulke, E., Patterson, M.Q.: Tactile acuity, aging, and Braille reading in long-term blindness. Experimental Psychology: Applied 2(2), 91–106 (1996)
14. Lee, G.S.: Low power haptic device: Ramifications on perception and device design. Ph.D. Thesis, University of Washington (2004)

Cross-Modal Frequency Matching: Sound and Whole-Body Vibration

M. Ercan Altinsoy and Sebastian Merchel

Chair of Communication Acoustics, Dresden University of Technology,
Helmholtzstr. 10, 01069 Dresden, Germany
ercan.altinsoy@tu-dresden.de

Abstract. Interest in human responses to whole-body vibration has grown, particularly due to the increasing usage of vehicles, e.g. cars, trucks, and helicopters etc. Another reason for growing interest in recent years is the importance of the vibrations generated by the performance of music for multimedia reproduction systems. There is a strong relationship between the frequency of the auditory stimulus and the frequency of the tactile stimulus, which simply results from the physical processes that generate the stimuli. The recordings in different vehicles or in different concert situations show that the whole-body vibration signal is like a low-pass filtered audio signal. The spectral contents, particularly low frequencies, are matched with each other. This correlation plays an important role in our integration mechanism of auditory and tactile information and in the perception of an immersive multimodal event.

In this study, psychophysical experiments were conducted to investigate, if subjects are able to match the frequencies of two different sensory modalities with each other. In this experiment, sinusoidal sound and vibration signals were used. The auditory stimuli were presented to the subjects via headphones and the tactile stimuli were presented through a vibration seat. The task of the subject was to match the frequency of the whole-body vibration to the frequency of the auditory stimuli. The results show that the subjects are able to match the frequency of both modalities with some tolerances.

Keywords: Whole-body vibration, frequency, cross-modal-matching, audiotactile perception.

1 Introduction

Human response to vibration (or to tactile feedback) and sound is strongly dependent on the frequency of the stimulus. Measurements in vehicles and in concert situations confirm that the spectra of sound and whole-body vibration have strong correlations at low frequencies [1,2]. It has been shown that synchronous presentation of vertical whole body vibrations during concert DVD reproduction can improve the perceived quality of the concert experience [3]. From the view of a sound engineer, the following question arises: how sensitive are humans to the content of the vibration stimuli? This question is also interesting for a vehicle acoustician who would like to optimize the vibration and sound in vehicles and provide a comfortable and enjoyable environment

R. Nordahl et al. (Eds.): HAID 2010, LNCS 6306, pp. 37–45, 2010.
© Springer-Verlag Berlin Heidelberg 2010

to driver and passengers. Noise and vibration play an important role in what is called the overall harmony of the vehicle.

Sounds that are audible to the human ear fall in the frequency range of about 20-20,000 Hz, with the highest sensitivity being between 500 and 4,000 Hz. Our perception of music is influenced by how the auditory system encodes and retains acoustic information [4]. Auditory perception of frequency is logarithmic in nature. It is well known in acoustics that, given any note as a starting point, subjects can single out certain others, which bear a definite relationship to the first, and are known as its octave, etc. In order to determine the sensory capacity of the auditory system, measurements of the human ability to discriminate the changes in frequency of a pure tone were conducted. Just-noticeable frequency differences for the auditory system were reported e.g. by [5]. Zwicker and Fastl found that, at frequencies below 500 Hz, we are able to differentiate between two tone bursts with a frequency difference of only about 1 Hz. This value increases in proportion to frequency and is approximately 0.002*f above 500 Hz.

The range of frequencies most often associated with effects of whole-body vibration in the context of health, activities and comfort is approximately 0.5 to 100 Hz [6]. However the vertical whole-body vibrations in the frequency range of about 1-500 Hz can be perceived by the human body. The tactile sense is rather poor at discriminating frequency in comparison to the ear (auditory system). Just-noticeable frequency differences for whole-body vibrations were measured by Bellmann [7]. Humans are able to differentiate between two vibrations of 5 and 5.4 Hz ($\Delta f = 0.4$). Above 5 Hz Δf increases in proportion to frequency and is about $0.34 * f - 1.25$ Hz. This equation is applicable for reference frequencies between 5 and 40 Hz.

Two recent studies have discussed cross-modality frequency matching between audio and tactile stimulation of the hand [8,9]. They found that the subjects tend to prefer pairs having the same frequency for the auditory and tactile stimuli. In most cases, subjects judge also the second harmonic of the vibration frequency to be suitable for the auditory frequency. Are people able to match the frequency of whole-body vibration to the frequency of auditory stimuli, although they have poor tactile frequency discrimination? The purpose of this study is to explore how accurate is the cross-modal frequency matching capability of human for sound and whole-body vibration. In order to approach this aim in a systematic way, psychophysical experiments were conducted.

2 Experiment

2.1 Subjects

Eighteen subjects, eight men and ten women, aged between 20 and 49 years, participated in the experiment. The subjects were undergraduate students and university staff. They were paid on a hourly basis. All subjects had normal hearing, with no known back disorders.

2.2 Experimental Set-up

Whole-body vibrations have been reproduced using a self build electro-dynamical vibration seat (Fig. 1). The system is capable of producing vertical vibrations in a frequency range from 5 Hz to 1000 Hz. The transfer characteristic of the shaker loaded with a seated person has been measured using a semi-rigid pad with a triaxial accelerometer (B&K 4322). This frequency response depending on the individual test person is called the Body Related Transfer Function (BRTF) [10]. All stimuli have been compensated for the transfer characteristic of the seat in vertical direction by using inverse filters in MATLAB.

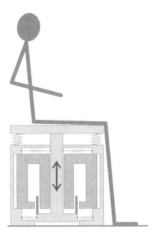

Fig. 1. Electro-dynamical vibration seat. The participant was sitting on a flat hard wooden seat with both feet standing on the ground.

The auditory stimulus was presented from a PC. The noise was amplified and delivered diotically through Sennheiser HDA 200 closed-face dynamic headphones which has a very high sound isolation level and therefore damped the sound radiated by background noise of the shaker. The experiments were conducted in a sound-attenuated room.

2.3 Stimuli and Procedure

In this experiment, sinusoidal sound and vibration signals were used. Auditory stimuli were pure tones at nine different frequencies (50, 63, 67.5, 80, 100, 112.5, 125, 160, 200 Hz). To avoid an influence of stimuli intensity, the loudness of the stimulus for different frequencies was equalized according to ISO 226:1987. The loudness level was 60 phon.

The task of the subjects was to match the vibration frequency to the frequency of the auditory tone. A Matlab graphical user interface was used for the experiment. Subjects could increase or decrease the frequency of the tactile stimulus pressing two buttons. The step size of the frequency increment and decrement was one-third- octave frequency intervals (0,26*f) which is comparable to the JNDF for whole-body vibrations. The acceleration level of the vibration stimuli was equalized for different frequencies to a reference vibration level (100 dB for 50 Hz). If the subject felt that she/he found the best matched vibration frequency, she/he should press a decision button. The decision was recorded after each adjustment and a next stimulus was presented in different random order for each subject.

Tactile and auditory stimuli were presented simultaneously. Each comparison was repeated eight times for each test person. Two different initial frequencies were chosen to avoid the secondary effects of initial value (low or high). For four repetitions, the initial frequency was 8 Hz. For other four repetitions, the initial frequency was 300 Hz. Before the start of the experiment, three anchor stimuli were presented to the subjects so that they could become familiar with the system and the experiment (The anchor stimuli don't belong to the stimuli dataset of the experiment. Frequencies: 30 Hz, 90 Hz, 200 Hz). Each experimental session lasted approximately half an hour including the training session.

3 Results and Discussions

In this study subjects can control the frequency of the vibration, but not continuously, rather in steps (quasi-continuously). Therefore the results of the experiment are plotted in histograms for each auditory frequency separately. The percentages of cross-modality frequency matching responses are shown in Fig. 2 to 9 as a function of the whole-body vibration frequency. Since the histograms have frequently two peaks, a check of the data regarding the Gaussian distribution makes little sense.

The maximum of the responses histogram for a 50 Hz auditory signal is found at vibration frequency of 50 Hz with a percentage of 35 (Fig. 2). Although 35% is very small in comparison to expected higher matching rates (75% or higher), it is possible to say that the participants have a tendency to match the same frequency in both modalities. Interestingly the results show that 25 Hz (an octave lower than the test frequency of 50 Hz) was found as best suitable vibration frequency after 50 Hz.

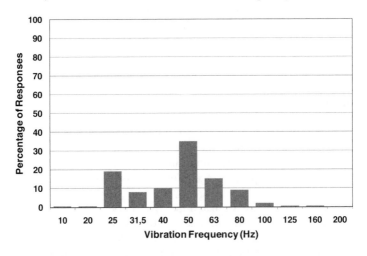

Fig. 2. The percentage of cross-modality frequency matching responses for auditory frequency 50 Hz

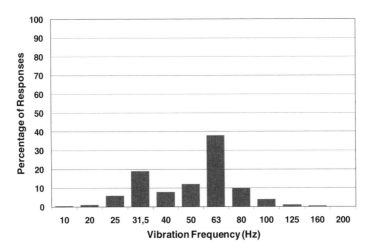

Fig. 3. The percentage of cross-modality frequency matching responses for auditory frequency 63 Hz

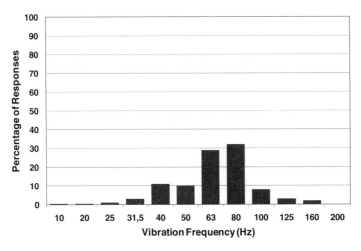

Fig. 4. The percentage of cross-modality frequency matching responses for auditory frequency 80 Hz

The results of the 63 Hz (Fig. 3) have very similar character in comparison to the results of the 50 Hz (Fig. 2). Figure 3 shows that 63 Hz vibration signal was found as the most suitable for the 63 Hz auditory stimuli. The lower octave of 63 Hz (31,5 Hz) shows an increase of the percentages of responses as neighboring 1/3 octave band frequencies.

The results for 80 Hz show some differences in comparison to the results of 50 and 63 Hz (Fig. 4). The maximum of the responses histogram is found at vibration frequency of 80 Hz with a percentage of 32. However the 63 Hz vibration signal also obtained a comparable matching percentage (28%). One reason for this phenomenon can be the high JNDF values for 80 Hz. The subjects cannot easily differentiate both signals. However 100 Hz vibration signal which is also very near to the 80 Hz, did not obtain comparable matching percentage. Interestingly the lower octave of 80 Hz (40 Hz) has very low matching percentage (11%).

The histogram of 100 Hz auditory stimuli is shown in Figure 5. A distinct peak is not recognizable in this histogram, the results have ambiguous character. High JNDF values in high whole-body vibration frequencies can be a reason. The participants have found that the vibration signals in the frequency range of 63-125Hz are suitable for 100 Hz auditory stimulus.

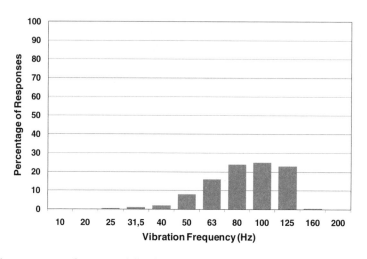

Fig. 5. The percentage of cross-modality frequency matching responses for auditory frequency 100 Hz

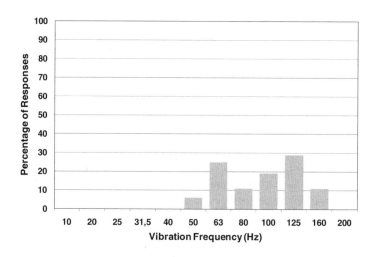

Fig. 6. The percentage of cross-modality frequency matching responses for auditory frequency 125 Hz

The histogram of 125 Hz auditory stimuli is shown in Figure 6. There are two peaks which are found 125 Hz (29%) and 63 Hz (25%). 100 Hz signal has also relatively high matching rate (19%).

The participants have found that 160 Hz vibration is the most suitable signal for the 160 Hz auditory stimuli (Fig. 7). Again 80 Hz (an octave lower of 160 Hz) has obtained high matching rate as neighboring 1/3 octave band frequencies.

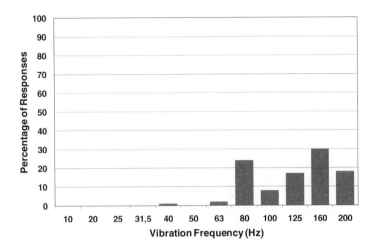

Fig. 7. The percentage of cross-modality frequency matching responses for auditory frequency 160 Hz

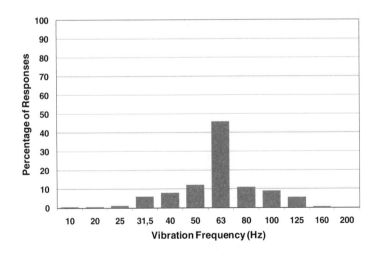

Fig. 8. The percentage of cross-modality frequency matching responses for auditory frequency 67,5 Hz

The cross-modality frequency matching experiment was conducted for an additional auditory frequency 67,5 Hz. However the exact same frequency was not in the pool of vibration stimuli. The reason for this additional investigation was to check if the lower octaves became higher matching rates rather coincidentally. The results of this additional investigation are shown in Figure 8. In this case the participants have selected the next 1/3 octave neighbor as suitable vibration signal. 63 Hz vibration signal was the most suitable one for 67,5 Hz tone (Fig. 8). Interestingly other signals did not obtain a comparable high rating. A possible reason for that can be the lower octave of 67,5 Hz was not in the stimuli pool.

4 Summary and Outlook

It is possible to observe interesting tendencies for cross-modality frequency matching. To find the most suitable frequency for the vibration signal in comparison to auditory signal, the subjects tend to prefer pairs having the same frequency for the auditory and tactile stimuli. In most cases, subjects judge also the lower octave of the auditory frequency to be suitable for the vibration frequency. One reason for that can be that in concert or in vehicle driving situations, we are used to perceive low frequency content mainly through tactile modality and high frequency content mainly through auditory modality. Rao has conducted an investigation on the perception of whole-body vibration frequency and found that if two whole-body vibration stimuli in different octave frequencies were presented, subjects can estimate the frequency ratio [11]. The results of this study confirm his results that octave perception is possibly existent for whole-body vibration similar to auditory octave perception. The results have extensive similarities with the results of audiotactile frequency matching studies for sound and hand vibration. They have also found that subjects tend to prefer pairs having the same frequency for the auditory and tactile stimuli [8,9] and there were some evidences for the octave perception in tactile modality [8].

For further research, it might be interesting to compare the obtained results with another experiment, in which the vibration frequency can be continuously controllable. Another aspect would be to expand the investigated frequency range.

Acknowledgment

The authors wish to thank Prof. Ute Jekosch for her support and informative discussions.

References

1. Daub, M., Altinsoy, M.E.: Audiotactile simultaneity perception of whole-body vibrations produced by musical presentations. In: Proceedings of the CFA/DAGA 2004 (Congrès Joint/Joint Congress 7ème Congrès Français d'Acoustique CFA/30th German Annual Meeting for Acoustics DAGA), Strasbourg, France, March 22-25 (2004), ISBN-10 CD-ROM: 2-9521105-3-0

2. Altinsoy, M.E., Merchel, S.: Einfluss der zeitlichen Frequenzveränderung auf die audio-taktile Integration im Fahrzeug. In: Proceedings of the DAGA 2008 – 34th German Annual Conference on Acoustics, Dresden, Germany, March 10-13 (2008)

3. Merchel, S., Altinsoy, M.E.: Vibratory and Acoustical Factors in Multimodal Reproduction of Concert DVDs. In: Altinsoy, M.E., Jekosch, U., Brewster, S. (eds.) HAID 2009. LNCS, vol. 5763, pp. 119–127. Springer, Heidelberg (2009)

4. McDermott, J.H., Oxenham, J.A.: Music perception, pitch, and the auditory system. Current Opinion in Neurobiology 18, 1–12 (2008)

5. Zwicker, E., Fastl, H.: Psychoacoustics: Facts and models, 2nd edn. Springer, Berlin (1999)

6. Griffin, M.J.: Handbook of Human Vibration. Academic Press, London (1990)

7. Bellmann, M.: Perception of whole-body vibrations: From basic experiments to effects of seat and steering-wheel vibrations on the passenger's comfort inside vehicles. Ph.D. Thesis. Carl von Ossietzky Universität Oldenburg (2002)

8. Altinsoy, M.E.: The influence of frequency on the integration of auditory and tactile information. In: Proceedings of the 18th International Congress on Acoustics (ICA), Kyoto, Japan (2004)

9. Occelli, V., Gillmeister, H., Forster, B., Spence, C., Zampini, M.: Unimodal and Crossmodal Audiotactile Frequency Matching in the Flutter Range. In: Altinsoy, M.E., Jekosch, U., Brewster, S. (eds.) HAID 2009. LNCS, vol. 5763. Springer, Heidelberg (2009)

10. Altinsoy, M.E., Merchel, S.: BRTF - Body related transfer functions for whole-body vibration reproduction systems. In: Int. Conf. on Acoustics (NAG/DAGA 2009), Rotterdam, The Netherlands (2009), ISBN-13: 978-3-9808659-6-8

11. Rao, B.K.N.: Some Studies on the Subjective Doubling of Low Frequency Whole-Body Vibrations. Journal of Sound and Vibration 51(2), 308–310 (1977)

Audioworld:
A Spatial Audio Tool for Acoustic and Cognitive Learning

André Melzer[1], Martin Christof Kindsmüller[2], and Michael Herczeg[2]

[1] Université du Luxembourg, Campus Walferdange, L-7201 Walferdange, Luxembourg
andre.melzer@uni.lu
[2] University of Luebeck, Institute for Multimedia and Interactive Systems,
Ratzeburger Allee 160, D-23538 Luebeck, Germany
{mck,herczeg}@imis.uni-luebeck.de

Abstract. The present paper introduces *Audioworld*, a novel game-like application for goal-oriented computer-supported learning (CSL). In *Audioworld*, participants localize sound emitting objects depending on their spatial position.
Audioworld serves as a flexible low cost test bed for a broad range of human
cognitive functions. This comprises the systematic training of spatial navigation
and localization skills, but also of verbal skills and phonetic knowledge known
to be essential in grammar literacy, for example. The general applicability of
Audioworld was confirmed in a pilot study: users rated the overall application
concept novel, entertaining, and rewarding.

Keywords: Audio-based localization, computer-supported learning, human
cognitive functions, spatial navigation.

1 Introduction

Multimodal human-computer interfaces make use of the synergetic effects of human
vision and auditory perception. In visual tasks, for example, sound enables the user to
monitor the state of background processes while remaining focused on the visual task
[1, 2]. Sound thus reduces the demands on visual attention and increases the efficiency in common multiple task situations during computer use (e.g., [3]). In addition
to the complementary function of hearing, audio enhanced interfaces grant access to
digital information when visual input is either not available or impossible (e.g., text-
to-speech utilities for users with special needs [4]).

The present study continues and extends the latter line of research, yet focuses on
intact vision. We introduce Audioworld, a software application for standard consumer
hardware, which aims at providing a tool for multifaceted audio-based learning in a
game-like environment. In Audioworld, sound is the main sensory mode for navigation and orientation. By using their spatial hearing abilities, players navigate a desk-
top virtual environment to localize sound emitting objects (e.g., musical instruments
or verbal information).

R. Nordahl et al. (Eds.): HAID 2010, LNCS 6306, pp. 46–54, 2010.
© Springer-Verlag Berlin Heidelberg 2010

2 Binaural Hearing, Modeling, and Rendering Spatial Audio

Processing spatially presented auditory cues requires binaural hearing, which mirrors stereoscopic vision [5, 6]. Interaural Time and Level Differences (ITD, ILD) are the essential cues in human binaural source localization. These cues arise from the separation of the ears on the head and their resonant and reflective anatomical characteristics. ITDs and ILDs are affected by stimulus features like frequency and intensity, offsets in the interaural baseline, and imposition of amplitude modulation.

Spatial audio in virtual 3D environments (VE) is either based on the perceptual systems or the physical systems approach [7, 8]. Physical auditory VE systems require direct sound and early reflections to be calculated on the basis of environment geometry and acoustic properties of the individual listener. Perceptual auditory VE systems employ signal-processing algorithms without specific individualized physical models. Volume panning methods model a sound field with different intensities according to the direction of the virtual source [7, 8]. Volume panning is implemented in most toolkits targeted at the consumer entertainment market (e.g., Microsoft's DirectSound®).

Though volume panning has certain limitations (e.g., see [7]), the *Audioworld* application presented in this paper is based on this method. This was mainly done because we were focusing on evoking specific auditory perceptions, not on physical accuracy. In addition, it was our goal to use only off-the-shelf hardware.

3 The *Audioworld* Concept

The main task in *Audioworld* requires localization of meaningful sound emitting objects distributed across a spatial 2D array. Sound localization is the result of complex cognitive processing. It requires binaural hearing in order to determine the direction and distance to a target object. Additionally, distracting noise or competing sounds need to be suppressed in order to maintain the focus of attention on the auditory target dimension specified by the task. Finally, actions have to be initiated towards the target object location (i.e., moving one's own body or the body of an avatar). At the same time, movements towards lures (e.g., irrelevant sound emitting objects) have to be avoided.

3.1 Technological Aspects

We designed *Audioworld* using the 3D Game Studio (3DGS; Conitec, http://www.conitec.com) authoring suite for 2D and 3D real-time applications based on Microsoft's DirectX® graphics rendering standard. *Audioworld* uses a first person camera perspective. In addition to its binaural hearing requirements, the first person perspective specifically engenders psychological identification with the main acting character, a major aspect of cognitive and emotional learning (i.e., perspective taking [9]).

3.2   Main Function

The center of the *Audioworld* GUI's main menu shows a level preview, and two level select buttons. The button row located at the bottom of the screen comprises start, options, name of player, and quit (Fig. 1). Options refer to level and sound options. Level settings include an adjustable counter for a time limit, the item positioning function, and the sound item list that includes an "add" button. Additional wave files for sound items may be loaded into the system. *Audioworld* automatically loops wave files for continuous playback.

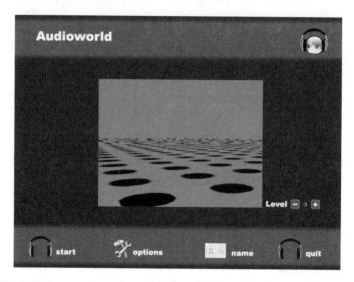

Fig. 1. Main menu in *Audioworld* with a preview of the Syllables game level

Sound item positioning may be done by randomly distributing items across the two-dimensional level map ("random"), or by using automatic positioning according to a fixed spatial array ("default"). Manually placing ("drag-and-drop") selected sound items on the 2D map preview supports systematic individual learning ("rearrange", c.f. Fig. 2). The volume panning in *Audioworld* models a sound field with different intensities according to the direction of each sound item, which renders a realistic spatial audio impression.

Sound options were conceived to enable gradual and individual learning by adjusting task difficulty. Hence, sound options comprise a three-step adjustment of the sonic radius for sound items, and a collection of distracting sounds (e.g., street noise, pink and white noise, schoolyard noise), which are independent of the player's spatial position. Like sound items, new distracting sounds may also be loaded into the system.

We included distracting sounds because sound localization requires suppression of competing sounds. Hence, additional processes are needed to focus attention. The detrimental effect of additional noise or competing sound on various cognitive tasks is well documented (e.g. [10]). Thus, and compared to a control condition, additional distracting sounds make localization of target sounds more difficult. This is typically reflected by behavioral dependent measures. Hence, distracting sounds both prolong the time needed for task completion and increase the number of errors compared to a control condition without distracting sounds. We tested this hypothesis and the overall applicability of *Audioworld* in a pilot study.

Fig. 2. Manual "drag-and-drop" positioning in Audioworld

4 Pilot Study

A total of fourteen participants took part in the pilot study. By using the arrow keys on the computer keyboard, they navigated game levels and localized sound emitting target objects as quickly as possible. Time needed for completion and errors were logged automatically. At the end of the experiment participants answered a questionnaire. Participants rated the playability for each game level. Also, they estimated the game's effect on their personal level of motivation. Finally, participants rated how difficult it was to localize sound objects on the basis of auditory perceptions.

4.1 Design, Stimuli, and Apparatus

The pilot study used a 2x2 mixed factorial design. Distracting sound was the between-subjects factor. Half of the participants were presented with a task-irrelevant distracting sound (schoolyard noise) throughout levels, while the other half was not distracted by irrelevant sound. Game level (nonspeech-based: Music World, speech-based: Syllables) was manipulated within subjects, that is, each participant played both game levels.

We designed two different game levels and one training level (see below). Four different sound emitting objects were used per level. Objects (i.e., instrument sounds or syllables, see below) were distributed across each level map such that a square-like configuration would have resulted if objects had been interconnected. Hence, item positioning was fixed and nearly identical across levels.

4.1.1 Dark World (Training Level)

This level was exclusively used for training purposes. Players navigated an open arena, which was surrounded by an enclosure. Both enclosure and floor consisted of abstract and dark textures. The four target sound objects were invisibly placed on the map (i.e., copier, water tap, telephone, and washing machine). Hence, object localization in Dark World required participants to rely on their hearing sense. Each target location emitted the typical sound of the assigned object (e.g., water dripping from the tap, telephone ringing). Characteristic object sounds were therefore used as auditory icons (earcons) [1, 11, 8].

4.1.2 Music World (Game Level 1)

This game level was also based on the map of Dark World. Yet, it provided even less visual information. This was achieved by adding plain white textures to the level. Therefore, the only visual information came from a ground evenly textured with black dots (c.f. Fig. 1). Every movement of the player caused an immediate and coherent displacement of the dots. The resulting optical flow induced an impression of "walking".

In Music World, sound objects were again invisible and presented as auditory icons. We used prerecorded sounds of musical instruments (e.g., drums, guitar, and vibes). The target sound objects were presented as isolated musical instruments that were part of a looped musical pattern. Participants listened to this instrumental pop tune played by all instruments together before starting Music World.

4.1.3 Syllables (Game Level 2)

The second game level was a variation of Music World. It also provided only minimum visual information, but appeared in light blue color (Fig. 1). Instead of using instruments as constituents of a coherent song, the German word "Missverständnis" (i.e., misconception) was split into its syllables "miss–ver–ständ–nis" that formed four different target objects. The syllables were spoken by a male voice and then looped. Before collecting the syllables, participants listened to the intact word several times.

4.1.4 Apparatus

Standard 14" notebooks (HP Compaq Evo N620C) equipped with stereo headphones (Stagg SHP-2200) were used.

4.2 Participants

Participants were randomly assigned one of two experimental conditions. In the distracting sound condition, participants' (2 female and 5 male) mean age was 28. In the non-distracting condition, participants' (7 males) mean age was 34. All participants were naïve to the subject of the experiment. They reported normal hearing abilities and spoke German as first language. No participant indicated problems with reading or writing skills (e.g., dyslexia).

4.3 Procedure

In a training session, participants made themselves familiar with Audioworld. This included the handling of game controls for navigation and the game's GUI. Most importantly, they learned to localize sound objects on the basis of their binaural hearing. Participants moved forward (up arrow on standard keyboard), backward (down arrow), turned left (left arrow), or turned right (right arrow) depending on their acoustic perceptions of sound intensity and direction. Localizing (i.e., "running into") one of the invisible target sound objects immediately triggered verbal feedback (e.g., "excellent") spoken by a pre-recorded male voice.

At test, participants started either with Music World or Syllables. In the distracting sound condition, participants selected "schoolyard noise". Participants in the non-distracting condition turned off the distracting sound function.

In Music World, two additional musical instruments (i.e., sitar and double bass) appeared as lures. These "false instruments" fitted the harmonies of the song, but sounded inappropriate for the pop tune. In Syllables, two extra spoken German syllables (i.e., "ge" and "da") were added as lures. "Running into" lures always triggered an immediate short two-tone failure sound and was coded as an error. After participants had finished test levels, they were instructed to fill in the questionnaire.

5 Results

First, level completion data will be reported. Then, results of the questionnaire will be presented.

5.1 Time Needed for Level Completion

The 2x2 mixed factorial analysis of variance performed on the mean time scores needed for game level completion indicated no significant result[1] ($Fs \leq 1.73$). It took participants longer, albeit not significantly, to complete Syllables ($M=205$ sec, $SD=75.80$) compared to Music World ($M=175$ sec, $SD=77.63$). Participants in the distracting sound condition ($M=192$ sec, $SD=87.71$) were not slower than participants in the non-distracting condition ($M=189$ sec, $SD=67.34$). Figure 4 illustrates the mean time scores in the different conditions. The failure to observe significant effects, especially with game level, is probably due to the small overall number of participants.

5.2 Errors

For Music World, there were only 6 errors in the non-distracting condition and only one error in the distracting sound condition. For Syllables, 4 errors were recorded in each distracting condition. Due to the overall low number of errors we cannot rule out the possibility that participants might have applied different strategies that caused a distortion in time scores. Hence, careful avoidance of lures (i.e., false instruments or syllables) may have resulted in slow game play. Again, further testing with a greater number of participants is needed.

5.3 Questionnaire

Participants' responses were coded for quantitative analyses. A four-point Likert scale was used. Lower numerical values indicated stronger agreement (e.g., 1=*strongly*

---

[1] For all statistical analyses, the alpha value was set at .05.

agree to 4=*strongly disagree*). Scores were calculated by taking the mean of the scores given for each condition. Preliminary analyses indicated no substantial differences between distracting sound conditions. Therefore, data were collapsed across conditions.

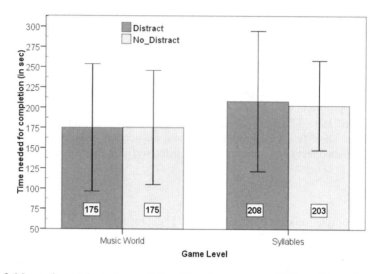

Fig. 3. Means (in sec) for task completion. Error bars represent 95% confidence intervals.

5.3.1 Navigation

Participants reported that it was *"very easy"* to *"easy"* to use the arrow keys for navigation (M=1.64, SD=0.74). This is important, because it suggests that transferring already existing navigation skills to game controls in *Audioworld* was easy for participants. The findings from the behavioral data thus seem to reflect the intended task of locating sound objects via the auditory sense, rather than the participants' struggle with game controls.

5.3.2 Gaming Enjoyment, Motivation, and Overall Concept

Participants apparently enjoyed playing *Audioworld* (M=1.50, SD=0.52). In addition, they felt motivated to continue playing the game with additional levels (M=1.71, SD=0.73). Finally, the overall concept was considered novel (M=1.57, SD=0.65).

6   Discussion

Results clearly indicated a good acceptance of *Audioworld*. The concept received good to excellent ratings in terms of handling, degree of difficulty, and navigation. There was only a numerical advantage for the non-speech sounds in Music World compared to the verbal information in Syllables: it took participants slightly longer to "collect" the target syllables than the musical instruments. Based on the literature, we had expected an advantage for non-speech sounds because these sounds are good at giving rapid feedback on actions, and quickly presenting continuous data and highly structured information. In contrast, speech in general is preferred for giving instructions and absolute values [1]. In addition, the verbal task in Syllables was even more difficult, due to the higher mental workload. That is, participants had to keep in mind the correct sequence of the syllables, and they had to recall which syllable would come next. As mentioned above, this finding might reflect overall low power of the experiment.

Finally, we have to address the null finding in the analyses performed on the distracting sound variable. Localizing sound objects requires active and effortful suppression of distractive noise or competing sounds (e.g., [10]). Hence, we had speculated that additional time-consuming and error-prone processes would be needed to focus attention on the acoustic target object. Apparently, this is not true for distractive noise per se. We may speculate that the distracting sound in our study was simply unobtrusive. Therefore, if we (a) had increased distracting noise level, or (b) had devised a more difficult task, we might have obtained a negative effect of distracting sound. However, this will be subject to future testing.

7 Future Work and Conclusion

Interestingly, though instructions were intentionally lacking any information on efficient strategies to localize target sound objects, participants uniformly reported having developed an almost identical strategy. By using the arrow keys they adjusted their position so that both ears received simultaneous sound of similar intensity. Then, they increased the perceived volume level by pressing the arrow keys to approach the sound source. Clearly, participants were actively and deliberately using the hallmarks of binaural hearing, namely the ITDs and ILDs [5]. *Audioworld's* game controls led to a high sense of perceived achievement, which fitted the natural form of sound localization.

We believe that the *Audioworld* concept fits the demands of different learning contexts. First, *Audioworld* may be adapted for entertainment purposes. Several audio games have been successfully introduced recently [12]. Most importantly, *Audioworld* may be used in various learning scenarios. In our pilot study, Music World and Syllables seem particularly promising in this regard. Music World, for example, refers to the learning of music concepts and structures. By using Audioworld, students may learn to differentiate musical instruments, pitch, or scales on the basis of their hearing sense. Using Syllables, *Audioworld* may support the acquisition of reading and writing skills. In a playful context, students may learn to focus on the phonetic and spatial aspects of verbal material (i.e., the individual sounds of verbal constituents), which has emerged as a key component in grammar literacy and is considered to be deficient in dyslexia, for example [13].

Taken together, the innovative and generic audio game concept of *Audioworld* supports learning because it induces continuous high levels of motivation needed for learning; an important, and often neglected, quality factor not only in experimental research but particularly in CSL.

References

1. Brewster, S.: Nonspeech auditory input. In: Jacko, J.A., Sears, A. (eds.) The Human-Computer Interaction Handbook, pp. 220–239. Lawrence Erlbaum Associates, Inc., Mahwah (2003)
2. Fang, X., Xu, S., Brzezinski, J., Chan, S.C.: A Study of the Feasibility and Effectiveness of Dual-Modal Information Presentations. International Journal of Human-Computer Interaction 20, 3–17 (2006)
3. Shneiderman, B., Plaisant, C.: Designing the User Interface, 4th edn. Pearson, Boston (2005)
4. Kennel, A., Perrochon, L., Darvishi, A.: WAB: World Wide Web Access for Blind and Visually Impaired Computer Users. In: Proc. of ACM SIGCAPH, vol. 55, pp. 10–15. ACM Press, New York (1996)
5. Blauert, J.: Spatial Hearing: The Psychophysics of Human Sound Localization. The MIT Press, Cambridge (1997)
6. Braasch, J.: Modelling of Binaural Hearing. In: Blauert, J. (ed.) Communication Acoustics, pp. 75–103. Springer, Berlin (2005)
7. Naef, M., Staadt, O., Gross, M.: Spatialized Audio Rendering for Immersive Virtual Environments. In: Proc. of VRST 2002, pp. 65–72. ACM Press, New York (2002)
8. Novo, P.: Auditory Virtual Environments. In: Blauert, J. (ed.) Communication Acoustics, pp. 277–297. Springer, Berlin (2005)
9. Flavell, J.H., Botkin, P.T., Fry, C.L., Wright, J.W., Jarvis, P.E.: The development of role-taking and communication skills in children. Wiley, New York (1968)
10. Baddeley, A.: Working Memory. Oxford University Press, Oxford (1986)
11. Mynatt, E.D.: Designing with Auditory Icons: How Well Do We Identify Auditory Cues? In: Proc. of CHI 1994, pp. 269–270. ACM Press, New York (1996)
12. Friberg, J., Gärdenfors, D.: Audio Games: New Perspectives on Game Audio. In: Proc. of ACE 2004, Singapore, June 3-5, pp. 148–154. ACM Press, New York (2004)
13. Snowling, M.J.: Phonemic Deficits in Developmental Dyslexia. Psychological Research 43(2), 219–234 (1981)

Exploring Interactive Systems Using Peripheral Sounds

Saskia Bakker, Elise van den Hoven, and Berry Eggen

Eindhoven University of Technology, Industrial Design Department, P.O. Box 513, 5600MB Eindhoven, The Netherlands
{s.bakker,e.v.d.hoven,j.h.eggen}@tue.nl

Abstract. Our everyday interaction in and with the physical world, has facilitated the development of auditory perception skills that enable us to selectively place one auditory channel in the center of our attention and simultaneously monitor others in the periphery. We search for ways to leverage these auditory perception skills in interactive systems. In this paper, we present three working demonstrators that use sound to subtly convey information to users in an open office. To qualitatively evaluate these demonstrators, each of them has been implemented in an office for three weeks. We have seen that such a period of time, sounds can start shifting from the center to the periphery of the attention. Furthermore, we found several issues to be addressed when designing such systems, which can inform future work in this area.

Keywords: Calm Technology, Periphery, Attention, Sound design, Interaction design.

1 Introduction

As a result of the upcoming of pervasive technologies, the role of computers in everyday life is rapidly changing. This development has lead to a broad discussion on how digital technologies can fit into everyday life. Weiser [14] envisioned the computer of the future vanishing into the background. By this, he aimed not only at the technology 'disappearing' by being hidden in artifacts or surroundings, computers will also be perceived and interacted with in the background, so that "we are freed to use them without thinking and so to focus beyond them on new goals" [14, p. 3].

This vision refers to the way we naturally perceive information in the physical world. We do not have to consciously look out the window for an impression of the current weather, or count the papers on our colleague's desk to know that he is busy. We know these things without specifically focusing our attention on them. Computing technology however, is generally designed to be in the center of the attention. Weiser and Brown introduced the term *calm technology*, "technology that engages both the center and the periphery of our attention and in fact moves back and forth between the two" [15, p. 8]. In other words, skills acquired through (inter)action in the physical world are used to interact with or perceive information from the computer. These skills, allowing us to perceive information in the periphery of our attention or focusing on it in the center, regard all our senses. However, as sound can be perceived without having to look at the source [6], we particularly see potential for the audio to

R. Nordahl et al. (Eds.): HAID 2010, LNCS 6306, pp. 55–64, 2010.
© Springer-Verlag Berlin Heidelberg 2010

be used in calm technology. In this paper we describe an explorative study on design of systems that use audio as calm technology. We have created three such systems and placed each of them in a shared office environment for three weeks, in order to evaluate how users perceive audible information and how this perception changes over time. Focus group interviews with people working in this office have been used as input for a discussion on interactive auditory systems designed for the periphery.

2   Theoretical Background and Related Work

In almost any situation, multiple auditory channels will reach the ear. Although all these channels are heard simultaneously, we are able to focus our attention on one channels while ignoring others [3]. We can have a conversation, while at the same time we hear music, noise outside and someone closing a door. We are thus actively, but implicitly, selecting which channel to attend to [10]. This cognitive phenomenon is commonly called the *cocktail party effect* [3] and has been extensively studied in the area of cognitive psychology [2][12]. Theories of selective attention [10] describe a selective filter in the perceptual process, which selects one channel to attend to and blocks [2] or attenuates [12] others. In a normal situation, the channel you consciously choose to attend to is selected and the attention is focused on it. The other channels are not perceived in detail. However, the selection is not only influenced by conscious choice, but also by the *salience* [10] of the incoming stimuli as well as by a cognitive process known as *priming* [12]. A loud noise for example has such distinct physical properties that it becomes salient and therefore overrules conscious choice; when a sudden loud noise is heard, it is immediately attended to and thus selected. Priming is a process that makes the selection of certain stimuli more likely. One's own name is a common example of a primed stimulus. When someone mentions your name, even in a channel you were not attended to, this will likely attract your attention. The detection of the primed stimulus in an unattended channel causes the filter to select this channel over the attended channel. See Figure 1 for an overview of this theory.

Sound is used in many interactive systems, such as for alerts, notifications, warnings, status indication, or as feedback to support interaction [13]. Although most of these sounds are designed to be in the center of the attention, some systems have been designed for the periphery. 'Audio Aura' [9] for example, uses background auditory cues to provide office workers with relevant information such as the number of unread emails or the availability of colleagues. 'Birds Whispering' [4] uses ongoing bird-sounds to subtly communicate information about the activity in the office. The 'AmbientRoom' [8] makes stock information audible through ongoing soundscapes of bird and rain sounds. Hermann et al. [7] used auditory weather reports broadcasted on the radio to provide users with awareness of the upcoming local weather. Schloss and Stammen [11] present a three art installations that make information about the current weather conditions audible in public indoor spaces.

Although all these examples aim at background monitoring of information through sound, hardly any have experimented with over a longer period of time. However, a learning period will often be needed to get used to audio of such systems. In order to find issues to address when designing peripheral audio, evaluating them over a period of time is therefore crucial.

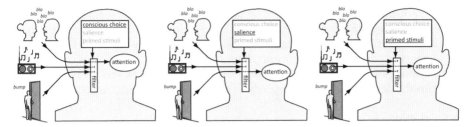

Fig. 1. An overview of selective attention theory: normal situation where the attention is focused on a conversation (left), a situation where a (salient) loud noise is heard (middle) and a situation where the listener's name (primed stimulus) is heard on the radio (right)

3 Demonstrators and Experiments

In this paper, we present three working demonstrators, named AudioResponse, EntranceSounds and RainForecasts, each of which uses sound to convey information, intended to allow users to attune to it, but also ignore it if desired. The demonstrators, which should be considered research tools, implement a diverse range of sounds and types of information, enabling us to compare different functionalities and sound designs among each other. We have evaluated these demonstrators in three separate experiments to gain new insights in how informative sounds can play a role in interactive systems as well as to find issues to address when designing such systems and their sounds and mappings, particularly regarding longer term use.

All three experiments took place in an open office in which 12 researchers work, including the first author, of which nine actively participated in the experiments. The participants (4 female, 5 male, age 23 to 32) have diverse cultural backgrounds and none have extensive knowledge in audio related topics. Other than people entering, talking and working, PCs, lights humming, doors opening and closing, there are no significant sounds already present, e.g. there is no music playing. Footsteps are softened because of carpet on the floor. Each demonstrator ran in this office for three weeks continuously. At the start of each experiment, the participants were explained about the working of the demonstrator. See Figure 2 for an impression of the location.

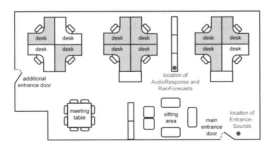

Fig. 2. Lay-out of the open office used in the experiments, indicating the desks of our nine active participants in grey, and the location of the demonstrators

To evaluate the use of sound in these demonstrators, we were mainly interested in the experiences of the participants. Therefore, we gathered qualitative data to inform a discussion on this topic. All comments made by either participants or by visitors were carefully noted during the experiments. Furthermore, after each period of three weeks, a group interview was conducted with 4 to 5 participants. In this section, we will describe the demonstrators and the analysis of the experiments and interviews.

3.1 AudioResponse

Design. The AudioResponse is a simple interactive system that plays an ongoing soundscape of piano tones with semi-randomized pitch. The AudioResponse system constantly monitors the loudness (in decibel) of the sound registered by a microphone, located in the center of the room (Figure 2). This loudness determines the amplitude of the piano tones; the higher the registered loudness, the larger the amplitude of the tones. The information communicated through this sound can provide awareness of the loudness of sounds the participants and their surroundings produce. This may provide awareness of 'what is going on around you' in a broad sense.

Results. From reactions during the experiment and the group interview, we extracted 44 quotes regarding experiences with the AudioResponse interactive system. To analyze these data, the quotes were clustered topic-wise by the first author.

When the AudioResponse experiment ran in the office, four participants indicated that it made them aware of the loudness of certain everyday sounds. For example, a door in the hallway triggered a loud sonic response from the system, while the sound of this door was normally not experienced as very loud. Furthermore, two participants found the system useful as it warned them when they were too loud, which also caused them to attempt working more quietly to avoid triggering the system.

All participants agreed that the information conveyed by the system was not relevant. However, some participants found the system 'fun' at certain moments, as it triggered laughing or conversation. Others experienced it as being annoying, because already disturbing sounds were enhanced to be even more disturbing. Regarding the piano sounds used in this design, the randomness of the pitch of tones caused some confusion, as some participants expected the pitch to be linked to certain information.

3.2 EntranceSounds

Design. The EntranceSounds is an interactive system located at the main entrance door of the open office (see Figure 2). A motion sensor located above the entrance registers if someone passes through the door (see Figure 3). Whenever a person is detected, a short piano chord is played. The pitch of the root of this chord indicates the number of people detected in the last hour. For example, if someone enters at 11.32h, the number of people registered between 10.32h and 11.32h is represented. Low pitch means that few people have passed and high pitch means that many people have passed. Since the EntranceSounds system does not register the direction in which people pass through the door, entering or leaving the room is not distinguished.

This system provides information about how busy the office was in the last hour, but also informs the people working in the office that someone is entering or leaving. The door used was always open during the experiment. As the office floor is covered with carpet, one will normally hardly hear someone entering or leaving.

Fig. 3. Picture of the EntranceSounds system, located at the main entrance of the open office

Results. The 39 quotes gathered regarding the EntranceSounds system were processed in a way similar to the approach used in the AudioResponse experiment. With the EntranceSounds system, there are clearly two types of users; people that enter or leave the room and thus trigger the sounds to be played (direct users) and people working in the open office hearing the sounds triggered by others (indirect users). Most indirect users noted that the system mainly informed them that someone is entering or leaving. This was not always experienced as relevant information, as many people can directly see the door, or are just not interested in this information unless the person entering comes to visit them. However, these participants also noted that it was easy to ignore the system and that they even experienced moments where someone had come to visit them, while they had not noticed the sound.

The information conveyed through the pitch of the chord was generally considered most useful by direct users; it made them realize that it was a busy hour in the office, or that "they had not been active enough". When knowing the routines in this office, the information turned out to be rather useful in some cases. For example: one participant came in at 10.00h one morning and noticed that the sound was higher than expected, while the office was empty. This informed her that her colleagues must have gone for a coffee break. To indirect users however, the information about the number of people having entered or left did not turn out to be relevant; none of them felt the need to be informed of this each time someone passed the door. However, the sound was not experienced as annoying or disturbing by any of the participants.

All participants could clearly recognize the pitch changes when multiple people passed the door together. However, small differences were not noticed when the time in between two chords was bigger (say 5 minutes or more). This also became apparent from an experience of one of the participants who entered the office when the sound was much higher than normal, due to an event in the room. When this participant entered the office, she noted "this is not my sound, normally it always gives me the same sound, but now it is totally different". Apparently, she usually did not notice pitch differences, even though small differences must have been present.

3.3 RainForecasts

Design. The RainForecasts system provides audible information about the short term rain forecasts for the city in which the experiment was held. Every half hour, the system sonifies the rain forecast for 30 minutes in the future. This data is extracted from a real-time online weather forecast [1] in terms of an 8 point scale (0 meaning no precipitation and 7 meaning heavy thunderstorm). This value is represented by a specific auditory icon [5] (see Table 1), played in the center of the room. The sounds were selected to resemble the natural occurrence of each level precipitation, but also to be recognizable as such while presented out of context. This last consideration motivated our choice for drop sounds rather than recordings of actual rain, as short samples of such recordings played at an unexpected moment sound like white noise.

The RainForecasts system differs from the systems that sonify weather information mentioned previously, by providing short term forecasts rather than real-time information [11], or forecasts for 24 hours [7]. This information may in a different way be relevant to users as it may influence their short term planning.

Table 1. Sound used in the RainForecasts system, indicating different levels of precipitation

Level of precipitation	Precipitation in mm per hour	Auditory icon
0	0	Bird sounds
1	< 1	Three rain drops
2	< 2	Four rain drops
3	< 5	Six rain drops
4	< 10	Eight rain drops
5	< 50	Mild thunder sound
6	< 100	Medium thunder sound
7	> 100	Heavy thunder sound

Results. The 56 quotes gathered regarding the RainForecasts system were processed in the same way as the previously described experiments. All participants agreed that they could easily recognize the rain forecast based on the sounds produced by the system. However, some participants felt that it was difficult to distinguish the different levels of rain when the sounds were played with 30 minute intervals. All participants agreed that the sound indicating 'no precipitation' was not distracting at all, whereas one participant indicated that the rain-drop sounds were more distracting as they seemed louder than the no-rain sounds. The participants indicated that they noticed the sounds less often towards the end of the three weeks of the experiment. Most participants mentioned that they did not hear it when working concentratedly.

From the group interview, it became evident that the information conveyed by the RainForecasts system was not of equal relevance for all participants. Some were just not interested in the weather, while one participant, who traveled by bicycle, even based the time of going home on the weather. The information was therefore very relevant for this latter participant, who noted that it was exactly the information she needed: "The internet provides a lot of information, which makes it hard to find the specific information I need". Another participant however, wanted more detailed information (e.g. temperature) and preferred using the internet to look up forecasts.

The participants also indicated that the system provided them with information other than the rain forecasts, namely the time. The system makes a sound every half hour, which often resulted in reactions such as "did another half hour pass already? I must have been very focused!" Furthermore, some participants mentioned that the sound caught their attention more often at noon, which is the time of their usual lunch break. This indicates that the sound is more noticeable, or moves to the center of the attention, when the conveyed information (time in this case) is more relevant.

4 Discussion

In this paper, we have described the design and evaluation of three working demonstrators that use sound to subtly communicate different kinds of information. In this section, we will discuss the insights we gained regarding *types of information* and *sound design* suitable for such systems and the *perception of audible information*.

4.1 Types of Information Conveyed by the Demonstrators

When comparing the three systems, all participants agreed that the RainForecasts system was most useful as they found the conveyed information most relevant. The AudioResponse system was considered least useful as the information provided was of no direct relevance to the participants. For this reason, some participants also experienced the AudioResponse system as being disturbing, while the other two systems did not disturb them. Interestingly, the volume of the AudioResponse sounds was not higher than that of the other sounds, and the used piano tones were similar to those used in the EntranceSounds. This indicates that the relevance of the information is related to the extent to which the sound representing it is experienced as disturbing.

Although the relevance of the audible information seems to be of importance, we have also seen that it is difficult to predict which information is relevant at which moment. For example, when one participant heard that many people had passed the door, she knew that her colleagues had gone for a coffee break. Another participant noticed the sounds of the RainForecasts system more clearly at 12.00h than at other times, as this indicated lunch time. The information that users take from such systems, is thus not always related to the information that is intended to be communicated. When and what information is relevant highly depends on the context as well as on the interests, state of mind and knowledge of the user. As multiple users are provided with the information at the same time, it can be relevant in one way to one user, in another way to another user and not at all to a third user. Given this difficulty in selecting relevant information, an iterative approach seems to be valuable for the design of such systems. Only if demonstrators are evaluated in an everyday context and with the intended users, one can assess when and how they will be useful.

When we look at the RainForecasts system, the conveyed information seemed relevant to many of the participants. However, some noted that the system did not provide enough information regarding the weather forecasts. For these participants, the information may have been too relevant to be conveyed in such 'limited' form. Although more sophisticated sound design could partly solve this (e.g. [7]), it points out an interesting issue regarding the choice of information to be made audible. This information should be relevant, but in case it is that relevant that users require more detail, the interactive system should provide easy access to a layer of detailed information. This way, general information can be monitored in the periphery via audio, and details can be examined in the center of the attention when desired. The layer of details could be displayed through audio or by other means such as visual display.

When audio is used however, it would be advisable to implement a different sonic character than the peripheral sounds. Using similar sound may confuse indirect users, who are listening to but not directly interacting with the system.

4.2 Sound Design

The presented demonstrators implemented three different sound designs and mappings. The AudioResponse used an *ongoing soundscape* of piano tones, the EntranceSounds played short *auditory cues* when users passed through the door and the RainForecasts conveyed information through *auditory icons* every half hour.

The pitch changes realized in the AudioResponse system were random and did therefore not convey any information, which caused confusion. The pitch differences in the EntranceSounds system however, revealed the number of people detected in the last hour. This has shown to be valuable at certain distinct moments. However, experiences with the EntranceSounds system have also shown that smaller pitch differences were not recognized, particularly when two tones were played with some time in between. The same issue was seen in the RainForecasts system, where participants found it hard to distinguish sounds indicating different levels of rain. If two sounds are not played successively, the differences between the sounds should therefore be clear enough to be perceived and remembered.

The sounds we used in the demonstrators presented in this paper were intended to be unobtrusive, so that they can be perceived in the periphery of the attention. The participants in the RainForecasts experiment noted that the rain-sounds were much more distracting, and thus in the center of the attention, than the sound indicating no rain. When comparing these two sounds, the rain-sounds were impact sounds and the no-rain sound was not. Using the same style of sounds may support them being perceived in the periphery and shift to the center of the attention only when required. Furthermore, impact sounds may be less suitable for these kind of applications.

4.3 Perception of Audible Information

All three experiments ran for three weeks successively, which enables evaluation of how the perception of audible information changed over time. In each experiment, the sounds were perceived in the center of the attention at the start. This means that the participants consciously heard them and often also reacted to them by looking at the demonstrator. However, in both the EntranceSounds and the RainForecasts experiments, we saw that the sounds shifted more to the periphery towards the end of the three weeks. This may indicate that getting used to the sounds can support the process of them moving back and forth between periphery and center of the attention, which is the intention of calm technology. The sounds of the AudioResponse indicating above average loudness did not shift to the periphery but were always in the center of the attention. This may be explained by the fact that many participants linked the information to themselves being loud, which annoyed them.

As mentioned before, we have seen that the information that participants took from the sounds often different from what was intended by the design. For example concluding that colleagues went for coffee based on the pitch of the chord in the EntranceSounds system. These kind of events occurred more often toward the end of the experiment period, even though the participants were informed about the meaning of the sounds at the start of the experiments. This may indicate that a learning period is needed to get used to the direct meaning of the sounds, before users can interpret them to gain additional information. This also emphasizes the need for iterations involving longer term use of prototypes when designing such systems.

In the results described in this paper, we see that the systems were most useful when the information conveyed by the sounds differed from what the user expected. This happened for example with the EntranceSounds system when the colleagues of the direct user had already gone for a coffee break. In such cases, the sounds were clearly in the center of the participants' attention and were experienced as relevant. However, this only occurred in a small number of cases. In all other cases, the information conveyed by the sounds were as expected and did therefore not add to the knowledge of the participants. In fact, it is likely that in over 95% of the cases that a sound was played, no new information was conveyed. Though this may appear to be useless, it is exactly the intention of our designs. When comparing this to sounds in our physical environment, we see the same thing; when driving a car, the engine will sound as usual in most cases. Only in case of a problem, the sounds will be different. This conveys new and relevant information and immediately shifts to the center of the attention. When the sounds are only relevant in a low number of cases however, it is crucial to design them such that they only shift to the foreground when required.

As we have seen, at times the sounds were in the periphery and at other times they were in the center of the attention. Relating this to selective attention theory [2][12], we see that most cases when sounds shifted from the periphery to the center related to *salience*. For example, when the rain sounds were experienced as louder than the no-rain sounds. However, sometimes participants attuned to the system for other reasons. For example, when the RainForecasts sound at 12.00h attracted the attention more than the sounds at other moments, as it indicated lunch time. This could have been the result of *priming*; the participant likely knew in the back of her mind that it was almost time for lunch, so stimuli indicating time may have been *primed*.

5 Conclusions

In this paper, we have described three interactive demonstrators that use audio to convey information in the periphery of the user's attention. We evaluated each demonstrator in a three week experiment. As a result of our studies, we have found that the participants did perceive some of the sounds used in our designs in the periphery of their attention, though getting used to the systems was required to achieve this. Furthermore, the kinds of information that participants picked up from the sounds differed depending on the context, interests, knowledge of the user, as well as on their experience with the system. As this is difficult to predict, we propose that an iterative approach, in which systems are experimented with for a period of time, is most suitable when designing such systems. This will also ensure the relevance and unobtrusiveness of the design. Although the unobtrusiveness of sound may differ per participant and depends on the relevance of the information, using a set of sounds that is consistent in style will support it being perceived in the periphery of the attention.

This paper adds to existing work by describing longer term evaluations with systems using unobtrusive sounds, which provides new insights in how sound may play a role in calm technology and what issues to address when such sounds are aimed to be perceived in the periphery of the attention.

References

1. Buienradar.nl, http://www.buienradar.nl/ (Last accessed 15-06-2010)
2. Broadbent, D.E.: Perception and Communication. Pergamon Press, London (1958)
3. Cherry, E.C.: Some experiments on the recognition of speech, with one and with two ears. J. Acoust. Soc. Am. 25(5), 975–979 (1953)
4. Eggen, B., Mensvoort, K.: Making Sense of What Is Going on 'Around': Designing Environmental Awareness Information Displays. In: Markopoulos, P., De Ruyter, B., Mackay, W. (eds.) Awareness Systems, Advances in Theory, Methodology and Design, pp. 99–124. Springer, London (2009)
5. Gaver, W.W.: The SonicFinder: an interface that uses auditory icons. Human-Computer Interaction 4(1), 67–94 (1989)
6. Gaver, W.W.: What in the World Do We Hear? An Ecological Approach to Auditory Event Perception. Ecological Psychology 5(1), 1–29 (1993)
7. Hermann, T., Drees, J.M., Ritter, H.: Broadcasting auditory weather reports - a pilot project. In: Proceedings of the International Conference on Auditory Display, pp. 208–211 (2003)
8. Ishii, H., Wisneski, C., Brave, S., Dahley, A., Gorbet, M., Ullmer, B., Yarin, P.: ambientROOM: integrating ambient media with architectural space. In: CHI 1998 conference summary on Human factors in computing systems, pp. 173–174. ACM, New York (1998)
9. Mynatt, E.D., Back, M., Want, R., Baer, M., Ellis, J.B.: Designing audio aura. In: Proceedings of the SIGCHI conference on Human factors in computing systems, pp. 566–573. ACM Press, New York (1998)
10. Pashler, H.E.: The Psychology of Attention. MIT Press, Cambridge (1998)
11. Schloss, W.A., Stammen, D.: Ambient media in public spaces. In: Proceeding of the international workshop on Semantic Ambient Media Experiences, pp. 17–20. ACM, New York (2008)
12. Treisman, A.M.: Verbal Cues, Language, and Meaning in Selective Attention. Am. J. Psychol. 77(2), 206–219 (1964)
13. Walker, B.N., Nees, M.A.: Theory of Sonification. In: Hermann, T., Hunt, A., Neuhoff, J. (eds.) Handbook of Sonification. Academic Press, New York (in press), http://sonify.psych.gatech.edu/~mnees/
14. Weiser, M.: The computer for the 21st century. SIGMOBILE Mob. Comput. Commun. Rev. 3(3), 3–11 (1999)
15. Weiser, M., Brown, J.S.: The Coming Age of Calm Technology. In: Denning, P.J., Metcalfe, R.M. (eds.) Beyond Calculation: the next fifty years of computing, pp. 75–85. Springer, New York (1997)

Basic Exploration of Narration and Performativity for Sounding Interactive Commodities

Stefano Delle Monache[1], Daniel Hug[2], and Cumhur Erkut[3]

[1] IUAV - University of Venice, Italy
[2] Zurich University of the Arts, Zurich, Switzerland
[3] Aalto University, Dept. Signal Processing and Acoustics, Espoo, Finland
stefano.dellemonache@gmail.com, daniel.hug@zhdk.ch, cumhur.erkut@tkk.fi

Abstract. We present an exploration in sonic interaction design, aimed at integrating the power of narrative sound design with the sonic aesthetics of a physics-based sound synthesis. The emerging process is based on interpretation, and can represent a novel tool in the education of the future generation of interaction designers. In addition, an audio-tactile paradigm, that exploits the potential of the physics-based approach, is introduced.

Keywords: Sonic Interaction Design, Aesthetics, Physics-based Synthesis, Methodology, Narrative Sound Design.

1 Introduction

From physical guidance in training activities, to expressive control in novel interfaces and affective computing, interaction designers are exploring the potentials of sonic and haptic feedback. DIY haptic devices are sufficiently robust and valuable tools for rapid prototyping of design ideas in an exploratory way [22,27]. Sound can be understood as "touch at a distance", and auditory attributes can influence the tactile perception of surfaces, thus enhancing aesthetic experiences [7,2]. Explorations in *sonic interaction design* (SID) investigated means to establish continuous negotiations with interactive artifacts, and affect the interplay between the sensory channels [24,17]. As designers, we search for ways to embed and articulate intentions in computational artifacts, that is providing them with expressional, performative qualities [18]. Sound is a potential mediator of such qualities and contributes to the socio-cultural dimension of artifacts [15].

In this paper we present a pilot study aimed at integrating the power of narrative sound design with the sonic aesthetics of a physics-based sound synthesis. We set up a proof-of-concept, and an exploratory framework wherein expressive qualities, that are distilled from a systematic analysis of film sound cases, are transferred to the specific possibilities afforded by a physics-based approach.

The paper has the following structure: Section 2 frames the theme and introduces a narrative approach to SID; in Section 3, we introduce the Sound Design

R. Nordahl et al. (Eds.): HAID 2010, LNCS 6306, pp. 65–74, 2010.

Toolkit (SDT), a software for physics-based sound synthesis; Section 4 presents our pilot experiment; in Section 5 we discuss the outcomes; in Section 6, future work is discussed; in Section 7, we draw our conclusions.

2   Background

Sketching and prototyping are fundamental means of research through design, be it visual, sonic or haptic [6,20,28]. In SID there are only few established design heuristics or existing cases to work with in an early phase of design work.

Recent work has proposed a structured, iterative process, which uses *narrative metatopics* for informing the design of experience prototypes of sonic interactions [16]. Narrative metatopics are abstracted themes and attributes associated with narratively significant artifacts and interactions in fictional media, like film or games. They were established in structured sessions of discussions, coding and clustering of extracts from over thirty films and games, in which sound played a significant interpretive role [16]. For instance, the sounds associated to the wand in Harry Potter movie are a pointer of magic, expressional and interactional properties of the artifact and its usage. Thus, narrative metatopics provide a means of navigating a complex semantic space, and can be associated with a collection of specific sound design strategies which serve as material to build grounded SID hypotheses.

In this study, this narrative sound design strategy is combined with a basic approach to physics-based sound design [24,12]. Originated in post-Bauhaus design schools, the basic approaches design problems in terms of exercises constructed around specific themes, with well defined objectives and constraints [1]. Observations are constructively shared, similarly to what experimental phenomenologist do when tackling phenomena that cannot be reduced to collections of separate and measurable variables [25]. In physics-based sound synthesis, sound generation is described in terms of elementary actions and correspondent physical events. This approach strongly complements Foley, a common design practice for audiovisual media [26,3]. Like Foley artists, sound designers are provided with a palette of virtual sounding objects that can be combined, to create compound, elaborated sound events.

3   The Sound Design Toolkit

The Sound Design Toolkit (SDT) is a complete front-end application running on Max/MSP (www.cycling74.com), providing a palette of virtual lutheries, that can be exploited in SID research and education. The application includes polyphonic features and connectivity to multiple external devices and sensors in order to facilitate the embedding of sonic attributes in interactive artifacts [8]. A physics-based approach is close to designers thinking: sounds are described in terms of shapes, properties of materials, and dynamics of gestures. It allows a certain immediate "visualization" of the sketched sound with its interactive context, and an intuitive sensory connection with touch. Hence, augmented objects can be provided with an expressive acoustic behavior in the sense of ecological hearing [13]. The SDT has been extensively used in various interactive installations, workshops and research activities [24]. Here, we explore further and challenge the physics-based sound design with specific narrative contents.

4 Experiment: Sound Design Process

In this paper we aim at probing if and how a narrative strategy can be transferred to a physics-based sound design. In doing that, our domain of interest focuses on 1) interactions that are continuous and that involve human manipulation; 2) making use of a cheap and off-the-shelf interface in the sensing process (Nintendo Wii-remote http://en.wikipedia.org/wiki/Wii_Remote); 3) generating the sound feedback in the SDT environment solely, without further processing. For this purpose, the three above-mentioned conditions are set as general constraints that frame the design process. The goal is to re-design the narratives associated with some metatopics using the SDT environment, and to evaluate the narrative sound transfer. Two of the authors took part to the process as Participant 1 (P1) and Participant 2 (P2). Hence, we set up the following process, paying attention to track each single step.

1. P1 provides narrative metatopics and associated filmic sound designs;
2. P2 analyses the filmic sounds and implements the resulting design idea about how to recreate the metatopics, in a prototype using the SDT;
3. P1 explores the SDT setups, producing an audiovisual think aloud protocol;
4. P1 provides a post-task interpretation of the sound design experience;
5. The design idea is compared against the interpretation and the design strategies used by P2.

The tests were conducted with Max/MSP 4.6 and Osculator (http://www.osculator.net/) on a Mac Powerbook G4, using a Nintendo Wiimote, and consumer-level loudspeakers with subwoofer.

The video documentation of the process is available at: http://www.acoustics.hut.fi/~cerkut/temp/design_report/index.html.

4.1 Filmic Sound Designs and Associated Metatopics (P1)

The film material provided by P1 is part of the corpus previously used to produce the catalog of narrative metatopics, as described above [16]. It was selected together with P2, according the general constraints set to the design process, and the following acted as corollaries and selection criteria: 1) there had to be an observable relationship between a continuous sound and a represented action; 2) the sound-action relationship had to be re-creatable using the SDT, at least in principle; 3) it had to be possible to use the narrative elements of the filmic examples in a specific design scenario. For this pilot test, three narrative metatopics were selected:

Fig. 1. Squizdajuice: the implementation of the design concept

Quality of energy refers to a general aesthetics of the sonic identity of the forces behind the processes in the device, and also relates to a judgement of the artifact in the process.

Quality of use, in particular in relation to a notion of stability. This refers to attributes and affordances associated with the artifact as experienced in the interaction process.

Quality of control refers to the user-artifact relationship, and the negotiatons established in the interaction loop. The articulation of energy and control becomes semantic and expressive values are embedded in the artifact.

P2 was instructed on the methodology based on narrative metatopics [16], provided with a list of metatopics and related filmic examples, and was asked to formulate a design concept, based on his analysis of the fictional sounds. In practice, P2 acted as a designer, interpreting the filmic examples and prototyping a design idea, accordingly. This methodical choice allowed a cross-evaluation of both narrative and physics-based approaches.

4.2   Design Concept and Prototyping (P2)

Squizdajuice exploits the human energy put into a squeezing action. It can be used for crumpling trash paper while encouraging physical activity. The device is worn as a glove and considerably reduces the cognitive effort to operate it while optimizing the energy flow of the crumpling action. For a correct operation, a first sound feedback helps the user to find a balanced posture, while a second sound conveys information about the process, affecting the perceived effort. Incorrect posture and energy dissipation are expressed by a sound as well. Figure 1 shows the implementation with the Wiimote.

As mentioned, the goal of this exploration is to recreate the narrative sound designs associated with the three metatopics using the SDT environment, and to compare it with the formulated design concept. In the following, the design approach to narrative metatopics is described. According to the basic design approach, the metatopics are incorporated in the concept as general themes to be explored. Thus, design problems are constructed around an objective to achieve, within well defined constraints.

Quality of Use. Stability as articulation of a *quality of use* can be brought back to something characterized by a regular pace, or a balanced physical state, and thus formulated as a case of balancing task.

Theme: *supportive and expressive feedback in balancing task.*

Objective: *design the feedback for a balancing task, in such a way to define the boundaries of the functional-actional space and a comfortable posture can afford the exploration of the interface.*

Constraints: *the feedback should be continuous, and convey the semantic value of stability.*

The design of the balancing task makes use of the friction model [5], available in the SDT. The rubbing force and the pressure on rubber are coupled and mapped around the Y-axis of the Wiimote, in order to achieve a balanced posture located in the silent state, holding the hand horizontally. The friction sound defines an imaginary circular space around the hand. Deviations from the balanced posture up to the vertical position generates a sort of glass harmonica sound. Two timbral configurations are provided, respectively sound A_High_Res and sound B_Low_Res, that differently affect the perceived stability and resolution of the playable space. In sound A_High_Res, the interaction properties of the friction model are configured in order to generate a smoother sound attack and slower timbral evolution, with slighter motion of the hand. On the contrary, in sound B_Low_Res, the dynamic evolution of the friction is much more responsive, with faster sound attacks, and a louder region of rough sound.

Quality of Energy and Control. In everyday interactions, such as hitting a spoon on the table, or charging a mechanism, the acoustic percept of energy, its qualities and control is given by the dynamic evolution of pitch, amplitude, and harmonic content of the generated sound [11]. To exert continuous control on such events means to get acquainted with the tools, and learn to practice appropriate gestures. The previous balancing task is incorporated in a energy control task with respect to the squeezing action.

Theme: *expressive and supportive continuous feedback in squeezing action.*

Objective: *design the feedback for a squeezing action, in such a way to afford a comfortable control over the energy flow (regular pace).*

Constraints: *The feedback should be continuous, non-symbolic, immediate to catch (or pre-attentional), and yet divisible into three clear stages (active space, critical state, breakdown)*

The pace and depth of the squeezing action are detected as variations on the Z-axis of the Wiimote, and mapped on the velocity parameter of the rolling model [23]. The continuous squeezing motion makes a virtual ball starts rolling. When the hand posture enters the critical state and the breakdown position, the rolling sound is combined with the glass harmonica. The velocity of the virtual ball decreases abruptly, generating bouncing and scratchy sounds.

The pace and the speed of the ball are explored in four control maps, as means to support the squeezing action. The *pace* is defined along the continuum *fast to slow*, and affects the energy transfer function of the squeezing. It means that to keep a same constant velocity a higher or lower effort is needed. The *speed* attribute describes the perceived inertia of the system, from *rapid to delaying*.

4.3   Exploration of the Interaction and Interpretation (P1)

P1 explored the design implementation provided by P2, in three different test conditions. In *test condition 1*, he was not aware of the design concept, and proceeded to a blind exploration of the sound-gesture relationship. In *test condition 2*, he was provided with the instructions related to the balancing and squeezing tasks. In *test condition 3*, he was provided with all the necessary information about the design concept, e.g. posture, use and function. All explorations were conducted thinking aloud, audio-visually protocolled, and are summarized in the following subsections. The written protocol of the experiment can be found at: http://www.acoustics.hut.fi/~cerkut/temp/design_report/index.html.

Test Condition 1: Blind Exploration of the Sound-gesture Relationship. P1 freely explored the friction sound feedback, looking for a relationship with the notion of stability. He observed the dynamic evolution of the sound feedback, and associated the timbral space of a "singing glass". The silence state associated with the horizontal position of the Wiimote was well noticed, but not related to the notion of stability. Instead, the participant framed the symmetry of the sound feedback evolution around the roughness states. He interpreted the rough and scratchy regions as unwanted or broken edges, and the resonant singing glass sound, produced by repeating rocking motions of the Wiimote, as stable.

Test Condition 2: Exploration of the Balancing and Squeezing Tasks. In combining balancing with stability, P1 interpreted the rough regions as "something in the device's energy source which was overloaded". The coupling of the rolling and friction sounds afforded P1 to assume the balanced posture in the silent region of the friction feedback: at this position the virtual ball was responsive and fed back the energy that was exerted in the squeezing movement. The delayed response of the virtual ball supported the image of a reactive artifact. The combination of rolling and friction sounds in circular hand motions reinforced the notion of "correct use". Abrupt stops of the virtual ball and hard irregular impacts were interpreted as breakdown and an energy signature could be clearly perceived. The rocking movement around the roll axis of the arm provided the highest interpretive consistency: "I'm keeping up an energy level while avoiding the breakdown of the rolling sound". Application scenarios were constructed, for example as a kinetic charging device.

Test Condition 3: Exploration of *Squizdajuice*. P1 was fully instructed about the design concept, the usage of *Squizdajuice*, and provided with a revised version of the sound models configuration, as summarized in subsection 4.2 . He explored the combination of friction sounds (e.g. A_High_Res and B_Low_Res) with the four interaction strategies proposed for the rolling sound. Unlike the previous explorations with free, unguided squeezing movements, P1 used a metal spaghetti tong. The knowledge of the context now focused the interpretation process. In general, sound A_High_Res was judged more effective for locating the correct posture. The dynamic evolution of the sound when leaving the correct, silent position conveyed a continuous deviation from the correct posture. However, the simplified timbral space didn't foster exploration too much. Sound B_Low_Res conveyed a better perception of the critical states. The hand motion was much more abrupt, and the device seemed more sensitive and fragile.

In this configuration, to find the silent position again, required to maintain a specific harmonic sound. This was interpreted as an "overload" condition, which could be overcome by "relaxing" the device. This increased the interest and curiosity in the timbral space, and the expressiveness of the interaction. P1 noticed the improvement of the control maps, that now allowed a smooth rolling behavior of the virtual ball only for a correct squeezing gesture.

Bumping sounds suggested that the squeezing frequency might be too low or too fast or hectic. The correspondence of the friction sound with suddenly increasing bumping facilitated the interpretation of the border of "correct use". The combination *fast pace and delaying speed* was judged as most playful and effective as it sparked off a clear image of a physical process behind the interaction with the artifact. This observation was confirmed by an independent thinking aloud test carried out by P2.

5   Discussion

A central insight concerns the individual roles that a) sound, b) control maps, and c) interpretation play in the experience and evaluation of sounding interactive artifacts. While strongly intertwined in shaping aesthetic experiences, the experiment procedure shows that changes to one of the three elements can significantly affect the interactive experience.

Sound is a powerful means to define a gestural semantics even when a clear understanding of the intended gestural pattern is not given (test condition 1). Subtle, expressive and dynamic variations foster exploration and willingness to learn. Sound becomes often meaningful in *relation* to another sound, more or less independently from the specific spectro-temporal quality. Despite the simplified glass harmonica timbre, slight changes in the interaction configuration of the friction model resulted in very different aesthetic experiences (test condition 3).

The rolling case showed that a narrative approach to control maps design can provide the designer with effective tools for shaping interactions, as well as sparking the imagination. Rhythm, anticipation, pace, resolution are possible attributes that can be modulated in order to shape interaction [19,4,21].

The interpretive approach, described here, retains the holistic, experiential quality of the interactive experience, but still allows to dissect it into its expressional, interactional and technical aspects. For instance, in the rolling sound case the general experience of a breakdown of control and energy flow was correctly interpreted. However, the specific event of abrupt breakdowns of the rolling sound was reported as an interpretive conflict between an informative display function and an actual technical error. This observation helped to identify the problem in the control map: what is questioned is not the identification of the breakdown, but its cause. In addition, the structured iterative process with pro-tocoled interpretations was effective for sparking new design ideas, in particular in the blind test condition.

5.1   Persistence of the Metatopics in the SDT Implementation

Despite the use of only two sound models (friction and rolling) without fur-ther processing, and simple control maps, the three metatopics, quality of use, energy and control transferred well to the SDT implementation. P1 found an appropriate, meaningful gesture-sound relationship, and constructed a semantic that related strongly to the designer's intention. Particularly in test condition 1 (blind), the dissonant, rough state of the friction model was always interpreted as an altered, overloaded state of the system. In test condition 2 and 3, the coupling of the friction and rolling sounds was correctly related to the notion of stability, as a specific quality of use. In test condition 3, the rolling sound was linked to the energetic state of the mechanism and the quality of control, while the resonating, intermittent bumping sounds were referred to the narratives of destabilization and breakdown.

6   Towards Audio-tactile Interaction with the SDT

It is our intention to explore more systematically the design process here ap-proached. The knowledge about related design strategies will help to inform the design of virtual lutheries and Foley pits. We expect to produce a descriptive matrix of metatopics, interaction attributes, and dynamic properties of sound models, thus contributing to the formulation of SID design heuristics.

So far we emphasized the importance of the auditory modality, and considered the haptic channel only for its possible role in sensory substitution. However, the experiment reported here reveals two important aspects of our approach in relation to the haptic channel. First, both the balancing and the squeezing tasks we have constructed have rich haptic affordances. The second is related to the physicality of our approach; as we have pointed out in [10], we can link a physics-based sound synthesis environment such as the SDT to a haptic interface by the direct exchange of physical variables. This section elaborates these aspects.

The interpretation and evaluation of the experiments indicates that both tasks were constructed with associated tactile qualities. The notion of a physical space, proffered in the first task, was interpreted as determining several regions and their boundaries within this space, although only indicated by sonic feedback in our experiments. The tactile feedback could enhance these structures. In the second task, a simple object, the spaghetti tong, helped to clarify the gestural space, thus confirming a valuable use of haptic feedback.

Previously in [10], we have investigated how to link a physical model for digital sound synthesis with a haptic interface [14]. Physics-based models preserve the interaction fidelity in synthetic sound, and can naturally be controlled by our gestures and actions. These properties have made physical models, such as the SDT, favorable in integrated haptic and audio interfaces [9]: we can transform audio signals in a dual variable pair of force and displacement, define the notions of energy, impedance, and admittance for object blocks, and manage their physically-based interaction. This approach will be used in our future work.

7 Conclusion

We have presented a pilot study aimed at combining the power of a narrative sound design with the sonic aesthetics of the physics-based approach. The study aimed at setting the foundation for a systematic investigation of connections between narrative discourse, aesthetic attributes and sonic dynamic properties of interactive commodities. The emerging process allows intuitive explorations, embraces interpretation, and is easy to implement. In addition, it is a promising method for exploiting the potential of physical modeling in the design of audio-tactile interactions. It can represent a novel tool in interaction design education.

References

1. Albers, J.: Interaction of Color, 1st edn. Yale University Press, New Haven (2008)
2. Altinsoy, M.E.: The effect of auditory cues on the audiotactile roughness perception: Modulation frequency and sound pressure level. In: Pirhonen, A., Brewster, S. (eds.) HAID 2008. LNCS, vol. 5270, pp. 120–129. Springer, Heidelberg (2008)
3. Ament, V.T.: The Foley Grail. Focal Press (2009)
4. Aschersleben, G.: Temporal control of movements in sensorimotor synchronization. Brain and Cognition 48(1), 66–79 (2002)
5. Avanzini, F., Serafin, S., Rocchesso, D.: Interactive simulation of rigid body interaction with friction-induced sound generation. IEEE Transactions on Speech and Audio Processing 13(5), 1073–1081 (2005)
6. Buxton, B.: Sketching User Experiences: Getting the Design Right and the Right Design. Morgan Kaufmann, San Francisco (2007)
7. Chang, A., O'Sullivan, C.: An audio-haptic aesthetic framework influenced by visual theory. In: Pirhonen, A., Brewster, S. (eds.) HAID 2008. LNCS, vol. 5270, pp. 70–80. Springer, Heidelberg (2008)
8. Delle Monache, S., Devallez, D., Drioli, C., Fontana, F., Papetti, S., Polotti, P., Rocchesso, D.: Sound design toolkit. Deliverable of Project CLOSED, University of Verona (2009)
9. DiFilippo, D., Pai, D.: The AHI: An audio and haptic interface for contact interactions. In: Proc. ACM Symp. UIST, San Diego, CA USA, pp. 149–158 (November 2000)
10. Erkut, C., Jylhä, A., Karjalainen, M., Altinsoy, E.M.: Audio-tactile interaction at the nodes of a block-based physical sound synthesis model. In: Pirhonen, A., Brewster, S. (eds.) HAID 2008. LNCS, vol. 5270, pp. 25–26. Springer, Heidelberg (2008)

11. Farnell, A.: Designing Sound. Applied Scientific Press, London (2008)
12. Franinovic, K.: Basic interaction design for sonic artefacts in everyday contexts. In: Focused - Current Design Research Projects and Methods, Bern, Switzerland, pp. 95–112. Swiss Design Network (2008)
13. Gaver, W.W.: What in the world do we hear? an ecological approach to auditory event perception. Ecological Psychology 5, 1–29 (1993)
14. Hayward, V., MacLean, K.: Do it yourself haptics: Part I. IEEE Robot. Automat. Mag. 14(4), 88–104 (2007)
15. Hug, D.: Genie in a bottle: Object-sound reconfigurations for interactive commodities. In: Proceedings of Audiomostly 2008, 3rd Conference on Interaction with Sound (2008)
16. Hug, D.: Investigating narrative and performative sound design strategies for interactive commodities. In: Ystad, S., Aramaki, M., Kronland-Martinet, R., Jensen, K. (eds.) Auditory Display - 6th International Symposium, CMMR/ICAD 2009, Copenhagen, Denmark, Revised Papers, May 18-22. LNCS, vol. 5954. Springer, Heidelberg (2010)
17. Jylhä, A., Erkut, C.: A hand clap interface for sonic interaction with the computer. In: CHI EA 2009: Proceedings of the 27th international conference extended abstracts on Human factors in computing systems, pp. 3175–3180. ACM, New York (2009)
18. Krogh, P.G., Petersen, M.G.: Design articulation for aesthetics of interaction. In: DPPI 2009: Proceedings of the 2009 conference on Designing pleasurable products and interfaces (2009)
19. Lim, Y.K., Stolterman, E., Jung, H., Donaldson, J.: Interaction gestalt and the design of aesthetic interactions. In: DPPI 2007: Proceedings of the 2007 conference on Designing pleasurable products and interfaces, pp. 239–254. ACM, New York (2007)
20. Lim, Y.-K., Stolterman, E., Tenenberg, J.: The anatomy of prototypes: Prototypes as filters, prototypes as manifestations of design ideas. ACM Trans. Comput.-Hum. Interact. 15(2), 1–27 (2008)
21. Löwgren, J.: Toward an articulation of interaction esthetics. New Review of Hypermedia and Multimedia 15(2), 1361–4568 (2009)
22. MacLean, K., Hayward, V.: Do it yourself haptics: Part II. IEEE Robot. Automat. Mag. 15(1), 104–119 (2008)
23. Rath, M., Rocchesso, D.: Continuous sonic feedback from a rolling ball. IEEE MultiMedia 12(2), 60–69 (2005)
24. Rocchesso, D., Polotti, P., Delle Monache, S.: Designing continuous sonic interaction. International Journal of Design 3(3), 13–25 (2009)
25. Sinico, M.: Demonstration in experimental phenomenology. Theory & Psychology 18(6), 853–863 (2008)
26. van den Doel, K., Kry, P.G., Pai, D.K.: Foleyautomatic: physically-based sound effects for interactive simulation and animation. In: SIGGRAPH 2001: Proceedings of the 28th annual conference on Computer graphics and interactive techniques, pp. 537–544. ACM, New York (2001)
27. Visell, Y., Law, A., Smith, S., Rajalingham, R., Cooperstock, J.: Contact sensing and interaction techniques for a distributed, multimodal floor display. In: IEEE 3D User Interfaces (2010)
28. Zimmerman, J., Forlizzi, J.: The role of design artifacts in design theory construction. Artifact 2(1), 1749–3463 (2008)

Tactile Web Browsing for Blind Users

Ravi Kuber[1], Wai Yu[2], and M. Sile O'Modhrain[3]

[1] UMBC, 1000 Hilltop Circle, Baltimore, MD 21250, USA
[2] Thales, Alanbrooke Road, Belfast, BT6 9HB, UK
[3] Queen's University Belfast, University Road, Belfast BT7 1NN, UK
rkuber@umbc.edu

Abstract. Recent developments in tactile technologies have made them an attractive choice to improve access to non-visual interfaces. This paper describes the design and evaluation of an extension to an existing browser, which enables blind individuals to explore web pages using tactile feedback. Pins are presented via a tactile mouse to communicate the presence of graphical interface objects. Findings from an evaluation have revealed that fifteen participants were able to learn the tactile HTML mappings developed, and were able to perform a range of web-based tasks in a less constrained manner than using a screen reader alone. The mappings presented in this paper, can be used by web developers with limited experience of tactile design, to widen access to their sites.

Keywords: Blind, human factors, tactile, web browsing.

1 Introduction

Tactile technologies play a vital role in supporting exploration of an interface by blind individuals. In contrast with speech-based output, which mainly provides an overview of the textual content present on a graphical user interface (GUI), tactile cues can be used to communicate the layout of objects (e.g. icons, textboxes and buttons) through cutaneous stimulation of the skin. Examples include the non-visual system described by Petrie et al. [1], where a touch-sensitive pad is used to provide a spatial overview of a GUI, while a Braille display enables direct manipulation of objects at a finer level. Wall and Brewster [2] have represented graph-based data using a tactile mouse. Pins are presented underneath the fingertips to indicate the presence and height of bars, providing the user with an alternative to raised paper graphs. BrailleSurf [3] has been developed to browse the Web. The tool synthesizes the contents of a page directly through to a Braille or a speech output device. The HTML source code is analyzed by the application, graphical objects are filtered and the page is restructured in a textual way to aid effective comprehension of page content. Rotard et al. [4] have presented text, graphics and other interface objects (e.g. tables, lists and frames) from web sites on a tactile graphics display. The content is presented in Braille format, while images are displayed in tactile pin format. The solution has addressed the issue of limited graphical information presented via screen readers. However, it still remains to be seen whether users can access the tactile information coherently, or whether the user will be overloaded with the amount of stimuli present.

R. Nordahl et al. (Eds.): HAID 2010, LNCS 6306, pp. 75–84, 2010.
© Springer-Verlag Berlin Heidelberg 2010

The limited number of tactile web browsing interfaces is rather surprising owing to the fact that touch is used by a number of blind individuals for both communication (e.g. Braille) and understanding graphical concepts (e.g. raised paper diagrams). Exploring a web page using an device such as a tactile mouse, would enable blind users to explore the page freely, rather than dealing with the constraints of navigation using a screen reader where the user is required to move sequentially through objects. It would also enable the structure of the web page to be retained, aiding a range of tasks which can pose challenges when using existing assistive technologies. Examples of these tasks include moving through unfamiliar pages where content is tightly-packed, filling out web-based forms, and collaborative tasks with sighted users (Murphy et al., [5]). In this paper, we describe the development and evaluation of tactile cues for a non-visual browsing interface, to provide blind users with an overview of the layout of content and to provide assistance with the process of navigation.

2   Existing Non-visual Browsing System

A content-aware plug-in was developed for the Firefox browser, to overcome the challenges faced when using a screen reader. The solution enables blind individuals to explore web pages using a force-feedback mouse (Figure 1) [5]. Cues such as spatial textures, magnetic effects and vibrations were mapped to various graphical objects on the GUI [6]. Text-based content from the interface was also presented using the Microsoft Speech SDK. As the user moves around the interface, cues are presented via the mouse, enabling users to develop a mental representation of the layout of content.

Fig. 1. Logitech Wingman force-feedback mouse (www.logitech.com)   **Fig. 2.** VT Player tactile mouse (www.virtouch2.com)

To extend the research, we wanted to identify the ways in which tactile pin-based cues could be developed to offer the structural and navigational benefits achieved through the use of a force-feedback mouse. The aim was to develop a library of tactile sensations which web developers could reference, and integrate with their sites to make them more accessible to blind users. This would allow the users to utilize the type of feedback (e.g. tactile or force-feedback) that best suits their preferences.

3   Developing Tactile Cues for the Browsing System

The VT Player (Figure 2) has been chosen as a means of presenting tactile information to blind users. Two cells are positioned on top of the mouse, each containing a matrix of sixteen pins. These pins can be raised to form patterns, which are discretely presented underneath the fingertips. A series of tactile cues were integrated into a web page, to be presented via the tactile mouse. Patterns were developed by drawing inferences from the earlier workshops performed in the study by Kuber et al. [6], where blind screen reader users and haptic interface designers had worked together to advise on ways to convey the presence of icons using force-feedback. Examples are shown in Table 1, with a more definitive listing of other objects in Kuber [7].

Table 1. Inferences made to design tactile cues

Objects	Force-Feedback Representation	Inferences Drawn	Tactile Representation
Images	A slightly lowered or raised enclosure effect to encase the visual border. A spatial texture applied to the image's interior.	Border needed to convey outline, with interior texture to communicate body.	All pins raised on the left-hand contactor in the shape of a block.
Hyperlinks	A spring effect to direct the user towards the relative centre of a hyperlink. Optional use of distinctive spatial texture or weak periodic wave effect to communicate body.	Provide awareness of the length of the text string to be selected.	Middle two horizontal rows are raised on one contactor pad.
Textbox	A lowered enclosure effect applied to a text box, to enable the user to explore its contents.	Present the outline of a text box.	Pins raised in outline of a square with no interior.

A participatory-based approach was adopted to design tactile feedback tailored to the needs of blind web users. One blind screen reader user, one tactile interface designer, and one blind tactile interface designer who had participated in the workshop to determine the design of force-feedback cues (termed 'force feedback workshop'), were asked to participate in a new workshop (termed 'tactile workshop'), with the aim of suggesting and prototyping ideas for communicating graphical objects on a web page using tactile feedback. Participants were presented with a scenario of a blind employee using a tactile mouse to access a search engine. They were asked to comment on the different types of feedback that would benefit him in his particular situation. The researcher read aloud the scenario (*below*) to the group, with gaps where the character in the scenario encountered an object. Within each gap, the researcher asked each of the participants to evaluate the tactile mappings designed which were presented on the web pages developed.

John encounters a textbox underneath his fingertips. This is indicated by a pin pattern <<play tactile sensation>>. He then clicks the device when positioned over the box <<play tactile sensation>>. He feels a small stimulus from the pad of the device <<play tactile sensation>>, so knows that the cursor is positioned in the box and he is able to enter his search term.

The group was encouraged to suggest design ideas for communicating graphical icons, and had the option of mocking these up using a series of props. These included headed pins which could be quickly arranged to represent the patterns by placing into a sponge (Figure 3). Two sponges could be adjacently positioned to convey the stimuli presented by the two contactor pads of the mouse.

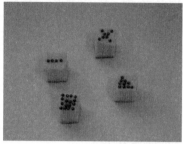 

Fig. 3. Headed pins are arranged into patterns, and inserted into sponges (props)

Fig. 4. Support aid for mouse enabling user to move vertically and horizontally in straight line

Participants from the tactile workshop stated the majority of design ideas presented to them were appropriate for use on a web page. For example, to convey the notion of a hyperlink, pins were arranged into the shape of a long bar on one contactor pad by raising the appropriate pins on the mouse. Further discussion by the group resulted in the strengthening of the idea. Participants suggested that additional feedback should be offered to indicate the status of the link when selected. Using an identical representation of a bar on the second contactor pad, would provide the user with the awareness needed of selection (Table 2).

The blind participants suggested that by providing a distinctive stimulus to indicate the presence that a textbox had been selected, valuable contextual information would be provided to a blind user when filling out a form. He/she would then know that text could be entered within the box, as the object was active. A sequence of pins raised and lowered in a time sequence, was thought by the group to grab the user's attention. This effect was mocked-up and presented for a period of two seconds. The group suggested that this 'animated stimulus' should be on-going as long as the user remains positioned inside the box, to heighten awareness of position on the interface. The user would have otherwise missed the cue due to its short duration.

Discussion continued until all members of the group achieved consensus on design ideas. Table 2 displays the tactile stimuli designed as part of the system, which originated from the tactile workshop. These tactile cues were developed and integrated into the non-visual browsing tool, enabling the user to perceive a tactile mapping when alighting over a graphical object.

The blind participants from the group found it difficult to move in a straight line both vertically and horizontally using the VT Player device, due to the lack of reference points available. Participants suggested that it was difficult to detect twisting or rotations of the mouse, also identified by Jansson and Pederson [8]. This prompted participants to suggest the design of a support structure for the mouse (Figure 4), which would allow the device to move along a slider both vertically and horizontally, enabling the user to maintain a straight path. This would enable the researchers to determine the usability of the tactile feedback, without having to consider problems with the device itself.

4   Evaluation

The aim of the evaluation process was to validate the benefit provided by cues which had been developed through the course of the tactile workshop. The main hypothesis examined was that the tactile cues designed, would be able to provide the structural and navigational support missing from presentation via a screen reader. The tasks selected were also used in an evaluation six months earlier, to validate the force-feedback plug-in (Kuber et al., [7]). However, web pages presented were manipulated (i.e. objects were arranged in different positions) to ensure that even if participants would have remembered the layout of content, it would have not assisted them in their tasks.

4.1   Participants and Training

Ten sighted and five fully-blind screen reader users, all aged between 20 and 68, were recruited for the study. None had previously made use of the tactile mouse for purposes of browsing. The sighted participants were blindfolded for the study. Participants were introduced to a web page containing all the tactile representations shown in Table 2. Speech icons were presented when hovering over blocks of text, hyperlinks, and alternative text associated with images. Participants were asked to explore the interface using the tactile mouse with support aid (Figure 4), and describe each pin-based cue presented by the mouse, followed by the object's respective location on the interface.

4.2   Procedure

Participants were asked to perform two main tasks to determine whether the hypothesis would be supported. The tasks selected were found by Murphy et al. [5] to pose a challenge to some screen reader users when performing them.

Task 1 - Determining the Layout of Objects
The pages used in the current study contained a larger number of interface objects (two images, eight hyperlinks and one image-hyperlink) (Figure 5 - left). Participants were provided with a maximum of three minutes to 'think-aloud', identifying any interface objects that were encountered. If participants were unable to explore the whole page, prompts were presented by the researcher to explore the remainder of content. For example, 'move the mouse to the left-hand side of the page and explore'. They were then asked to either draw or arrange tactile objects (Lego) to indicate the layout of content perceived.

Task 2 – Targeting Objects of Interest
A different web page was presented to participants. It contained thirteen hyperlinks, two images and text, all positioned in relatively close proximity to one another (Figure 6). Participants were asked to locate and retrieve information from three separate locations on the page:

- Counting the number of links presented horizontally at the top of the page (Q1).
- Naming the third hyperlink listed vertically under 'Further Information' (Q2).
- Targeting and selecting the email address of the named contact (Q3).

Table 2. Library of sensations to communicate the identity of web-based objects using tactile feedback

Interface Objects	Description of tactile representations	Tactile representations (Raised pins shaded)	Interface Objects	Description of tactile representations	Tactile representations (Raised pins shaded)
Images	All pins raised on the left-hand contactor in the shape of a block.		Text box	Pins raised in outline of a square. Animated stimulus to communicate that the box is active, when selected.	
Hyperlinks	Middle two horizontal rows of pins are raised on one contactor pad. May need additional directional support if moving horizontally through a series of links.	When located: When selected:	Buttons	Middle two horizontal rows of pins are raised on one contactor pad to represent button. Additional auditory icon required to differentiate from the hyperlink mapping. If selected, further feedback should be presented via a flashing pin pattern on second contactor.	When located: When selected:
Image-hyperlinks	All pins raised on the left-hand contactor in the shape of a block. Middle two horizontal rows are raised on right-hand contactor pad.		Adverts	The shape of a cross or X can be visualized when presented in tactile format under the fingertips. Ensure that it can be differentiated from outer border sensations.	
Page border	One line of pins raised on the contactor pad(s), reflecting the side of the page where cursor is located.		Headings	Pins raised in the outline of a rectangle over two contactor pads. Can be reduced in size to represent a smaller heading (e.g. a sub-heading).	
Area outside page border	Chessboard style texture (e.g. presentation of alternate pins forming a pattern).		Page Background	No feedback for background or text.	

A questionnaire was then presented, to solicit views on the experience using tactile feedback to explore the Web. Issues such as confidence in use of the tactile mouse and the ability to distinguish between stimuli were examined.

4.3 Results and Discussion

Task 1 - Determining the Layout of Objects
Participants were generally able to perceive and identify the majority of tactile feedback presented, as they had been exposed to these cues in the training process. They were then asked to explain the layout of objects on the page (Figure 5 - left). Participants were able to accurately identify the position of the image-link at the top left of the page, with two images aligned vertically underneath it. Other hyperlinks and text present on the page were also identified. It was clear from the descriptions provided, that participants were able to form a mental picture of page layout through the use of tactile feedback, and able to externalize this representation in diagrammatic form. Diagrammatic representations were generally thought to represent the visual nature of the web page, supporting the hypothesis.

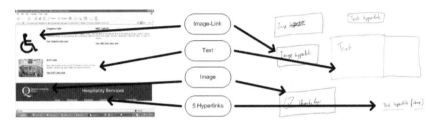

Fig. 5. Example of a blindfolded participant's spatial representation of web page

Inconsistencies were observed in some participants' diagrams. For example, in Figure 5 (right), the image and image-hyperlink are positioned incorrectly. This was not necessarily due to the quality of the tactile cues provided. It could have been attributed to the difficulties remembering the page layout to represent it diagrammatically. These same errors were not present when the participant provided a verbal description of the page layout.

Task 2 - Search and Targeting Tasks
In order to more comprehensively address the hypothesis, participants were asked to search and target objects. Results indicated that participants performed some subtasks faster than others, taking on average 94.9 seconds (SD: 58.5 seconds). The subtask which caused the most issues was counting the small hyperlinks present on the interface (Q1). Only nine out of fifteen participants were able to accurately identify the presence of five links, with others suggesting between three and four. Participants generally spent longer performing this sub-task compared to Q2 and Q3, with two spending over 180 seconds counting hyperlinks. Difficulties could have been due in part to the small size of the hyperlinks and their spatial proximity to each other. When moving the mouse quickly, it was difficult to identify gaps in between the hyperlinks. All fifteen participants were able to accurately complete Q2 and Q3.

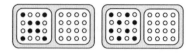

Fig. 6. Mapping for advert (left) and mapping for outer border (right)

4.4   Usability of the Interface

Fourteen out of fifteen participants expressed confidence in using tactile feedback to explore a web interface, as they thought that tactile information could be used to provide an effective overview of page layout. Participants described the tactile feedback to be more subtle compared to force-feedback which could on occasion be intrusive. The one participant who disagreed with the statement felt that further practice with the cues would have increased his levels of confidence in using the tactile device. While the majority of mappings could be distinguished from one another, some participants in the training stage encountered slight difficulties differentiating between adverts and the outer area around the border (Figure 6). This could have been attributed to limited human spatial resolution abilities, and the relatively short duration of the training period itself.

4.5   Blind Participants' Perceptions of Tactile Exploration

Results indicated that blind participants completed sub-tasks on average 33.2 seconds (SD: 23.2 seconds) faster than their blindfolded sighted counterparts. When questioned on their ability to manipulate the mouse, participants stated that controlled movements could be made using the device, simplifying the process of both focusing-in on an object, and enabling them to explore the relationship between items on a page. They suggested that the tactile browsing solution developed addressed the constrained method of navigation faced when using a screen reader. While the tactile mouse was larger than an ordinary mouse, it would not attract too much attention from others in the work environment. The main problem encountered was gauging object size. It was difficult for some participants to suggest whether images were large or small compared to the relative size of the page. This may have been due to the low resolution of the device, also discussed by Wall and Brewster [2].

4.6   Comparisons with Mappings from Other Studies

In terms of similarities, Rotard et al. [4] have used solid lines to represent the outline of borders of objects (e.g. tables). In the tactile workshop described in this paper, participants suggested that one line of raised pins would be able to indicate the edge of the page. The spatial position of this line when presented via the VT Player mouse, would provide further information about the location of the border (e.g. if the line is on the left edge of pin matrix, it would suggest that the user is positioned at the left-hand border of the page). Discussion prompted participants to extend the idea by suggesting using an animated directional effect to provide awareness of the edge of the page window. This would offer gentle persuasion for the user not to leave the confines of the page, unless he/she really wanted to do so.

Certain findings from our participatory-based approach differed from other work. For example, Rotard et al. [4] have represented headings through the use of Braille, providing information about the actual HTML tag used on the web page. Participants in our study believed that the user should not need to learn HTML code or Braille in order to explore a page. Instead participants felt that the heading should be conveyed using pins raised forming the outline of a bar. They suggested that the pin pattern should be varied in size depending on whether the object is a main heading or sub-heading. Braille has also been used to communicate contextual information on the GUIB interface. Mynatt and Weber [9] have suggested that text attributes such as font and color changes) can be presented in this way. Findings from our evaluation, revealed that while participants were able to learn the mappings presented, they suggested that too much tactile information on a page would lead to overload.

While some parallels can be drawn between findings from our study and other work, using a participatory-based design approach has led to the development of targeted feedback addressing the needs of blind users when performing web-based tasks which were difficult to perform solely using a screen reader [5].

5 Conclusion and Future Work

This paper has described the development of pin-based tactile cues for browsing the Web. Blind screen reader users and tactile interface designers were able to suggest and strengthen design ideas, using the novel design approach. Findings from the evaluation have helped to validate the tactile cues developed (Table 2), demonstrating that tactile information can be used to provide the structural and navigational support missing from speech-based screen reader presentation. These cues can be replicated by web developers, enabling them to provide an accessible representation of content for their blind users. In terms of future work, we aim to perform a more comprehensive comparative evaluation between the tactile and force-feedback cues, examining a number of browsing scenarios to determine whether one form of feedback is more appropriate for performing particular web-based tasks.

Acknowledgements

We would like to thank Emma Murphy, Philip Strain, Graham McAllister and Henry H. Emurian for their input into this work. This research was supported by Eduserv.

References

1. Petrie, H., Morley, S., Weber, G.: Tactile-based direct manipulation in GUIs for blind users. In: CHI 1995, pp. 428–429. ACM Press, New York (1995)
2. Wall, S., Brewster, S.A.: Feeling what you hear: tactile feedback for navigation of audio graphs. In: CHI 2006, pp. 1123–1132. ACM Press, New York (2006)
3. Hadjadj, D., Burger, D.: BrailleSurf: An HTML browser for visually handicapped people. In: Technology and Persons with Disabilities Conference (1999)

4. Rotard, M., Knodler, S., Ertl, T.: A tactile web browser for the visually disabled. In: ACM Conference on Hypertext and Hypermedia, pp. 15–22. ACM Press, New York (2005)
5. Murphy, E., Kuber, R., McAllister, G., Strain, P., Yu, W.: An empirical investigation into the difficulties experienced by visually impaired Internet users. Universal Access in the Information Society 7(1), 79–91 (2008)
6. Kuber, R., Yu, W., McAllister, G.: Towards developing assistive haptic feedback for visually impaired Internet users. In: CHI 2007, pp. 1525–1534. ACM Press, New York (2007)
7. Kuber, R.: Developing assistive haptic guidelines for improving non-visual access to the Web. Unpublished Ph.D. Thesis. Queen's University Belfast, UK (2008)
8. Jansson, G., Pederson, P.: Obtaining geographical information from a virtual map with a haptic mouse. In: 22nd International Cartographic Conference (2005)
9. Mynatt, E.D., Weber, G.: Nonvisual presentation of graphical user interfaces: contrasting two approaches. In: CHI 1994, pp. 166–172. ACM Press, New York (1994)

Reducing Reversal Errors in Localizing the Source of Sound in Virtual Environment without Head Tracking

Vladimir Ortega-González*, Samir Garbaya, and Frédéric Merienne

Arts et Metiers ParisTech, CNRS, Le2i
Institut Image, 2 rue T. Dumorey, Chalon-sur-Saône 71000, France
erikvladimir@gmail.com

Abstract. This paper presents a study about the effect of using additional audio cueing and Head-Related Transfer Function (HRTF) on human performance in sound source localization task without using head movement. The existing techniques of sound spatialization generate reversal errors. We intend to reduce these errors by introducing sensory cues based on sound effects. We conducted and experimental study to evaluate the impact of additional cues in sound source localization task. The results showed the benefit of combining the additional cues and HRTF in terms of the localization accuracy and the reduction of reversal errors. This technique allows significant reduction of reversal errors compared to the use of the HRTF separately. For instance, this technique could be used to improve audio spatial alerting, spatial tracking and target detection in simulation applications when head movement is not included.

1 Introduction

In this paper we present an approach to improve the accuracy of sound localization without human head tracking. Human auditory system has poor resolution in source localization [4]. However, according to the published research, the existing techniques of sound spatialization do not allow localizing sound sources with a resolution higher than provided by human natural hearing. The resolution could be very close to natural conditions depending on the employed model [21]. This leads to the conclusion that the existing techniques of spatial sound do not allow localizing sound source accurately.

Spatialized sound is used in different virtual reality applications for two main purposes: the simulation of acoustics in virtual environment. The second purpose is to enhance the quality interaction by means of spatial audio feedback.

The impact of 3D sound on presence and realism within the context of acoustics simulation has been already investigated (e.g. Hendrix and Barfield [9] and Larsson et al. [11]). The related studies concluded that the contribution of 3D sound is significant for the sensation of presence but not for realism.

---

* Corresponding author.

R. Nordahl et al. (Eds.): HAID 2010, LNCS 6306, pp. 85–96, 2010.
© Springer-Verlag Berlin Heidelberg 2010

The use of 3D sound in interactive applications has been studied by different authors. The main related applications are concerned with the audio spatial tracking, the audio spatial alerting and the assisted navigation.

The audio-assisted navigation refers to the use of 3D sound to provide the user with information to assist the navigation in unknown environment. This application of 3D sound has been subject of different research works (e.g. Lumbreras and Sánchez [13], Lokki et al. [12] and Walker and Lindsay [20]).

The audio spatial tracking refers to the capacity of detecting and following a moving target represented by a sound source. The effect of 3D sound for spatial tracking was studied by Mckinley et al. [15]. The authors found that the use of spatial auditory information contributes to better target detection. Bronkhorst el al. [3] presented a study of the effect of 3D sound for tracking targets in a flight simulator. They founded that 3D sound is suitable for complementing and for replacing visual displays such as the radar.

The audio spatial alerting refers to the displaying of spatially localized audio alerts. These spatial audio alerts can be more easily differentiated and they can convey spatial information. Ho and Spence [10] investigated on the benefits of audio spatial alerting in potentially dangerous situations in driving. According to their results, the use of spatial audio allows an effective way of capturing the attention of the driver better than non-spatial alarms.

The approach presented in this paper is based in the combination of the commonly used spatialization technique (HRTF: Head-Related Transfer Function) with additional sensory cues. The result is that 3D sound is enriched with additional audion cues. The existing techniques related to audio spatial tracking and alerting allow acceptable results but the reduction of reversal errors and the improvement of localization accuracy could produce better interaction quality.

The presence of reversal errors in audio spatial tracking and alerting can induce errors in the interaction and reduce human performance. These errors can be potentially important depending on the application. For instance, a target or an alert which is identified by the user as coming from a wrong direction. In these applications, the listener normally do not have time to make use of head movement to localize sound sources, for these reasons we focus our study on localization task when information about head movement is not provided.

2   Related Work

In this section two main issues are presented: the technique of reference of sound spatialization based on the HRTFs and the existing approaches to improve sound source localization by human user in virtual environment.

2.1   Sound Source Localization and the Head Related Transfer Function

The Head Related Transfer Function (HRTF) is a filter which expresses how an acoustic wave is affected by the anatomy of the listener. Begault [1] stated that HRTF represents the spectral filtering which occurs before the arrival of the sound to the internal ear drum. These filters recreate the natural altering effect on listened sounds caused by the morphology of each auricle as well as by the diffraction and reflection effects due to the head and shoulders respectively. These effects vary from individual to individual forcing systems designers to choose between the use of individualized or generalized filters.

Since interaural time and intensity differences are ambiguous under certain conditions, generalized HRTFs and more particularly customized HRTFs, are useful for reducing the presence of front-back and up/down (reversals) errors and of cones of confusion [1]. However, the implementation of customized HRTF requires specialized facilities, specialized equipment and specialized audio treatment processes. This is time consuming and relatively expensive. These elements make difficult the use of customized HRTF in virtual environment particularly considering that the cost of other immersive components is also high.

Wenzel et al. [21] conducted a series of experiments to evaluate the pertinence of non-individualized HRTF for virtual acoustic displaying. Authors observed that generalized HRTF makes users obtain a very similar angular accuracy in both real conditions and with 3D sound rendering. They also noticed that the use of generalized functions increases the rate of reversal errors.

Begault et al. [2] conducted an experiment to compare the effect of magnetic head-tracking, reverberation and generalized and individualized HRTF with non-speech sound for spatial displaying. They worked with a group of untrained subjects that indicated their judgements by using a graphic interface. According to their results, head tracking significantly helps to reduce angle errors and particularly to avoid reversals; reverberation helps azimuth precision; and the use of generic HRTF only affects slightly the perception compared to individualized HRTF. The reported mean angle errors vary from 15 to 25 degrees for both azimuth and elevation. This work is relevant to our study because the experimental conditions of the study described in this paper are similar.

2.2   Improving Sound Localization in Virtual Environment

There exist different approaches aiming at improving the localization accuracy of sound sources in virtual environment. Durlach et al. [4] presented the approach of supernormal auditory localization. This proposal is based on altering the azimuth of the used HRTF based on a transformation (mapping) function. A complement of this work can be found in Shinn-Cunningham et al. ([18] and [19]). This work is restricted to sound sources localized in the horizontal plane.

Gronh and Takala [7,8] presented an approach named MagicMikes for the sonification of localized data sets into a navigation context. This approach considers the use of audio cueing and audio spatialization. Gronh et al. [6] presented a study for evaluating localization accuracy in immersive environment with multichannel systems. The obtained results vary from 11 to 14 degrees in azimuth and from 22 to 27 in elevation.

Marentakis and Brewster [14] conducted an experiment of comparing different interactive audio cues for improving the efficiency of localization of sound sources. They tested different sources positioned in the horizontal plane. They obtained an accuracy error vary from 4 to 15 degrees in azimuth.

Lokki et al. [12] presented a study of the effect of spatial audio cueing on user performance for the navigation of virtual environments. The authors found that audio cueing have significant effect on performance (in terms of execution time) and that it is possible to navigate using audio cues only. One interesting point of this work is the combination of parametric cues with sound spatialization for improving sound source localization in elevation.

In contrast to the approach presented in this paper, the existing techniques relating to the improvement of sound localization are limited to the case where sound sources are located in the horizontal plane. The objective of our approach is to assist localization in both elevation and azimuth.

3   The Approach of HRTF and Additional Cues

The approach is based on spatial sound sources enriched with specialized cues. These cues provide the user with information which is intended to assist them in the execution of specific tasks. Each audio cue is associated to a parametrized sound effect. This association is determined by a mapping function defined by a behavior curve.

The proposed approach considers that the additional cues enrich the signal before the application of the HRTF model. In order to avoid the technical requirements of individualization, a generalized HRTFs is used. The HRTF database used in the work described in this paper is the KEMAR HRTF database created by Gardner [5] at the MIT Media Lab Machine Listening Group.

The used additional cues are detailed in Table 1. For each cue the associated audio effect as well as the corresponding parameter are specified. These parameters depend on the angular difference between the user head and the direction of origin of the sound source. The mapping of each effect and the corresponding parameter is specified by a behavior curve (Figure 1). These curves were defined empirically and adjusted during the pre-tests. The values of the parameters vary dynamically depending on the user activity.

The term of frontality refers to the ability to distinguish whether the sound source is localized in the front or at the back of the user. The technique is to use a lowpass filter that changes the character of the sound when it is localized at the back of the user. Thus, subjects perceive an occluded sound for absolute azimuth angles bigger than 90 degrees. The corresponding behavior curve is specified in figure 1a.

Table 1. Additional cues

Cue	Effect	Variable	Parameter	Range
Verticality	Reverb	Level	Elevation	$[-10k, 2k]mdB$
Horizontality	Attenuation	Factor	Azimuth	$[-40, 0]dB$
Frontality	Highpass	Cutoff Freq.	Azimuth	$[1, 22k]Hz$
Angular Proximity	Lowpass	Cutoff Freq.	Overall angle	$[200, 22k]Hz$

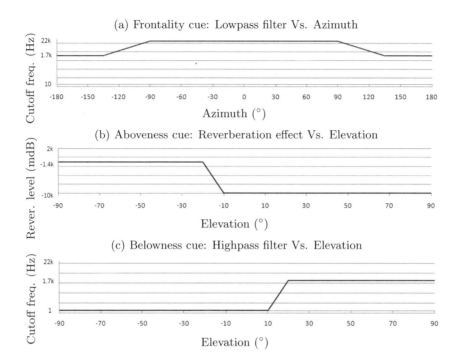

Fig. 1. Behavior curves characterizing the response of the different applied effects in terms of the defined parameters of the additional cues. The vertical axis of subfigures (a) and (c) are plot in logarithmic scale.

The term belowness refers to whenever the sound source is localized below the horizontal reference plane of the listener. For cueing this information we use the reverberation effect. In this manner, the sound sources in low elevations will be distinguishable by this extra reverberation. The corresponding behavior curve is shown in the figure 1c.

The term aboveness refers to whenever the sound source is localized above the listener. The technique is to use a highpass filter that changes the character of the sound when it is localized in high elevations. In this manner, the sound is more acute in high elevations. The behavior curve characterizing this cue is shown in the figure 1b.

The selected sound stimulus was obtained from the sound library Sound Rangers (2009) [16] and its waveform has a clink shape. It is a brief sound with a duration of 0.5 seconds approximately and it is reproduced continuously. The main criteria for selecting this kind of waveform is that brief stimuli have commonly less information to be decoded compared to a voice signals and that it could be more intelligible (easy to recognize), less diffused and probably less annoying than almost any kind of noise signal.

4   Experiment Design

The objective of the experiment is to determine the contribution of the additional cues when added to the HRTF in the localization accuracy and the rate of detected reversal errors. The source localization is made by a pointer. Head movement is not available. The employed HRTF is generalized. The sound display is made by closed headphones.

4.1   Task and Experimental Conditions

The task consists of localizing the provenance of a sound source with a pointer. The subject is asked to indicate the localization of the sound sound by Novint Falcon device produced by Novint Technologies [17]. The pointer is restricted to move over the surface of a localization sphere with fixed radius. The figures 2a and 2b show the graphic interface and a photograph of the experiment respectively.

Before executing the experiment, each subject has one minute approximately to get familiarized with the additional audio cues. Then, the mechanism of the additional cues is explained to the subject. The user has the possibility to test freely during one minute his sensation of a sound source which position is attached to the pointer. The table 2 presents the coordinates of the different fixed sound sources used in this experiment. The experimental variables are recorded for all these repetitions. These different localizations are presented to each subject randomly.

The experimental conditions are (1) HRTF and (2) Additional cues + HRTF. The condition (1) corresponds to the use of HRTF only. The condition (2) refers to the sound stimulus enriched by the cues and spatialized with the HRTF. Each

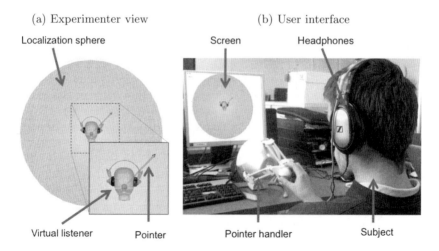

(a) Experimenter view   (b) User interface

Fig. 2. Experiment setup: (a) screenshot of the graphic interface and (b) photograph of a subject executing the task

Table 2. Different sound source locations

Rep.	Azimuth (φ_0)	Elevation (δ_0)	Rep.	Azimuth (φ_0)	Elevation (δ_0)
1	+0.00	+0.00	10	+180.00	+50.00
2	+60.00	+0.00	11	-60.00	+50.00
3	+120.00	+0.00	12	-120.00	+50.00
4	+180.00	+0.00	13	+0.00	-50.00
5	-60.00	+0.00	14	+60.00	-50.00
6	-120.00	+0.00	15	+120.00	-50.00
7	+0.00	+50.00	16	+180.00	-50.00
8	+60.00	+50.00	17	-60.00	-50.00
9	+120.00	+50.00	18	-120.00	-50.00

user performs the experimental conditions in random order. The random order of repetitions and experimental conditions is included to reduce the carry-over effects.

4.2 Group of Subjects

Fifteen subjects (thirteen male and two female) aged from 20 to 30 years old participated in this experiment. They are right-handed and did not report any visual or audio deficiency. They are university students without prior experience with 3D interaction devices.

Each user had to search for the localization of 18 different sound sources in 2 different experimental conditions, which makes 36 records of measures for each participant. The whole experiment, carried out by each subject, took approximately 25 minutes to be completed. Task execution in both experimental conditions are separated by a break of three minutes approximately.

4.3 Performance Measures

The user performance is measured in terms of the following objective variables: the execution time (in seconds) and the angular errors (in degrees). The angular errors are the azimuth, the elevation and the overall angular error. The overall angular error is the angle between the vectors $\overrightarrow{U}$ and $\overrightarrow{V}$ that represent the localization of the sound source and the orientation of the listener's head respectively.

5   Results and Data Analysis

The evaluation of the user performance is based on the measurement of the task execution time, the absolute angular errors (azimuth, elevation and overall angular error) and the percentage of reversal errors (front/back, up/down and left/right). In order to determine the effects of each audio stimulation technique, we performed a Generalized Linear Equations (GEE) model using the collected data.

The table 3 presents the descriptive statistics of the variables of execution time and angular errors for both experimental conditions. Only the valid observations were taken into account. Because the distribution of the data was not assumed to be of normal type, the median and the quartile information were added to the typical statistics measures of mean value and standard deviation. This is carried out in order to provide a more general statistical characterization of the data. The use of the combination of additional cues and HRTF allows reducing the levels of the angular errors. The statistical significance of these difference will be verified later on.

Table 3. Descriptive statistics of the experimental variables for the different conditions (factors) of observations

Condition	Variable	N	Mean	Median	Quartiles			Std.
					Lower	Upper	Range	dev.
1 HRTF	Execution time (s)	252	9.02	7.57	4.94	11.65	6.71	5.49
	Overall error (°)	252	66.64	56.36	37.17	87.97	50.80	41.27
	Azimuth error (°)	252	60.67	39.13	20.41	84.62	64.21	55.21
	Elevation error (°)	252	33.44	31.07	11.50	50.27	38.77	26.40
2 Additional	Execution time (s)	252	9.87	8.46	5.72	12.43	6.71	5.95
cues &	Overall error (°)	252	39.33	35.75	20.59	47.98	27.39	27.14
HRTF	Azimuth error (°)	252	28.50	18.77	4.70	35.32	30.63	35.00
	Elevation error (°)	252	25.79	21.88	9.95	38.70	28.76	19.72

Note: All the statistics measures of the angular errors (azimuth, elevation and overall) were calculated using the absolute values of the corresponding datasets.

The figure 3a shows the boxplots and the mean values of execution time for the experimental conditions. The descriptive values and the dispersion are similar for both conditions. The figure 3b shows the boxplots and the mean values of overall angular error. It is noticed that the descriptive values and the dispersion of data are lower for the condition of combining the additional audio cues and HRFT than for the HRTF only.

The table 4 shows the percentage of the different types of reversal errors for the two experimental conditions. The use of the combination of additional audio cues and HRTF allows reducing the presence of reversal errors. The figures 4a and 4b show the graphical representation of the detected reversals of front/back, and up/down for the experimental conditions respectively. The combined model reduces in approximately 38%, 16% and 10% the rates of front/back, the up/down and the left/right reversals respectively.

The table 5 shows the effects of combining the additional cues with the HRTF on the different experimental measures. The difference in execution time between the experimental conditions is not statistically significant ($p = 0.303$). The effects of the additional cues on the angular errors are statistically significants. The additional cues have statistically significant effects on the rates of detected reversal errors.

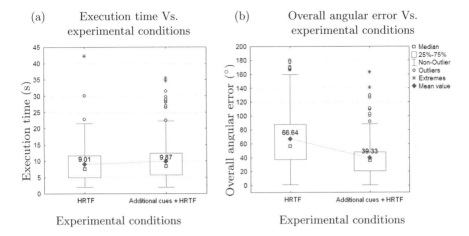

(a)   Execution time Vs.
        experimental conditions

(b)   Overall angular error Vs.
        experimental conditions

Experimental conditions

Experimental conditions

Fig. 3. Box plots and mean values of execution time (a) and overall angular errors (b) for the two experimental conditions

Table 4. Reversal errors for the experimental conditions

Exp. condition	Type of reversal	Observations w/o reversals	Detected reversals	Percent of reversals
1 HRTF	Front/back	129	123	48.81%
	Up/down	177	75	29.76%
	Left/right	216	36	14.29%
2 Additional cues & HRTF	Front/back	225	27	10.71%
	Up/down	218	34	13.49%
	Left/right	240	12	4.76%

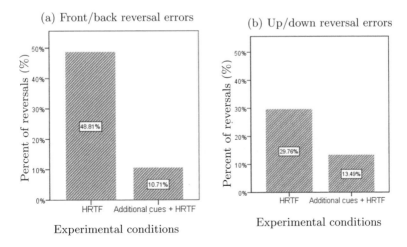

(a) Front/back reversal errors

(b) Up/down reversal errors

Experimental conditions

Experimental conditions

Fig. 4. Percentage of front/back (a) and up/down (b) reversal errors for the experimental conditions

Table 5. Analysis of the effect of factors by the Repeated Measurements Analysis under the Generalized Estimating Equations model

Factor	Variable	Model	Wald χ^2	DF	p	Sig.
Exp. conditions	Execution time (s)	Log-normal	1.061	1	.303	N
	Overall error (°)	Log-normal	34.177	1	.000	Y
	Azimuth error (°)	Exponential	34.478	1	.000	Y
	Elevation error (°)	Exponential	13.320	1	.000	Y
	Front/back reversals (%)	Binomial	94.316	1	.000	Y
	Up/down reversals (%)	Binomial	23.050	1	.000	Y
	Left/right reversals (%)	Binomial	16.525	1	.000	Y

Details of the model: The estimation of the effects is based on the Wald chi-square (χ^2) statistic. The test is of type III for which the order of aggregation of the factors is not relevant. The probability distribution model is indicated for each the variable in the column Model. The confidence level is 95%.

6   Conclusions and Future Work

In this paper we presented an evaluation work of the the approach of combining additional audio cues with the HRTF for sound localization task without the provision of information about head movement. The enriched 3D sound is based on the spatialization technique of HRTF and a group of additional cues associated to sound effects. These cues enrich the sound source with information that intends to assist the user in the localization task. The results show that the addition of audio cues to the HRTF has significant benefits for the improvement of the localization accuracy and the reduction of the rate of detected reversal errors.

Head tracking and customized HRTFs have been typically considered as means to reduce the presence of reversal errors. Nevertheless, head tracking and the use of customized HRTFs are relatively expensive and not suitable for applications of 3D sound of spatial alerting and tracking. The combination of the additional cues and HRTF allows reducing the rates of reversals errors in the absence of head tracking and customized HRTFs.

The future work includes different issues such as the use of head tracking and the comparison of different pointing gestures. The proposed technique is suitable for applications that intend to improve spatial tracking and alerting in simulation such as flight and driving simulation.

By adding information that do not exist in real conditions, the additional audio cues make spatial sound less consistent with the natural phenomena of spatial hearing. Nevertheless, the approach described in this paper and the related applications such as spatial tracking and alerting do not use spatial sound to simulate real acoustics. In these applications, spatial tracking and spatial alerting make use of spatial sound for cueing rather than to provide the user with meaningful spatial information. In this case, the consistency of spatial audio with real conditions is not important.

References

1. Begault, D.: 3D-Sound for Virtual Reality and Multimedia. AP Professional, USA (2005)
2. Begault, D.R., Wenzel, E.M., Anderson, M.R.: Direct Comparison of the Impact of Head Tracking, Reverberation, and Individualized Head-Related Transfer Functions on the Spatial Perception of a Virtual Speech Source. Journal of the Audio Engineering Society 49(10), 916 (2001)
3. Bronkhorst, A.W., Veltman, J.A., van Breda, L.: Application of a three-dimensional auditory display in a flight task. Human factors 38(1), 23–33 (1996)
4. Durlach, N.I., Shinn-Cunningham, B.G., Held, R.M.: Supernormal auditory localization. I. General background. Presence 2(2), 89–103 (1993)
5. Gardner, B., Martin, K.: HRTF Measurements of a KEMAR Dummy-Head Microphone. MIT Media Lab Perceptual Computing, USA (1994)
6. Grohn, M., Lokki, T., Takala, T.: Static and dynamic sound source localization in a virtual room. In: Proc. AES 22nd Int. Conf. on Virtual, Synthetic and Entertainment Audio, pp. 15–17 (2002)
7. Grohn, M., Takala., T.: MagicMikes - Multiple Aerial Probes for Sonification of Spatial Databases. In: Int. Conf. on Auditory Displays (ICAD 1994), Santa Fe, USA, p. 108 (1994)
8. Grohn, M., Takala, T.: MagicMikes - Method for Spatial Sonification. In: IS&T/SPIE Symposium on Electronic Imaging: Science & Technology, San Jose, USA, p. 108 (1995)
9. Hendrix, C., Barfield, W.: Presence in virtual environments as a function of visual and auditory cues. In: VRAIS 1995: Proceedings of the Virtual Reality Annual International Symposium (VRAIS 1995), p. 74. IEEE Computer Society, Washington (1995)
10. Ho, C., Spence, C.: Assessing the effectiveness of various auditory cues in capturing a driver's visual attention. Journal of Experimental Psychology: Applied 11(3), 157–174 (2005)
11. Larsson, P., Vastfjall, D., Kleiner, M.: Effects of auditory information consistency and room acoustic cues on presence in virtual environments. Acoustical Science and Technology 29(2), 191–194 (2008)
12. Lokki, T., Grohn, M.: Navigation with Auditory Cues in a Virtual Environment. IEEE MultiMedia 12(2), 80–86 (2005)
13. Lumbreras, M., Sánchez, J.: Interactive 3D sound hyperstories for blind children. In: CHI 1999: Proceedings of the SIGCHI conference on Human factors in computing systems, pp. 318–325. ACM, New York (1999)
14. Marentakis, G., Brewster, S.A.: A comparison of feedback cues for enhancing pointing efficiency in interaction with spatial audio displays. In: MobileHCI 2005: Proceedings of the 7th international conference on Human computer interaction with mobile devices & services, pp. 55–62. ACM, New York (2005)
15. McKinley, R., D'Angelo, W.R., Hass, M.W., Perrot, D., Nelson, W., Hettinger, L., Brickman, B.: An initial study of the effects of 3-dimensional auditory cueing on visual target detection. In: 39th Human Factors and Ergonomics Society Annual Meeting, USA, pp. 119–123 (1995)
16. Music, R.F.: Sound Rangers sound library (2009) (Sound Effect Refence: ding-wip01), http://www.soundrangers.com/
17. Novint Technologies Inc.: Novint Falcon User Manual (2007), http://home.novint.com/

18. Shinn-Cunningham, B.G., Durlach, N.I., Held, R.M.: Adapting to supernormal auditory localization cues. I. Bias and resolution. Journal of the Acoustical Society of America 103(5), 3656–3666 (1998)
19. Shinn-Cunningham, B.G., Durlach, N.I., Held, R.M.: Adapting to supernormal auditory localization cues. II. Constraints on adaptation of mean response. Journal of the Acoustical Society of America 103(6), 3667–3676 (1998)
20. Walker, B.N., Lindsay, J.: Navigation Performance With a Virtual Auditory Display: Effects of Beacon Sound, Capture Radius, and Practice. Hum. Factors 48(2), 265–278 (2006)
21. Wenzel, E., Arruda, M., Kistler, D., Wightman, F.: Localization using non-individualized head-related transfer functions. Journal of the Acoustical Society of America 93(1), 111–123 (1993)

Conflicting Audio-haptic Feedback in Physically Based Simulation of Walking Sounds

Luca Turchet, Stefania Serafin, Smilen Dimitrov, and Rolf Nordahl

Medialogy, Aalborg University Copenhagen
Lautrupvang 15, 2750 Ballerup, DK
{tur,sts,sd,rn}@media.aau.dk

Abstract. We describe an audio-haptic experiment conducted using a system which simulates in real-time the auditory and haptic sensation of walking on different surfaces. The system is based on physical models, that drive both the haptic and audio synthesizers, and a pair of shoes enhanced with sensors and actuators. Such experiment was run to examine the ability of subjects to recognize the different surfaces with both coherent and incoherent audio-haptic stimuli. Results show that in this kind of tasks the auditory modality is dominant on the haptic one.

1 Introduction

While several studies have investigated the interaction between touch and audition in hand based interactions, to our knowledge, the interaction of auditory and haptic feedback in foot based devices is still an unexplored topic.

A notable exception is the work of Giordano et al., who showed that the feet were also effective at probing the world with discriminative touch, with and without access to auditory information. Their results suggested that integration of foot-haptic and auditory information does follow simple integration rules [1].

In previous research, we described a system able to simulate the auditory and haptic sensation of walking on different materials and presented the results of a preliminary surface recognition experiment [2]. This experiment was conducted under three different conditions: auditory feedback, haptic feedback, and audio-haptic feedback. By presenting the stimuli to the participants passively sitting in a chair, we introduced a high degree of control on the stimulation. However, this method of delivery is highly contrived since it eliminates the tight sensorimotor coupling that is natural during walking and foot interaction. It is true for the auditory channel, but even more so for the haptic channel. In spite of these drastically constrained conditions, performance was surprisingly good.

In particular, the results indicated that subjects were able to recognize most of the stimuli in the audition only condition, and some of the material properties such as hardness in the haptics only condition. Nevertheless, the combination of auditory and haptic cues did not significantly improve recognition.

In a successive research we extended that work improving the developed technology which allowed subjects to walk in a controlled laboratory, where their

R. Nordahl et al. (Eds.): HAID 2010, LNCS 6306, pp. 97–106, 2010.

steps were tracked and used to drive the simulation [4]. Overall, results showed that subjects were able to recognize most of the synthesized surfaces with high accuracy. Results moreover confirmed that auditory modality is dominant on the haptic modality and that the haptic task was more difficult than the other two. Indeed such results showed that subjects performed the recognition task better when using auditory feedback versus haptic feedback, and that the combination of auditory and haptic feedback only in some conditions significantly enhanced the recognition.

Starting from those results, in this paper we investigate in a deeper way the role of dominance of the two modalities involved by means of a preliminary discrimination experiment. In particular, while in previous research we focused on providing coherent stimuli in the auditory and haptic modality, here we provide conflicting stimuli, to understand which modality is dominant.

The results presented in this paper are part of the Natural Interactive Walking (NIW) FET-Open project[1], whose goal is to provide closed-loop interaction paradigms enabling the transfer of skills that have been previously learned in everyday tasks associated to walking. In the NIW project, several walking scenarios are simulated in a multimodal context, where especially audition and haptic feedback play an important role.

2 Simulation Hardware and Software

We developed a system which simulates in real-time the auditory and haptic sensation of walking on different surfaces. A schematic representation of this system is shown in Figure 1. In order to provide both audio and haptic feedback, haptic shoes enhanced with pressure sensors have been developed. The way pressure sensors and actuators are embedded in the sandals can be seen in Figure 2, and a picture of a user wearing the shoes is shown in Figure 3. A complete description of such system and of all its components is given elsewhere in detail [5].

The hardware allows to control in real-time of a sound synthesis engine based on physical models. Such engine is illustrated in our previous research [3,7,6]. The same physical models have been used to drive the haptic and the audio synthesis.

As mentioned in section 1, the system has been evaluated by using it both offline and interactively. The complete results of this evaluation are described in [2,4].

3 Experiment

We conducted an experiment whose goal was to investigate the role of dominance of the audio and haptic modalities during the use of our walking system. Subjects were asked to interact with the system and to recognize the different walking sounds and vibrations they were exposed to.

---

[1] http://www.niwproject.eu/

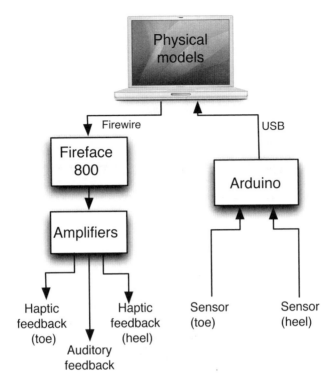

Fig. 1. Diagram illustrating the different hardware components of the system, together with their connections to the PC. The representation is for one shoe.

The experiment consisted of both coherent and incoherent audio-haptic stimuli. In presence of coherent stimuli the same surface material was presented both at audio and haptic level. Instead the provided incoherent stimuli consisted of different surface materials; in particular when at audio level a solid surface was presented, at haptic level an aggregate surface was modeled, and viceversa.

One of our hypotheses was that the audio modality would have dominated the haptic one. Another was that the recognition would have slightly improved using coherent stimuli rather than the incoherent ones. Similarly we hypothesized higher evaluations in terms of realism and quality in presence of coherent stimuli.

3.1 Participants

Ten participants, 7 male and 3 female, aged between 20 and 38 (mean = 25.81, standard deviation = 5.77), were involved in the experiment.

All participants reported normal hearing conditions and all of them were naive with respect to the experimental setup and to the purpose of the experiment.

The participants took on average about 11 minutes to complete the experiment.

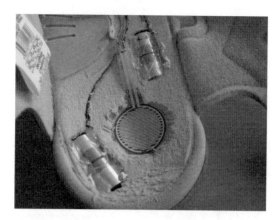

Fig. 2. A picture of one pressure sensor and two actuators embedded in the shoes

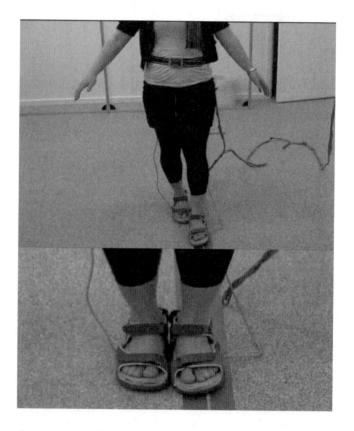

Fig. 3. Top: A user wearing the sandals enhanced with sensors and actuators. Bottom: the sandals.

3.2 Setup

The experiment was carried out in an acoustically isolated laboratory. The walking area was approximately 18 square meters, delimited by the walls of the laboratory.

The setup consisted of the pair of sandals mentioned in section 2, an Arduino board, a Fireface soundcard, a laptop and a set of headphones[2]. In order to facilitate the navigation of the subjects, the wires coming out from the shoes in all setups, as well as the wires connecting the headphones to the soundcard, were linked to a bumbag or to snaplinks attached to trousers.

3.3 Task

During the experiment participants were asked to wear the pair of sandals and the headphones described in sections 2 and 3.2, and to walk in the laboratory.

During the act of walking they listened simultaneously to footsteps sounds and vibrations on a different surface according to the stimulus presented. The task consisted of answering, by writing on a paper, the following three questions after the presentation of the stimulus:

1. Which surface do you think you are walking on? For each stimulus choose a material.
2. How close to real life is the sound in comparison with the surface you think it is? Evaluate the degree of realism on a scale from 1 to 7 (1=low realism, 7=high realism).
3. Evaluate the quality of the sound on a scale from 1 to 7 (1=low quality, 7=high quality).

As opposed to our previous research, participants were not provided with a forced list of possible choices. This was due to the fact that we wanted subjects to be somehow creative in their recognition of the surface, without guessing from a predefined list.

Subjects were informed that they could use the interactive system as much as they wanted before giving an answer. They were also told that they could choose the same material more than one time. When passed to the next stimulus they could not change the answer to the previous stimuli.

At the conclusion of the experiment, participants were asked some questions concerning the naturalness of the interaction with the system and to comment on its usability and possible integration in a virtual reality environment. In particular the questionnaire was the following:

- Imagine that this is part of a system used to navigate in a computer game, answer to the following questions:
  1. How natural is the interaction? Evaluate on a scale from 1 to 7 (1=little natural, 7=very natural)

---

[2] Sennheiser HD 600, http://www.sennheiser.com

2. How normal do you feel during the act of walking? Evaluate on a scale from 1 to 7 (1=little normal, 7=very normal)
3. How constrained do you feel during the act of walking? Evaluate on a scale from 1 to 7 (1=little constrained, 7=very constrained)

In addition they were also given the opportunity to leave an open comment on their experience interacting with the system.

3.4   Experimental Plan

Participants were exposed to 12 trials consisting of 4 coherent stimuli and 8 incoherent stimuli. The 12 audio-haptic stimuli were presented once in randomized order.

The modeled surfaces were 4 (2 solid and 2 aggregate): wood, metal, snow and gravel. In presence of incoherent stimuli the conflict was rendered providing on the one hand one of the solid surfaces by means of auditory feedback, while at haptic level one of the aggregate surfaces was presented. On the other hand, analogously, another set of incoherent stimuli consisted of aggregate surfaces at auditory level while a solid surface was presented by means of haptic feedback.

4   Results and Discussion

Table 1 shows the confusion matrix resulting from the experiment. In such table are illustrated the participants answers gathered according to three material categories: solid, aggregate and liquid.

The first noticeable element emerging from the table is that none of the participants classified as liquid the simulated surfaces. Moreover it is very evident that in presence of conflicts the auditory modality is strongly dominant on the haptic one. This result is more clearly illustrated in table 2, and it seems to be confirmed by the answers concerning the names of the chosen materials (see table 3). Indeed, participants had the tendency to answer with the same names chosen when a same material was presented at auditory level both in presence of coherent and incoherent stimuli. In other words they were driven in their choice by the auditory feedback.

This does not mean that they completely ignored the haptic part of the bimodal stimulus; indeed in the comments two participants reported that they noticed that only some of the haptic stimuli where appropriate for the sound they were listening. Moreover results show that in two cases participants seemed to be driven in their choices, at least partially, by the haptic feedback; this is the case of the audio-haptic stimulus metal-snow for which one participant surprisingly gave the answer "mud" which can be considered appropriate for the haptic stimulus. Concerning the stimulus snow-wood one participant chose the answer "carpet" which seems to consider both the two components of the bimodal stimulus since the sound of snow could be interpreted as the sound on carpet in presence of an haptic feedback expressing a solid surface like wood. Both the participants, like all the others, were asked, at the conclusion of the experiment,

Table 1. Confusion matrix of experiment

Stimulus		Answer			
Audio	Haptic	Solid	Aggregate	Liquid	I don't know
Wood	Wood	7	1		2
Wood	Snow	7			3
Wood	Gravel	6	1		3
Metal	Metal	9			1
Metal	Snow	6	1		3
Metal	Gravel	8			2
Gravel	Gravel		9		1
Gravel	Wood		10		
Gravel	Metal		7		3
Snow	Snow		10		
Snow	Wood		9	1	
Snow	Metal		9		1

Table 2. Percentages of dominance of the auditory and haptic modalities in presence of incoherent stimuli

Stimulus		Dominance	
Audio	Haptic	% Audio	% Haptic
Wood	Snow	70	0
Wood	Gravel	60	0
Metal	Snow	60	10
Metal	Gravel	80	0
Gravel	Wood	100	0
Gravel	Metal	70	0
Snow	Wood	90	10
Snow	Metal	90	0

to explain their answers and they confirmed their choices. In particular all the participants were asked at the end of the experiment to classify their answers as belonging to the categories of solid, aggregate or liquid materials.

For the stimulus wood-gravel one participant reported the answer "not solid plastic" which could be addressed as haptic dominance, but the same participant chose the same answer also for the coherent stimulus wood-wood and for this reason we did not consider such answer as haptic dominance in table 2.

Regarding the percentages of "I don't know" answers, although the number is low, it is an indication of the difficulty of the proposed task. This fact was also confirmed in numerous comments left by participants who on average reported that the task was very difficult. Although the comparison between coherent and incoherent stimuli with the same auditory stimulus do not reveal any statistically significant difference (confirming from another point of view the dominance of the auditory feedback), the percentages of "I don't know" answers is on average higher for the incoherent stimuli.

Table 3. Names of the materials chosen for each audio-haptic stimulus. In bold the choices which seem to be driven by the haptic feedback.

Stimulus		Answer
Audio	Haptic	Names of chosen materials
Wood	Wood	wood, concrete, plastic, not solid plastic
Wood	Snow	wood, concrete, plastic, gum
Wood	Gravel	wood, concrete, plastic, not solid plastic
Metal	Metal	metal, iron, steel, wood, glass
Metal	Snow	metal, iron, steel, wood, glass, **mud**
Metal	Gravel	metal, iron, steel, wood, glass, plastic
Gravel	Gravel	gravel, little stones, sand
Gravel	Wood	gravel, little stones, sand
Gravel	Metal	gravel, little stones, sand
Snow	Snow	snow, ice, gravel, sand, leaves, not solid plastic, paper
Snow	Wood	snow, ice, gravel, sand, leaves, not solid plastic, **carpet**
Snow	Metal	snow, ice, gravel, sand, not solid plastic

Table 4. Average realism and quality scores from a seven-point Likert scale and relative standard deviation

Stimulus		Realism		Quality	
Audio	Haptic	μ	σ	μ	σ
Wood	Wood	2.75	1.488	3.25	1.2817
Wood	Snow	2.7143	1.496	3.2857	1.2536
Wood	Gravel	2.5714	1.8127	2.7143	1.3801
Metal	Metal	2.8889	1.6159	4	2
Metal	Snow	3.8571	1.496	3.5714	1.1339
Metal	Gravel	2.625	1.3025	2.875	1.5526
Gravel	Gravel	3.2222	1.0929	4	1
Gravel	Wood	4	0.9428	4.4	0.9661
Gravel	Metal	3.7143	1.8898	4.1429	1.4639
Snow	Snow	3.7	1.567	3.8	1.3984
Snow	Wood	3.6	1.4298	3.7	1.567
Snow	Metal	4	1.5	4.1111	1.453

Table 5. Questionnaire results. Average scores from a seven-point Likert scale and relative standard deviation.

	μ	σ
Naturalness	3.5	1.6499
Normality	4	1.5635
Constriction	4.2	1.3166

Table 4 shows the degree to which participants judged the realism and the quality of the experience. Such parameters were calculated by looking only at the answers different from "I dont know". Contrary to our hypotheses we did not find higher evaluations of these parameters for the coherent stimuli compared to the incoherent one. Surprisingly for some stimuli the evaluations are even higher for the incoherent stimuli. Anyways an in depth statistical analysis performed with the t-test revealed that all these differences are not significative.

Finally, as concerns the questionnaire conducted at the conclusion of the experiment, results in table 5 show that that subjects judged the interaction with the system not too much natural (mean = 3.5), and that they felt quite normal (mean = 4) but at the same time quite constrained (mean = 4.2) during the act of walking.

Indeed, more than one subject commented on the need of a wireless system able to convey vibrations to the shoes and sounds to the headphones set.

5 Conclusion and Future Work

In this paper, we describe an experiment conducted with a real-time footsteps synthesizer able to provide audio and haptic feedback, and which is controlled by the user during the act of walking by means of shoes embedded with sensors and actuators.

In the experiment, both coherent and incoherent audio-haptic stimuli were provided. Results confirm that auditory modality is dominant on the haptic one. This can be due to the low sensitivity of the foot when exposed to haptic signals.

The developed system is ready to be integrated in computer games and interactive installations where a user can navigate.

In future work, we indeed plan to utilize the system in multimodal environments, and include visual feedback, to understand the role of the different sensorial modalities to enhance sense of immersion and presence in scenarios where walking plays an important role.

Acknowledgment

The research leading to these results has received funding from the European Community's Seventh Framework Programme under FET-Open grant agreement 222107 NIW - Natural Interactive Walking.[3] The authors wish also to thank Amir Berrezag and Vincent Hayward who provided the shoes used in the experiments.

References

1. Giordano, B.L., Mcadams, S., Visell, Y., Cooperstock, J., Yao, H.Y., Hayward, V.: Non-visual identification of walking grounds. Journal of the Acoustical Society of America 123(5), 3412–3412 (2008)

---

[3] www.niwproject.eu

2. Nordahl, R., Berrezag, A., Dimitrov, S., Turchet, L., Hayward, V., Serafin, S.: Preliminary experiment combining virtual reality haptic shoes and audio synthesis. In: Proc. Eurohaptics (2010)
3. Nordahl, R., Serafin, S., Turchet, L.: Sound synthesis and evaluation of interactive footsteps for virtual reality applications. In: Proc. IEEE VR 2010 (2010)
4. Serafin, S., Turchet, L., Nordahl, R., Dimitrov, S., Berrezag, A., Hayward, V.: Identification of virtual grounds using virtual reality haptic shoes and sound synthesis. In: Proc. of Eurohaptics Symposium on Haptics and Audio-Visual Environments (2010)
5. Turchet, L., Nordahl, R., Berrezag, A., Dimitrov, S., Hayward, V., Serafin, S.: Audio-haptic physically based simulation of walking sounds. In: Proc. of IEEE International Workshop on Multimedia Signal Processing (2010)
6. Turchet, L., Nordahl, R., Serafin, S.: Examining the role of context in the recognition of walking sounds. In: Proc. of Sound and Music Computing Conference (2010)
7. Turchet, L., Serafin, S., Dimitrov, S., Nordahl, R.: Physically based sound synthesis and control of footsteps sounds. In: Proceedings of Digital Audio Effects Conference (2010)

The Influence of Angle Size in Navigation Applications Using Pointing Gestures

Charlotte Magnusson, Kirsten Rassmus-Gröhn, and Delphine Szymczak

Department of Design Sciences, Lund University, Box 118,
221 00 Lund, Sweden
{charlotte,kirre,delphine.szymczak}@certec.lth.se

Abstract. One factor which can be expected to influence performance in applications where the user points a device in some direction to obtain information is the angle interval in which the user gets feedback. The present study was performed in order to get a better understanding of the influence of this angle interval on navigation performance, gestures and strategies in a more realistic outdoor setting. Results indicate that users are able to handle quite a wide range of angle intervals, although there are differences between narrow and wide intervals. We observe different gestures and strategies used by the users and provide some recommendations on suitable angle intervals. Finally, our observations support the notion that using this type of pointing gesture for navigation is intuitive and easy to use.

Keywords: Non-visual, pointing, gesture, audio, mobile, location based.

1 Introduction and Related Work

The introduction of compasses in more and more hand held devices has opened the way for applications making use of pointing gestures to provide information about objects or locations in the real world. With geo tagged information on a device which knows where it is (through GPS or other means) and also knows in which direction it is pointing (through a compass) it is possible to show the user information on important buildings, restaurants, future or past events etc etc in the direction the device is pointing (http://layar.com). Using non-speech sound or vibration in a handheld device to guide pedestrians in a wayfinding situation has been studied previously but not extensively. One group of proof-of-concept systems make use of spatial audio for navigation purposes and thus require headphones. AudioGPS by Holland et al. [1] displays the direction and the distance to a target uses stereo together with a repeated fixed pitch tone and a repeated varying pitch tone to give the user the directional information. A Geiger counter metaphor is used to convey distance from target (more frequent tone bursts the closer to the target the user is). In gpsTunes created by Strachan et al. [2] the user's preferred music was placed with spatial audio to provide bearing and distance information. As long as the user kept walking in the direction of the goal, the music was played at the desired volume. Stahl's The Roaring Navigator [3] guides visitors at a zoo by playing the sounds of the three nearest animals. The system also uses speech recognition for interaction

R. Nordahl et al. (Eds.): HAID 2010, LNCS 6306, pp. 107–116, 2010.
© Springer-Verlag Berlin Heidelberg 2010

and speech to display further information about the animals to the user. Jones et al. modify the volume of music stereo playback to guide users toward their destination in the ONTRACK system [4]. The full sound is given in both ears within an angle of 90 degrees around the target. Between 90 and 180 degrees, the sound is shifted 45 degrees to the left or right, and it is completely shifted to the left or right ear for angles above 180 degrees. Their field trial also showed that visual distraction may interfere with audio guiding.

The AudioBubbles concept by McGookin et al. [5] is similar to AudioGPS, but does not require the use of headphones. The context is somewhat different in that is not specifically targeted to navigation, but to support tourists to be aware of and locate points of interest while wandering freely. The SoundCrumbs application described by Magnusson et al. in [6] enables the user to place virtual spheres of sound in a virtual georeferenced system and locating them again to support finding ones way back to a starting location, or to create virtual trails to share with others. It is possible to locate the next soundcrumb on the trail by pointing - when the magnetometer points in the direction of the next sound crumb, it will be played with adjusted volume, depending on whether the user points directly at the target or beside it.

Instead of using audio as a beacon at the target, tactile feedback such as vibration has also been used. In the SweepShake system presented by Robinson et al. [7] the user point in a direction and receives vibratory feedback when the device is pointing at the target. The targets are different in size depending on their information content (a larger target indicates more information content) and the use case described is primarily browsing and selecting geolocated information while standing still. Ahmaniemi & Lantz [8] similarly use vibratory feedback to investigate target finding speed in a laboratory set-up. The user scans or sweeps a handheld device while standing still. The study considered feedback angles between 5 and 25 degrees, concentrating on the speed of the sweeping movement. The possibility of missing the target at high speeds for smaller angles is stated. The results show that reaching a target with a vibratory angle of 5 degrees is significantly more difficult than with larger angles. The Social Gravity system described by Williamson et al. [9] intends to guide a group of people toward a common meeting point, called a "centroid" that adjusts its position according to the individual members of the group, using vibration feedback. The users are also here expected to scan for the target (centroid), and a 60 degree target indication angle was used in the field trial. Before choosing the field trial angle a simulations was made with angles from 5 to 180 degrees.

A more detailed study on the influence of angle size on performance, gestures and strategies in a more real outdoor navigational setting is still missing. The present study is aimed at improving this state of affairs.

2   Test Description

The present study was set up to answer the following questions: What happens when you vary the angle interval? Is there a preferred angle? What kind of strategies/gestures do the users adopt when interacting with this type of pointing application?

For the test we used an external magnetometer (a SHAKE SK 6 device) connected via Bluetooth to a Sony Ericsson Xperia mobile phone running Windows Mobile. The test was done within a limited space outdoors. Most test rounds were done in a park like area outside our department which contained open areas, foot/bike paths, trees, bushes and some artistic installations. We had decided on this type of fairly open environment for several reasons:

- A road network would impose a limited number of possible directions making it harder to discern the effect of the angle interval alone.
- One can expect users to visit parks and open squares, and the test environment contained elements natural for that type of environment.
- This type of environment allows more freedom in the design of different trails.

To see what happens in a completely open environment we also carried out three tests in an open field further away. The test tracks at both locations were based on a grid structure (see Fig. 1 A).

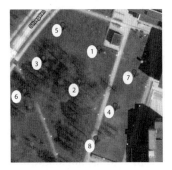 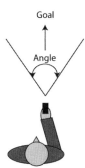

Fig. 1. A) The grid points for the test trails. B) The angle interval

The four different tracks available can be worked out from Fig 1A. Each track started at point 1 and went on to point 2. At 2 you could turn either left or right. The same would happen at the points 3 or 4. The track ended at one of the corner points 5,6,7 or 8. The turns at the points 2, 3 and 4 were made in an alternating fashion so that if you turned left at the first turning point the first trial, you turned right during the next trial. Thus if your first trail was 1, 2, 3, 6 and your second trail 1, 2, 4, 8 your third trail would be 1, 2, 3, 5. The same design was used for the following turn. The initial values for the turns in the sequence were assigned randomly. Since there were four tracks and eight tests each track occurred twice. Due to both GPS inaccuracy as well as deviations due to different angle intervals the users did not walk the same way every time even though the underlying GPS track was the same. When asked about it after the test, none of the users had noticed that some paths were the same. Furthermore the order in which the angle intervals were presented was randomized to cancel out possible learning effects.

The grid distance in the (5,1,7) direction was 37 m while the distance in the perpendicular direction (1,2) was 33 m. Each point in the track was surrounded with a circle of an approximate[1] radius of 10 m. If the user was inside this radius the application would lead the user towards the next point in the sequence. When the user was within an approximate radius of 20 m of the goal waypoint the phone started to vibrate slowly. When the user was 10 m (or closer) to the target the goal was considered reached and the phone started to vibrate quickly.

The user got information about which direction to go by pointing the device in different directions (as was done in [6] and [9]). If the device was pointing in the right direction audio feedback playing a wave file (the sound of waves against the shore) was played. The volume did not change – the sound was either on or off. The direction was considered to be right as long as the device was pointed to a direction within a specified angle interval as shown in Fig 1B.

The angle intervals tested were 10°, 30°, 60°, 120°, 150° and 180°. The order in which these were presented to the test person was randomized. A practice round at 30° was carried out before each test.

The users were observed during the test. After the test they were asked about which strategies they used for small and large angles, how much they felt they needed to concentrate or if they had any other comments about the interaction design. The test application logged time, GPS position and magnetometer heading. It also logged when the user passed different waypoints and when the goal was reached.

15 persons did the test. Of these users, 6 were female and 9 male. The age range was wide – our youngest test user was 13 while the oldest person who did the test was 70.

3   Results

Contrary to our expectations users were not very sensitive to the angle interval. Even for the 180° condition all test users found the goal.

Some differences were still seen. If we start by looking at the time to find the goals in table 1 we see that on the whole the 10° angle interval and the 180° angle interval takes longer. Statistical analysis using ANOVA showed significant differences ($p<0.0001$). A Bonferroni test showed significant differences with a confidence level of 95% between 10° and the angle intervals 30°, 60°, 90° and 120°. 180° was significantly slower than all other intervals except 10°. That the 10° and 180° conditions take longer to complete can be seen clearly if we look at the average times. We also note that there is little difference between the 30°, 60°, 90° and 120° angle intervals.

If we instead look at the trails we can pick up some general features. As expected the more narrow angles lead to more precise route following, while for the wider angles people would stray more and would even occasionally walk in circles for a while.

Looking at the three tests done on an open field we can see the trend quite clearly. In the top row of Fig. 2 we see the angles 10°, 30°, 60° and 90°. All these trails follow the intended path quite well, although we begin to see some deviations in the rightmost picture. In the bottom row of Fig. 2 we see the wider angles resulting in more deviations and finally also loops.

---

[1] The formula used in the implementation overestimated longitudinal distances with a factor of 1.19 compared to the haversine formula. For distances of 10 m this is within the GPS accuracy and should not influence the outcome of the test.

Table 1. Time in minutes to find the goal for different angles

Nr	10°	30°	60°	90°	120°	150°	180°
1	5,32	4,31	3,93	3,49	3,52	5,65	4,49
2	2,89	2,65	2,62	3,71	1,75	3,12	2,52
3	4,27	3,16	3,24	2,89	2,91	2,35	5,81
4	5,02	2,85	2,82	2,43	3,66	3,56	8,25
5	6,48	2,16	2,27	2,01	2,13	2,61	2,52
6	4,09	3,26	2,33	2,37	2,00	2,73	7,22
7	2,50	2,95	2,19	1,77	2,28	6,02	8,89
8	6,87	3,43	2,51	2,90	2,08	2,68	6,26
9	3,23	2,01	1,94	1,82	1,93	1,53	2,34
10	2,78	2,29	2,09	3,13	2,58	5,72	5,29
11	3,19	1,78	2,26	2,96	1,85	2,14	5,13
12	5,14	3,21	3,21	2,43	4,58	2,88	5,59
13	6,23	3,05	2,50	2,87	2,88	4,42	4,69
14	7,50	3,65	2,60	2,92	2,58	3,67	3,35
15	5,41	2,66	2,69	2,09	3,71	2,79	10,09
Av	4,73	2,89	2,61	2,65	2,69	3,46	5,50

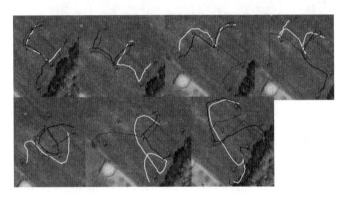

Fig. 2. Trails for 10°, 30°, 60°, 90° (top row), 120°, 150° and 180° (bottom row)

At the main (more realistic) test location there were objects such as trees, footpaths, cyclists etc that the test persons would have to avoid. In addition we also had more problems with the GPS signal. The trend is still the same, as can be seen from Fig 3. In the top row of Fig 3 we can see the intended paths quite clearly. In the bottom row things are getting less and less organized and the last picture at the bottom right shows a spaghetti like mess where several trails appear to make loops as well as deviating a lot from the intended paths. All these pictures were made with GPSVisualizer, http://www.gpsvisualizer.com/.

For the finding of the appropriate direction while standing still we saw three main types of gestures. The first, which basically all users made use of, was to hold the device out in front of the body, keeping the arm and hand position fixed relative to the body, and walk around on the spot (sometimes in a small circle). A second gesture which was used both while walking and while standing still was the arm scan. In this gesture the arm was moved to the side and back again. This gesture occurred to one side only or from side to side. The third type of gesture was hand movement only – the user moved the hand by flexing the wrist. Also this gesture was used both standing still and while walking. In addition two users also scanned by keeping the hand and arm still, but instead walking in a zig-zag/serpentine fashion forwards. One user also tried to scan by moving the device with the fingers (keeping the hand in the same position).

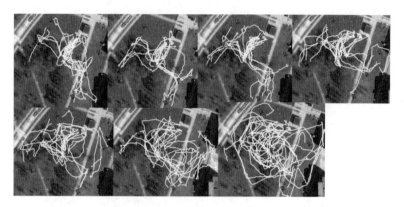

Fig. 3. Trails for 10°, 30°, 60°, 90° (top row), 120°, 150° and 180° (bottom row)

For finding the direction while standing still all the three main gestures were used. Some users preferred the whole body rotation only, while some started with the arm pointing and only made use of whole body rotation if this didn't give any result. The hand pointing was mostly used for the narrow angles (10° and sometimes also 30°).

In general our users would keep walking as long as they heard the audio feedback. When they lost it they stopped and checked the direction. The only exception was the 10° angle. As was noted already in [8] narrow angles make targets easy to miss, and for this angle it was really hard to keep a steady signal. This led either to the person stopping a lot, or to keep walking a while without signal and then stopping to check if he or she was walking the right way. Some users also tried to use arm or hand scan while walking to keep the signal, but given the noise in the signal, the limited update rate and the delays present this tended to work badly leading instead to a complete loss of signal.

For the wider angles we saw that we had two basic types of users. One group was more analytic and explored the width of the angle interval and then tried to walk towards the middle. The other group walked as soon as they felt they had a steady signal. The difference between the groups was most clearly seen in the 180° condition; although some of the more analytical users also had problems with this angle interval in general the analytical strategy made users better able to cope with the wider angles. In the analytical group we would often see the user trying to check the limits of the angle interval by doing a sideways scan (while walking) to find the border. The less analytic users would still tend to avoid the borders of the angle interval. Due to noise/jumps in the magnetometer signal the sound would start "hiccupping" near the border. All users made use of this info, although not everyone realized this was useful right from the start. While scanning standing still, this meant that the user would keep moving the device until the signal was steady (and often a little further) which meant that also the less analytic users would avoid walking right along the borders of the angle interval. While walking, the hiccup would either trigger a stop to scan a new direction, or the user would try to re-orient by doing an arm scan while walking.

In general users expressed that they felt more "secure" with the wider angles (although they didn't like the 180° which was said to be too wide). The 10° made users feel insecure, and they walked noticeable slower in this condition. We did not explicitly test cognitive load, but we did probe this by trying to talk to our subjects. Both from the responses to this, and also from answers to explicit questions it was clear that the narrow angles were more demanding. Particularly the 10° angle required a lot of concentration from the user. One user said "you have to concentrate so hard that you almost forget where you are". All users disliked the 10° and thought it was too narrow. With wider angles people were more relaxed and would often start talking spontaneously with the observer. They also commented that with larger angles you didn't have to concentrate that much, but could relax and enjoy the walk.

4 Discussion

Contrary to our expectations our test users were surprisingly insensitive to the size of the angle interval. Our results indicate that also wider angles such as 90° and to some extent even 120° can work reasonably well. Our test results confirm that we had included a sufficient range of angle intervals – we had both a too narrow angle (10°) and a too wide one (180°). In between those the recommendation for which angle to use depends on several factors:

- If it is important to get exact track following one should go for more narrow angles. This depends to some extent on the equipment at hand but from this test we would recommend 30° to 60°.
- If you want a design that puts small cognitive load on the user it is better to use wider angles. Judging from the results of this test 60° to 120° works for this purpose.
- In general people walk slower if the angle is too narrow. If you are targeting applications where the user wants to walk quickly or maybe even run (eg. jogging applications) wider angles are preferable.

The 60° used in [9] agrees with these findings. Even so, the task dependence of the recommendations indicates that angle interval is a variable which should be possible to customize.

The fact that the 10° angle is difficult is very much depending on uncertainties in the signal (a nice overview of this topic can be found in [10]) combined with a discrete sampling rate. When the heading value "jumps" due to noise it is easy to miss the goal completely. The risk of missing the target if it is narrow is also pointed out in [8]. Thus, one factor which influences these recommendations is the properties of the hardware. With faster and more precise equipment one can expect that smaller angles will be easier to deal with. The general trend that smaller angles favor more precise but also more cognitive demanding navigation can still be expected to hold.

We were a bit surprised that all users found the goal also in the 180° condition. Although they would sometimes walk in wrong directions and also on occasion walk in circles they would eventually converge on the target. Potentially this could be due to obstacles in the environment causing fortunate deviations, which is why we did a few tests also in a completely open environment – and also in the open environment users were able to get to the goal eventually.

The size if the track points was set to a size that initial tests showed resulted in smooth navigation. With smaller track point size we would expect a need for more exact navigation. It should be noted that the actual directions used for the angle feedback was calculated using the GPS point in the middle of the circle so the size of the circles would not have any effects on the direction information provided to the user - it influences only which track point the application thinks the user is looking for and when the user is considered to have reached the goal.

It should be noted that our results are for a fairly open environment. In a street grid environment the number of possible directions is limited, and wider angles can probably be used without loss of precision (as an example: if you are walking along a road even a 180° interval is likely to tell you if you are heading in the correct direction or not).

Another outcome of our study is an improved understanding of the strategies users employ. Some users are more analytical and will scan the extent of the interval and try to walk towards the center, while others will "just walk" when they get a signal. In general users find it quite natural to scan, which implies that it is important to make use of a compass that is fast enough to support this behavior. The device used for these tests (the SHAKE SK6) was fast enough to support scanning although very fast gestures had to be avoided. It also had a filtering mode that gave more steady headings – but pilot tests showed that this unfortunately slowed down the compass too much when used with the scanning gestures.

The pointing interaction used in this study appeared to be easily understood, and none of our users had any noticeable problems dealing with it. This is in agreement with the results in [7] and [9] who also find this type of pointing/scanning interaction easy and intuitive for users.

The audio used (a sound of waves against a shore) was well liked. It was quite easy to hear, but even more importantly it wasn't perceived as annoying or disturbing. Even the person who observed the tests and who listened to it for more than 17 hours found it nice to listen to. One further advantage of using a continuous sound was the "hiccupping" that happened near the borders of the angle interval which provided extra information. In a sense the continuous nature of the sound source made it easier to discern changes in signal. This agrees with the observation in [11] that changes in data are better mapped using continuous feedback – in this case audio. In the case of Geiger counter type designs (such as was used in [1]) you will miss this information. In cases where you want to mask irregularities in the signal this could be used to your advantage, but in the present case the border information is quite valuable.

In this study we used only sound on or off as feedback since adding different sectors in the angle interval would introduce more factors that might influence the results and we wanted to focus on the basic influence the width of the interval. This does not mean that it is not a good idea to vary the feedback to give the user the advantage of having both a more precise direction combined with the advantages a wider angle provides. One example of such a design can be found in [6] where a central interval of 30° with 100% volume was followed by an interval out to 90° where the volume was 40%. Outside this the sound played at 20% level all the way up to 180°.

5   Conclusion

The present study was performed in order to get a better understanding of the influence of angle size on navigation performance, gestures and strategies in a more realistic outdoor setting. We have been looking at what happens when you vary the angle interval, if there is a preferred angle, and what kind of strategies/gestures the users adopt when interacting with this type of pointing application.

We find that users are able to handle quite a wide range of angle intervals. The only intervals generating significantly slower completion times were the 10° and 180° angle intervals. Among the angle intervals that appear to be working reasonably well, we still find some differences. Narrow intervals provide more exact track following but may be slower and require more attention/concentration from the user. Wide angle intervals result in less exact track following, but allow users to walk faster and be more relaxed. Thus there is no single preferred angle interval – instead this depends on the task. If exact track following is important we would recommend an interval of 30° to 60° while we recommend an interval of 60° to 120° if low cognitive load is important. The 60° used in [9] agrees with these findings. The task dependence of our recommendations indicates that angle interval is a variable which should be possible to customize. It should be noted that the precise angle intervals in these recommendations depend both on hardware properties as well as the size of the circle around each track point within which the point is considered to be reached. The general trend indicated above should still be expected to hold.

In this test we observed three main scan gestures: the whole body scan, arm pointing and hand pointing. Users tended to keep walking as long as they had a signal and stop to scan for direction if they lost it. Some users scanned also while walking. For narrow angles this was done in order to keep the signal, while if it was performed for wide angles the scanning would be to check that the user was still heading roughly towards the middle of the angle interval. We have seen two basic types of strategies for dealing with the interaction: we have the analytic strategy where one checks the size of the interval and then tries to head for the center, and we have the direct strategy where you scan until you get a signal and then head in that direction.

Finally, our observations extend the observation made in [7] that this type of pointing gesture is intuitive and easy to use also for navigational purposes.

Acknowledgments. We thank the EC which co-funds the IP HaptiMap (FP7-ICT-224675). We also thank VINNOVA for additional support. The authors also gratefully acknowledge discussions with David McGookin and Stephen Brewster from the Multimodal Interaction Group in Glasgow.

References

1. Holland, S., Morse, D.R., Gedenryd, H.: Audiogps: Spatial audio in a minimal attention interface. Personal and Ubiquitous Computing 6(4) (2002)
2. Strachan, S., Eslambolchilar, P., Murray-Smith, R., Hughes, S., O'Modhrain, S.: GpsTunes: controlling navigation via audio feedback. In: Proceedings of the 7th international conference on human computer interaction with mobile devices & services, MobileHCI 2005 (2005)

3. Stahl, C.: The roaring navigator: A group guide for the zoo with shared auditory landmark display. In: Proceedings of the 9th international conference on Human computer interaction with mobile devices and services, MobileHCI 2007 (2007)

4. Jones, M., Jones, S., Bradley, G., Warren, N., Bainbridge, D., Holmes, G.: ONTRACK: Dynamically adapting music playback to support navigation. Personal and Ubiquitous Computing 12(5) (2008)

5. McGookin, D., Brewster, S., Prieg, P.: Audio Bubbles: Employing Non-speech Audio to Support Tourist Wayfinding. In: Altinsoy, M.E., Jekosch, U., Brewster, S. (eds.) HAID 2009. LNCS, vol. 5763, pp. 41–50. Springer, Heidelberg (2009)

6. Magnusson, C., Breidegard, B., Rassmus-Gröhn, K.: Soundcrumbs – Hansel and Gretel in the 21st century. In: Proceedings of the 4th international workshop on Haptic and Audio Interaction Design, HAID 2009 (2009)

7. Robinson, S., Eslambolchilar, P., Jones, M.: Sweep-Shake: Finding Digital Resources in Physical Environments. In: Proceedings of the 11th International Conference on Human-Computer Interaction with Mobile Devices and Services, MobileHCI 2009 (2009)

8. Ahmaniemi, T., Lantz, V.: Augmented Reality Target Finding Based on Tactile Cues. In: Proceedings of the 2009 international conference on Multimodal interfaces, ICMI-MLMI 2009 (2009)

9. Williamson, J., Robinson, S., Stewart, C., Murray-Smith, R., Jones, M., Brewster, S.: Social Gravity: A Virtual Elastic Tether for Casual, Privacy-Preserving Pedestrian Rendezvous. Accepted for publication in Proceedings of the 2010 Conference on Human Factors in Computing Systems, CHI 2010 (2010) (Private communication)

10. Strachan, S., Murray-Smith, R.: Bearing-based selection in mobile spatial interaction. Personal Ubiquitous Comput. 13(4), 265–280 (2009)

11. Sawhney, N., Murphy, A.: ESPACE 2: an experimental hyperaudio environment. In: Conference Companion on Human Factors in Computing Systems: Common Ground, Vancouver, British Columbia, Canada, April 13 - 18 (1996)

Audio-tactile Display of Ground Properties Using Interactive Shoes

Stefano Papetti[1], Federico Fontana[2], Marco Civolani[1],
Amir Berrezag[3], and Vincent Hayward[3]

[1] Università di Verona, Department of Computer Science
strada Le Grazie, 15 – 37134 Verona, Italy
{stefano.papetti,marco.civolani}@univr.it
[2] Università di Udine, Department of Mathematics and Computer Science
via delle Scienze, 206 – 33100 Udine, Italy
federico.fontana@uniud.it
[3] UPMC Universitè de Paris 06, Institut des Systèmes Intelligents et de Robotique
4 place Jussieu – 75005, Paris, France
amir.berrezag@isir.upmc.fr,hayward@cim.mcgill.ca

Abstract. We describe an audio-tactile stimulation system that can be worn and that is capable of providing the sensation of walking over grounds of different type. The system includes miniature loudspeakers and broadband vibrotactile transducers embedded in the soles. The system is particularly effective at suggesting grounds that have granular or crumpling properties. By offering a broad spectrum of floor augmentations with moderate technological requirements, the proposed prototype represents a solution that can be easily replicated in the research laboratory. This paper documents the design and features of the diverse components that characterize the prototype in detail, as well as its current limits.

Keywords: Interactive shoes, foot-based interfaces.

1 Introduction

As a recent complement to the design and engineering of machine interfaces for the study of human locomotion, balance and equilibrium in walking [1], researchers in human-computer interaction have begun to address questions concerning the interactive display to humans of psychophysical cues at ground level. Initially concentrating on the visual modality, with a focus on interaction scenarios ranging mainly between performing arts and gaming, researchers have then recognized the importance of non-visual ground cues as means to enrich the interaction with floors through the feet [2]. As a result, some radically novel paradigms have emerged enabling users to experience multimodal floor augmentations that – in addition to the mentioned application fields – are expected to play roles also in rehabilitation, critical labor environment simulations and for navigation aids for both normally gifted and impaired people.

R. Nordahl et al. (Eds.): HAID 2010, LNCS 6306, pp. 117–128, 2010.

Among such paradigms, those which are grounded on an *ecological* approach to interaction design appear to be especially promising [3]. For its strong potential to result into "natural" interactions that furthermore do not need any specific training or cultural probing, this approach has received specific attention especially by designers of non visual displays, in which implicit sonic and vibrotactile signals can be set to operate at the periphery of the focus of attention [4]. Notable results that can be ascribed to this approach include active floor installations using vibrotactile devices, capable of conveying realistic sensations of snow- and ice-covered grounds to users walking over them [5].

Floor-based setups offer virtually unlimited physical space where to locate sensors and actuators. Furthermore, the networking of different physical components just requires to connect them together via a wired communication infrastructure. Power connections are generally not a problem as well for non-mobile interfaces, such as active floors. Conversely, the realization of an infrastructure of this kind poses serious technical questions when the same interaction paradigm is exported to a mobile interface, that is, a pair of shoes.

In the mobile case basically all physical components need to be tailored in order to minimize size, weight and power consumption, meanwhile guaranteeing an acceptable performance of the interface. Moreover they must be robust, since they are moved around by users engaged in walking or running tasks. Under such working conditions, the measurement of the force exerted by the foot over a sole, the real-time computations which are needed to generate an output from time-varying force data, and the consequent display of realistic sound and vibrations from the shoes by means of active components become more difficult to be realized and kept stable across time.

In the following of this paper, the current development state of our project on interactive shoes is detailed so as to provide the reader with an in-depth vision on their design and engineering. Section 2 describes the concept. Section 3 forwards to a parallel publication in these proceedings, on the accurate measurement and analog-to-digital conversion of force data using cheap sensors and processing. Section 4 presents the software that is employed to generate feedback in real-time. Section 5 illustrates the characteristics and positioning of the haptic actuators and loudspeakers used for providing feedback. Finally, Section 6 briefly reports about the performances and current limits of the interface, furthermore outlining ongoing and future work.

2   Design Concept

During everyday walking tasks we are continuously exposed to changes in the floor properties. The perception of level and inclination allows walkers to maintain correct equilibrium and posture. In parallel, auditory and tactile ground cues provide significant detail about the floor characteristics [3]. By influencing gait and walking gestures, these cues determine our level of familiarity and confidence with ground surfaces. Blind persons make intensive use of such cues during their everyday way-finding and landmarking tasks across familiar environments.

Our interactive shoes aim at simulating changes in ground surface, by augmenting otherwise neutral (i.e., flat and homogeneous) floors. Augmented reality is receiving increasing recognition by interaction designers, for its potential to enrich our surrounding environments with additional information. As opposed to substitution, augmentation can smoothly alert of changing conditions and, if the warning messages are carefully designed, it can support user's decisions through the presentation of implicit (especially non-visual) signals [4]. Actuated shoes represent a significant instantiation of this concept, as they can display audio-tactile ground cues for purposes ranging from support to way-finding and landmarking, as mentioned before, up to rehabilitation, entertainment and simulations of immersive reality.

In a preliminary work, we have prototyped a pair of interactive shoes provided with force sensors and small loudspeakers, capable of generating auditory feedback in real-time by foot pressure data acquired during a walking task [6]. This prototype was able to concentrate all computational and power resources inside a backpack that could be worn by users. The interface, hence, could be made strictly mobile, and consequently it allowed total freedom of movement to users who could navigate, even for a long time, across an environment. We chose rubber clogs as they could be easily "hacked" by cutting, grooving, drilling their body. Thanks to these shoes we could test initial design ideas, especially concerning the choice and location of different types of sensors. On the other hand, the range of feet fitting with a single pair of clogs was limited to few sizes. This fact excluded a number of potential users from testing the prototype.

One important lesson that we learned from this preliminary prototype was that, as somehow expected already at the conceptual stage, substitution is far more difficult than augmentation. In other words, it is not easy to "cancel" the floor upon which one is walking meanwhile providing alternative ground surface properties. On the other hand, it is relatively easier to add simulated properties to the real floor by superimposing a layer of virtual material to it. So, for instance, turning a wooden floor into a marble surface would in principle require to mask the resonances coming from the wood, a goal that is clearly hard to achieve. As opposed to this, covering a "dry" material such as concrete with virtual gravel, dry leaves, or snow, is at reach of current feedback design techniques [2].

The recent introduction of vibrotactile actuators has resulted in a new prototype (see Fig. 1), that has dramatically improved the realism of the simulations. Furthermore, we have switched from clogs to sandals, as they can fit with a larger range of foot sizes. Thanks to a better positioning of the sensors – refer to Section 3 – we got satisfactory force detections by fastening feet sized between 38 and 44 (Italian standard scale) through the three buckles every sandal is provided with.

On the other hand, vibrotactile actuators are more demanding than small loudspeakers in terms of power consumption. For this reason a wired connection had to be planned in the current setup, to feed the actuators with high amplitude signals provided by a couple of power amplifiers. Holding this physical constraint, it was logical to locate all the physical components that do not need to reside

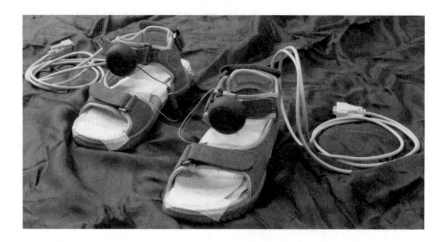

Fig. 1. Current shoe-based interface prototype

on the shoes (i.e., acquisition board, computer and output signal interface) off the wearable part of the interface.

A schematic of the components forming the prototype is illustrated in Fig. 2. Every shoe is provided with two force sensors, one small loudspeaker and two haptic actuators, all depicted within the rectangle in dashed line. The next sections detail such components, step by step.

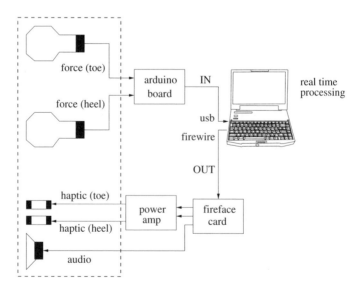

Fig. 2. Illustration of the prototype components. Sensors and actuators of one shoe are surrounded by the rectangle in dashed line.

3   Data Acquisition

The current implementation of the acquisition system presents a number of novelties that needed to expand this section into a self-contained paper, to which the reader is forwarded [7].

4   Real-Time Synthesis and Control

Interactive sounds are dynamic, informative, contextual, and occasionally bringing emotional content [8]. For this reason, sound design tools and systems should offer extensive control over the design process, generation, and interactive manipulation of sound.

Modern sound synthesis techniques, with their inherent parametric control, are able to handle continuous sound feedback in interactive contexts dynamically and effectively. In particular, physically-based synthesis models describe sonic interactions between resonating objects, and compute the resulting vibrations. Such vibrations are usually described in terms of signals accounting for local displacement and velocity of one or more objects. These signals can be directly sent to a loudspeaker. At the same time, they can drive a haptic device. Overall, physically-based models allow to maintain a tight coherence of the multimodal (in our case tactile and auditory) feedback.

For our specific purposes we made use of an open source software product called Sound Design Toolkit (SDT)[1] which is made of a set of physically-founded tools for designing, synthesizing and manipulating ecological sounds in real time. SDT consists of a library of external objects (*externals*) and programs (*patches*) for the real-time DSP environments Max/MSP and Pure Data (Pd). In particular, each external represents a physically-based or -inspired algorithm for sound synthesis or control, while the SDT patches combine those externals into complete control and sound models.

Below, first a brief description of the models providing audio-haptic feedback is given. Afterwards, an explanation is provided on how such models are controlled by making use of the data coming from the force sensors.

4.1   Physical Models of Contact Events

Contacts between solid bodies form a large class of sonic phenomena in everyday environments, and it has been shown that many contact interactions can be successfully simulated by using a flexible one-dimensional impact or friction model. Regarding this, short acoustic events like impacts can strongly gain or change in expressive content when set, for example, in an appropriate temporal sequence [9].

---

[1] The SDT is freely available from the following SVN repository: https://svn.sme-ccppd.org/svn/sobs/SoundDesignTools/

Soft Impact. The SDT *soft impact* model allows to synthesize the sound of impact on a soft surface, or of soft impact between two surfaces. The soft impact algorithm [10] exploits a rather simplified yet effective approach. Indeed the algorithm is physically-inspired, but it mainly focuses on the actual acoustic result: no actual interaction between objects is simulated, instead the algorithm exploits a filtered noise burst – representing a force signal – to excite a modal resonator [11]. The rationale behind the algorithm can be qualitatively justified considering that non-sharp contacts can be reduced to dense sequences of micro-impacts, thus in a sense discretizing the surfaces of the interacting objects as multiple contact areas. Also, the use of specifically filtered noise signals can be motivated considering that such micro-impacts can have a quasi-random character.

The available model parameters allow for full control of the modal resonator, an ADSR envelope (*attack time, decay time, sustain gain, sustain time, release time*), and the *cut frequencies* of two filters (respectively, high- and low-pass) which process the noise burst.

The *soft impact* model has been used to simulate the contact between a shoe and homogeneous floors or wet grounds, in particular providing two separate envelopes corresponding respectively to the heel and the toe. The aim was to add resonances to neutral floors in order to change the perceived ground material: for instance, a floor made of concrete can be augmented so as to resonate and vibrate like a wooden floor, or as a marshy ground.

Crumpling. The SDT *continuous crumpling* model [12,13] is the result of an *ad hoc* control layer superimposed to a low-level impact model. Similarly to the soft impact model, the crumpling algorithm does not actually model physical contacts between solid objects but, rather, time sequences of crumpling events, represented by groups of impact events. These sequences provide data that drive the evolution across time of the impact model parameters.

Both the temporal distribution of crumpling events and their own power follow stochastic laws which are derived from physics [14]. Such laws govern 1) the energy dissipation occurring during an impact, and 2) the temporal distribution of adjacent events. Each phenomenon exposes a characteristic parameter, resulting in the control of the average interval between events and the average power of impacts, respectively.

As for the actual implementation of the algorithm, the user is provided with several physically meaningful parameters, which allow to set: the applied *force* giving rise to crumpling events and being proportional to their average power, and the *resistance* put up by the material being crumpled, corresponding to the granularity of the latter.

In the perspective of simulating virtual aggregate grounds, the resistance parameter allows control of the compactness of the ground (the lower the resistance, the smoother and more uniform the sequence of crackling events), while the force parameter – being proportional to the energy of the micro-impact events – can be mapped directly to the pressure exerted by the foot on the ground.

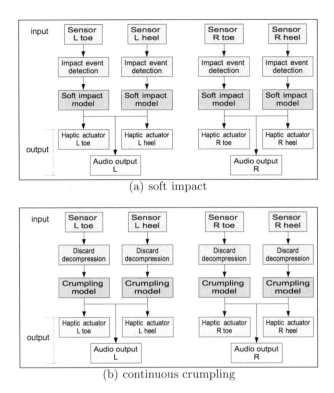

(a) soft impact

(b) continuous crumpling

Fig. 3. Diagram explaining the use of the *soft impact* and *continuous crumpling* models. The diagrams display connections, data conditioning and signal outputs driving both the audio and the haptic feedback.

These models have already been successfully exploited for synthesizing sounds and haptic feedback in simulations of walking on aggregate grounds [15], furthermore they have been adapted for simulating the sound of walking on icy snow, creaking floors, brushwood.

4.2   Data Conditioning and Synthesis Control

The high-rate data stream coming from the Arduino accounts for the force signals measured at each foot's toe and heel. These four signals are received by a Pd patch communicating with the Arduino, and then routed to the SDT model in use. Moreover, the same patch can save the force signals as text files (especially useful for e.g. offline analysis), and later reproduce such files in a way to control the SDT models with prerecorded data.

As for the *soft impact* model, the force signals coming from the sensors are used to trigger four individual noise bursts which excite a resonating object modeling the ground. More in detail, a simple algorithm is used which detects impact events occurring at both the heel and the toe. As soon as such an event is detected, the current force value is used to set the amplitude of the corresponding noise burst: the larger this amplitude, the more energetic the micro-impacts on the resonating object. See the diagram in Fig. 3(a) for an explanation of the use of the *soft impact* model.

Thanks to its external interface, the *continuous crumpling* continuously maps gestures into force parameters: in fact, the model reacts only to variations in the applied force, this way filtering out constant components that do not reflect active interactions. In this regard, the force signals coming from the four sensors have been mapped to the force parameters of four separate instances of the *crumpling* model. By considering that aggregate grounds dynamically respond to a foot falling on them or scraping over them, it was hypothesized that the model should provide energy proportionally to the changes in the force, accounting for corresponding variations of the foot compression. To this end, a gate function has been employed which filters out negative variations of the force, thus excluding feedback when the foot depresses the ground. See the diagram in Fig. 3(b) for an explanation of the use of the *continuous crumpling* model.

5   Vibrotactile and Audio Feedback

Vibrotactile feedback is produced by two vibrotactile transducers embedded in the front and the rear of the shoe sole respectively (Fig. 4(a)) [16] (Haptuator, Tactile Labs Inc., Deux-Montagnes, Qc, Canada). Two cavities were made in the soles to accommodate these broadband vibrotactile actuators. These electromagnetic recoil-type actuators have an operational, linear bandwidth of 50-500 Hz and can provide up to 3 G of acceleration when connected to light loads. They were bonded in place to ensure good transmission of the vibrations inside the soles. When activated, vibrations propagated well in the light, stiff foam. An improved type of such actuators is currently being deployed. This new type uses

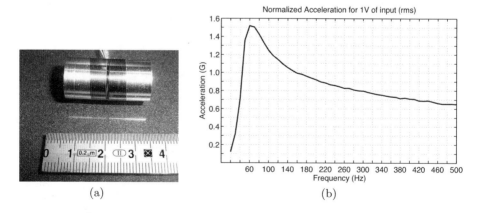

(a)   (b)

Fig. 4. Haptic actuator: (a) Architecture. (b) Characteristic response (from TactileLabs Inc.).

multiple magnets instead of just one, in a configuration designed to concentrate the magnetic flux on a small region. They also benefit from a new suspension design that expends the low-end response significantly and boost the vibratory power despite being of 10 mm in diameter. Such a small size makes it possible to embed them in a variety of objects. Due to their design and structure they can be immersed in the inside of a sole, meanwhile they are able to support the weight of a person with a very little vertical deflection, yet free to vibrate in the horizontal direction because of its anisotropic structure.

In addition to vibrations, each shoe emits sounds from one Goobay Soundball Mobile battery loudspeaker mounted on the top buckle (see Fig. 1). These devices are provided with on-board micro-amplifiers, hence they can be connected directly to the audio card. As any small, low-power loudspeaker device, they exhibit unavoidable performance limits both in the emitted sound pressure level (2.4 W RMS) and low frequency cutoff (about 200 Hz).

The former limit does not pose problems as far as an ecological loudness level of the walking sounds is set. Large levels can be obtained at the cost of audible distortion and faster discharge time of the battery.

The latter limit has perceptual implications instead, as walking interactions can give rise to acoustic energy also in the low frequency. This energy, however, is the result of resonances that are consequence of slowly decaying, large wavelength vibrations occurring in certain floors when they are excited by a shoe impacting over them—think of a floor made with a layer of large wooden bars or panels, for instance. In this sense, forcing a sonic shoe to reproduce low frequencies has no ecological meaning. Due to the aforementioned physical mechanism, it is in fact the floor that should display unlocalized low-frequency sounds on a large area while mimicking the dissipation of mechanical energy that has been transferred when someone walks over it.

5.1   Low and High Frequency Routing

For their efficiency in the high frequency band the small loudspeakers radiate acoustic waves that, by defining a shortest path to the listener's ears and for their strong directivity, create a neat localization of the sound source in correspondence of the shoes. By arriving at the ears later than such waves, any other auditory stimulus is aggregated to the same source location by the listeners due to the known *precedence* effect.

As opposed to small loudspeakers, the haptic actuators generate components in the low frequency. A look to Fig. 4(b) in fact shows that the response of the actuators lies approximately above 50% of the 60 Hz peak value in the range 50-300 Hz. Part of the mechanical energy that they emit, in the form of vibrations across this range, is transmitted to the floor through the shoe sole. Although not comparable with the vibrations of a floor surface that naturally resonates at those frequencies, this energy propagates across the ground and can be heard in the proximity of the walking area. In conclusion, the haptic actuators mitigate the absence in the interface of mid-range loudspeakers and woofers, capable of adding sound energy in the low frequency band.

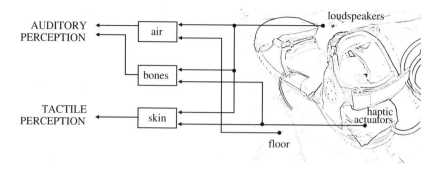

Fig. 5. Information paths connecting the actuated shoes to the auditory and tactile perception

In addition to this effect, a fraction of the vibrational energy that reaches the foot is probably transmitted to the auditory nerve through bone conduction. The set of potentially active information paths connecting the actuated shoes to our perceptual system are illustrated in Fig. 5.

To gain control of this information we have included some filters, all at software level, before routing the digital signal to the various channels in Fig. 2. Specifically, they include high-pass filters that cut off components below 20 Hz otherwise incoming to the output devices, and a smooth resonator that equalizes the response in Fig. 4(b) in the range 50-200 Hz, meanwhile cutting off the frequency components that lie outside the active range of the haptic actuator.

By significantly reducing the energy of the signal that is off the admissible band of the respective devices, these stages contribute to minimize the distortion artifacts and spurious frequency components otherwise introducing unpredictable effects in both the haptic actuators and small loudspeakers.

A systematic inspection of the contribution to listening and touch of the diverse sources of audio and vibrotactile signal, illustrated in Fig. 5, is far from being straightforward. If, on the one hand, their individual effects have been clearly experienced by anybody who informally tested the prototype, on the other hand a quantitative analysis of the perceptual impact of the vibrational energy propagating through the skin, in connection with the acoustic energy propagating through the air and conducted by the bones, would be worth opening another research chapter. In fact, not only the auditory and tactile percepts are difficult to be isolated in presence of a spatially concentrated audio and haptic stimulation, but also the coherence of the resulting (acousto-tactile) multimodal percept is probably conditioned by—perhaps even illusory—cross-modal effects occurring between the two modalities [17]. All this complexity at least does not affect the localization of sounds, for the precedence effect mentioned at the beginning of this section.

6 Conclusions and Future Work

One of the most important achievements of the proposed interface resides in the low latency of the feedback. Due to the excellent features of the audio card and its drivers, the efficiency of the real-time synthesis is not destroyed by bottlenecks encountered at the I/O stages of the system. More in general, this performance has come out as a result of trying many configurations among various operating and hardware systems, and by repeatedly refining the firmware of the acquisition board and the patches in Pd. Measurements made using an oscilloscope connected to the loudspeaker output, and triggered by an input from the audio card simulating a change in force signal, showed that this latency amounts to about 16 ms using the crumpling model.

The analysis of force data is not yet ready to resolve elaborate foot gestures and locomotion tasks that differ from simple walking. Improvements can be made on this analysis, but a general solution to the accurate detection of force during foot movement is not behind the corner if cheap sensors are employed. For instance, sensors like those we used in our prototype saturate at few hundred Newtons, corresponding to some tens of kilos. Hence, they cannot measure changes in the force occurring when users keep standing on the toes or the heel while moving their feet.

The cable connecting the shoes to the amplifiers represents a technological limit of the prototype, that will not be solved unless a new generation of power-efficient haptic devices becomes available.

In spite of these limits, the performance of the prototype is by all means encouraging. Ongoing research deals with the measurement of the skin displacement elicited by the haptic actuators, and with perceptual experimentation on a specific cross-modal effect induced by the multimodal feedback.

Acknowledgments

The research leading to these results has received funding from the European Community's Seventh Framework Programme under FET-Open grant agreement 222107 NIW - Natural Interactive Walking.

References

1. Iwata, H.: Haptic interface. In: Sears, A., Jacko, J.A. (eds.) The Human-Computer Interaction Handbook, 2nd edn. Lawrence Erlbaum Assoc., New York (2008)
2. Visell, Y., Fontana, F., Giordano, B., Nordahl, R., Serafin, S., Bresin, R.: Sound design and perception in walking interactions. Int. J. Human-Computer Studies, 947–959 (2009)
3. Giordano, B.L., McAdams, S., Visell, Y., Cooperstock, J.R., Yao, H., Hayward, V.: Non-visual identification of walking grounds. In: Proc. of Acoustics 2008 in J. Acoust. Soc. Am., vol. 123(5), p. 3412 (2008)
4. Norman, D.: The Design of Future Things. Basic Books, New York (2007)

5. Visell, Y., Cooperstock, J.: Design of a vibrotactile device via a rigid surface. In: Proc. of the IEEE Haptics Symposium, Waltham, MA (2010)
6. Papetti, S., Fontana, F., Civolani, M.: A shoe-based interface for ecological ground augmentation. In: Proc. 4th Int. Haptic and Auditory Interaction Design Workshop, Dresden, Germany, vol. 2 (2009)
7. Civolani, M., Fontana, F., Papetti, S.: Efficient acquisition of force data in interactive shoe designs. In: Proc. 5th Int. Haptic and Auditory Interaction Design Workshop (2010); Elsewhere in these proceedings
8. Bresin, R., de Witt, A., Papetti, S., Civolani, M., Fontana, F.: Expressive sonification of footstep sounds. In: Bresin, R., Hermann, T., Hunt, A. (eds.) Proc. of the Interaction Sonification workshop (ISon) 2010, KTH, Stockholm, Sweden (2010)
9. Rocchesso, D., Fontana, F. (eds.): The Sounding Object. Mondo Estremo (2003), http://www.soundobject.org/
10. Papetti, S.: Sound modeling issues in interactive sonification: from basic contact events to synthesis and manipulation tools. PhD thesis, University of Verona, Italy (2010)
11. Adrien, J.M.: The missing link: Modal synthesis, pp. 269–297 (1991)
12. Fontana, F., Bresin, R.: Physics-based sound synthesis and control: crushing, walking and running by crumpling sounds. In: Proc. Colloquium on Musical Informatics, Florence, Italy, pp. 109–114 (2003)
13. Bresin, R., Delle Monache, S., Fontana, F., Papetti, S., Polotti, P., Visell, Y.: Auditory feedback from continuous control of crumpling sound synthesis. In: CHI 2008 Workshop on Sonic Interaction Design, Florence, Italy. ACM, New York (2008)
14. Houle, P.A., Sethna, J.P.: Acoustic emission from crumpling paper. Physical Review E 54, 278–283 (1996)
15. Visell, Y., Cooperstock, J., Giordano, B.L., Franinovic, K., Law, A., McAdams, S., Jathal, K., Fontana, F.: A vibrotactile device for display of virtual ground materials in walking. In: Ferre, M. (ed.) EuroHaptics 2008. LNCS, vol. 5024, pp. 420–426. Springer, Heidelberg (2008)
16. Hayward, V., Dietz, G., Berrezag, A., Visell, N.O.Y., Cooperstock, J.: Haptic device engineering for walking interactions. Deliverable 2.1, NIW project (2009), http://www.niwproject.eu
17. Altinsoy, E.: Auditory-Tactile interaction in Virtual Environments. Shaker Verlag, Aachen (2006), http://www.ias.et.tu-dresden.de/akustik/Mitarbeiter/Altinsoy/data/15.pdf

Efficient Acquisition of Force Data in Interactive Shoe Designs

Marco Civolani[1], Federico Fontana[2], and Stefano Papetti[1]

[1] Università di Verona, Department of Computer Science
strada Le Grazie, 15 – 37134 Verona, Italy
{marco.civolani,stefano.papetti}@univr.it
[2] Università di Udine, Department of Mathematics and Computer Science
via delle Scienze, 206 – 33100 Udine, Italy
federico.fontana@uniud.it

Abstract. A four-channel sensing system is proposed for the capture of force data from the feet during walking tasks. Developed for an instrumented shoe design prototype, the system solves general issues of latency of the response, accuracy of the data, and robustness of the transmission of digital signals to the host computer. Such issues are often left partially unanswered by solutions for which compactness, accessibility and cost are taken into primary consideration. By adopting widely used force sensing (Interlink) and analog-to-digital conversion and pre-processing (Arduino) components, the proposed system is expected to raise interest among interaction designers of interfaces, in which the reliable and sufficiently broadband acquisition of force signals is desired.

Keywords: Force sensing, closed-loop interfaces.

1 Introduction

Assessment of human gait has been a well known issue in biomechanics and biomedical engineering. Early experiments in measuring and evaluating forces under the foot date back to the end of the 19th century (Beely, 1882; Momburg, 1908). Since that time, various techniques and methods have been implemented with the same purpose, involving the use of different kinds of floor-based electro-mechanic transducers [1,2,3].

Within this specific research topic, we are currently developing an instrumented shoe design that virtually reproduces ground surfaces, by interactively augmenting otherwise neutral (i.e., flat and homogeneous) floors [16]. By means of appropriate force sensing, real time signal processing, and final displaying of multimodal (audio and tactile) cues through portable loudspeakers and haptic actuators underfoot, this design is expected to serve purposes such as navigation in functional spaces, support to physical rehabilitation, and entertainment.

While planning the design of a sensing system for such shoes, we wanted to reach an acceptable trade off between accuracy of the recorded data and accessibility and cost of the technology. Furthermore, the same system had to deliver a

R. Nordahl et al. (Eds.): HAID 2010, LNCS 6306, pp. 129–138, 2010.

continuous data flow affording tight close-loop interaction with walkers through the real time processing of such data. Recently, small and light force sensing devices have been developed, allowing for within the shoe, online force measurements. In parallel, the exploitation of powerful integrated electronic devices has led to the design of portable and wearable data acquisition systems [4,5,6,7].

Unfortunately, there is a general lack of simple yet reliable wearable force measurement systems. It is true that biomechanical and biomedical researchers and engineers can choose commercial solutions providing integrated hardware and software platforms for accurate underfoot force measurements and gait analysis (see for example the Tekscan product line). Besides their quality, hardly these solutions can be adapted for prototyping novel, flexible concepts of foot-floor interfaces. Furthermore, integrated technologies like these do not always guarantee low-level accessibility to raw data, nor they specify exact figures of latency for the transmission of the related signals.

For these reasons, we have worked on the in-depth optimization of an architecture based on popular hardware in the interaction design field, made by Interlink[1] and Arduino[2] and overall costing few tens of dollars. Its performance depends on the number and characteristics of the sensors and the specifications of the acquisition board: together, they set the dynamic range and the band of the acquired information. Besides its applicability to instrumented shoes, the same architecture is of potential interest in all situations where accurate force data must be acquired and processed in real time.

This paper describes in detail its design and operation inside our prototype.

2   Sensors

Two Force Sensing Resistors (FSR) have been inserted between a sandal and a removable sole, forming an additional layer on top of the sandal itself (Fig. 1). Interlink equipment was chosen, for its versatility and popularity among interaction designers [8]. In this sort of "sandwich" configuration, the two sensors detect forces respectively in correspondence of the toe and the heel.

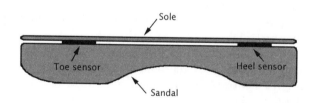

Fig. 1. Mechanical assembly of the shoe. For both toe and heel the Interlink FSR model 402 has been used.

---

[1] http://www.interlinkelectronics.com/
[2] http://arduino.cc/

Each FSR is connected in series with a fixed resistor. Together, they realize a voltage divider. The four dividers, two for each shoe, are finally connected to the first four analog inputs of an Arduino Duemilanove board, another quite popular device. Fig. 2 illustrates this connection.

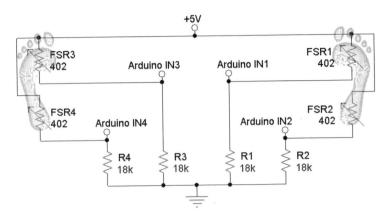

Fig. 2. Schematic of the conditioning circuit. The 5 V and ground pin are accessible from the Arduino board.

A previous version of the prototype used different sensor models and resistance values in the voltage divider [9]. In the following we will see that optimizing these two components leads to substantial improvements.

2.1   Characterization of the FSR

Interaction designers know that Interlink force sensors have good response in front of rapid and large changes in the applied force [10], and they are also especially robust [11]. Thus, they are suitable for detecting forces such as those typically exerted by the foot during gait. For their small size, the model 400 and model 402 are the only Interlink products that can find place inside a shoe without risk of breaking due to excessive mechanical deformation. Although quite similar, the model 400 overall exhibits a different behavior compared to the 402 [12]: in our previous prototype, a good balance between front and rear sensitivity had been achieved by placing a model 400 under the heel and a 402 under the toe.

While changing shoe model during the development of the current prototype, we found that the model 400 reaches mechanical saturation much faster than the 402. This overall unbalanced the acquisition of the data. Clearly, the foot pressure had a different distribution in the new sole.

Measurements have then been made to characterize their behavior. The same measurements furthermore proved useful to characterize the nonlinear behavior of the overall system, caused by the electrical coupling between the FSR and the

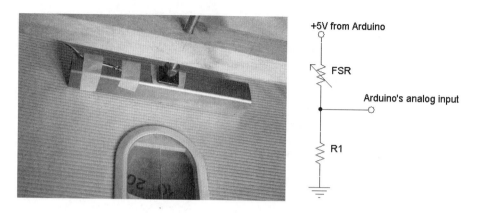

Fig. 3. Characterization of the FSR. (left) Mechanical setup. (right) Voltage divider for the acquisition of measured forces.

analog-to-digital converter (ADC) in the Atmel microcontroller on-board the Arduino [13].

A manual wooden press has been built, and mounted onto a weighing scale. This press had an interchangeable termination, providing mechanical matching with the active area of the sensor. With this simple setup, we could read the value of the force exerted by the press over the sensor. Fig. 3 (left) shows the setup.

The voltage divider containing the FSR was connected to the Arduino analog input as shown in Fig. 3 (right), then pressed. As a result of this simple test, several sets of curves have been obtained for each sensor mapping force into ADC values, for changing values of the resistance R1 in the voltage divider. In practice, each curve represents the relationship between the applied force and the ADC output (ranging from 0 to 1023) for a specific value of R1. Fig. 4 displays the corresponding plots, respectively for sensors model 400 (a) and 402 (b). Their inspection shows that the system is more linear when using the model 402.

All measurements were made by choosing standard resistance values for R1 below 100 kΩ. Smaller values result in a smoother response that furthermore reduces the dynamic range, particularly with the model 402. This means that when the FSR reaches mechanical saturation, the voltage across R1 is below the maximum input voltage of the ADC (5 V). Conversely, values amounting to more than 100 kΩ introduce a strong nonlinearity. Choosing R1 = 18 kΩ results in a good compromise between range and linearity of the system.

In conclusion, the model 402 has been preferred for all sensing points and the resistance in the voltage dividers has been set to 18 kΩ: these choices have substantially improved the sensitivity of our instrumented shoes. Besides our specific application case, a simple measurement experience like the one described here can reward each time an FSR must be coupled to an ADC in an acquisition system of interest.

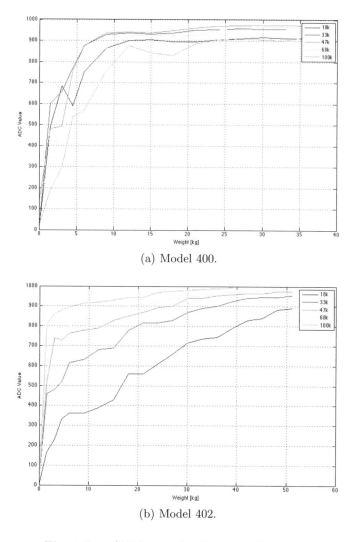

(a) Model 400.

(b) Model 402.

Fig. 4. Force/ADC maps for changing values of R1

3   Firmware

A good firmware program can enable the cheap hardware on-board the Arduino
to perform as an effective front-end for data acquisition from the sensors. A
reliable analog-to-digital conversion along with a low-latency transmission of the
acquired data are in fact necessary to achieve this goal, when designing a real
time interactive system providing instantaneous feedback. The essential tasks of
the Arduino are illustrated in Fig. 5.

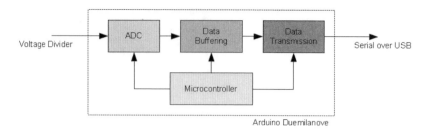

Fig. 5. Blocks of the data acquisition module

The firmware employed in the previous prototype of the interactive shoes included an application program, that repeatedly read the four values coming from the respective analog inputs through a traditional polling procedure nested inside a main loop [9]. Then, data were filtered in such a way that a packet containing the values was sent only if two subsequent samples differed at least by a given threshold. Concerning the serial transmission, we sent to the host packets made of four ADC values separated by a space character. Each packet ended with a separator (end of line) character.

Both the polling sequence and the transmission routine have been written using functions and procedure calls provided by the Arduino SDK. The use of this framework allows to write code very easily, thanks to the good level of abstraction provided by the embedded C++ API. Unfortunately the compiled program is often not efficient enough, especially if running on applications requiring a constantly low latency during the acquisition of uniform data flows.

In our case, the unconditioned use of the API affected the reliability of the analog-to-digital conversion and the constancy of the transmission rate of the serial connection over USB from the Arduino to the host. In fact, the previous firmware used the `analogRead` function, which, as a normal practice in acquisition procedures of this kind, was called for every channel during polling. As a consequence, the sampling frequency could not be kept stable: the main loop in fact can be interrupted at any moment, and it takes an unpredictable time for the system to return to the application program.

The transmission was managed using the `Serial.print` function, which prints out data to the serial port in the form of ASCII characters. In particular, every number digit was printed using the respective character. Once again, the API-based solution is quite standard and easy to be coded, but poorly performing. For instance, transmitting four 10-bit values requires, in the worst case (i.e., all the four values greater than 1000), $8 \cdot 4 \cdot 4 + 8 \cdot 4 = 160$ bits.

Interrupts can introduce heavy jitter. In the Arduino this problem is a consequence of the weak control of the low level structures inside the microcontroller through the API. In essence, the Arduino is not provided with resources capable to handle both processes in parallel:

- the ATMega168 is a single-thread machine, thus when the CPU is handling the ADC interrupt it cannot (among other things) transmit data over the serial connection;
- the Arduino USB connection is controlled by a FTDI FT232RL chip, which *emulates* a serial RS-232 connection over a USB line.

A consequence of the first point is that sampling with an exceedingly high frequency is unsafe since some values would be inevitably lost. The second point deals with the buffers that are present on the transmitter (inside the FTDI chip) and the receiver (in the USB controller driver, run by the operating system of the host computer). These buffers are governed by independent schedulers and procedures [14], and a low-level debugging of their mutual activity is a hard task.

As it often happens in this kind of architectures, the best performance is achieved by writing part of the code in assembly language at the cost of decreased readability and portability. A solution in between, that can be adopted with AVR-compliant microcontrollers like the ATMega168, is to write programs encoding API calls and AVR Libc instructions[3] together.

In the current firmware, we have set the ADC to work in *free-running* mode. Under this mode, the ADC interrupts the program only when the acquisition on the selected channel is completed. The sampling frequency can be selected by setting the ADC *prescaler* bits (ADPS) in the ADCSRA register. In free-running mode, a single conversion takes 13.5 CPU cycles, thus the sampling frequency turns out to be equal to $Fs = (16/13.5)/P$ MHz, where P represents the value of the prescaler.

Furthermore, a custom transmission protocol has been implemented [15]: binary data are transmitted instead of ASCII values using the `Serial.write` function. Every packet is formed by two bytes, B_{MSB} and B_{LSB}, such that their juxtaposition is $B_{MSB} B_{LSB} = 1CCCCVVV\ 0VVVVVVV$. In this structure, the four bits denoted with C encode the channel number (16 channels are allowed), whereas the ten bits denoted with V encode the measured value thus guaranteeing sufficient accuracy for the acquired force. In the end, each sensor is assigned to a different channel. Hence, sending four values (one for each channel) using this protocol occupies a constant packet size, equal to $8 \cdot 2 \cdot 4 = 64$ bits.

3.1   Uniform Sampling of Force Data

We opted for a reliable, although not necessarily optimal assignment of the system variables in the new firmware, by empirically determining the transmission rates of in absence of drop-outs.

An oscilloscope was connected to a digital pin of the board. The pin was set at the beginning of the ADC routine, and was reset at the end of the same routine. The ADC routine called the transmission procedure only when the transmission buffer was full.

---

[3] http://www.nongnu.org/avr-libc/

When sending a cluster of bytes (i.e., a buffer) with the `Serial.write` function, the Atmel performs a serial transmission of data to the FTDI chip's buffer. For what we said above, data are sent on the USB line according to specific handshaking and buffering policies that in principle vary with the transmitter/receiver protocol.

The observations made on the oscilloscope uncovered that the serial transmission from the Atmel to the FTDI chip requires a large amount of CPU time. The values coming from the ADC which fall into this bottleneck are lost. For this reason we set the prescaler to $P = 128$, even if lower values are allowed.

By setting the buffer size to 2 bytes we obtained a regular sequence of impulses from the probed pin, testifying uniform sampling. In practice, this buffer size ensured that the transmission time is shorter than the sampling time. At this point, a linear relationship between the transmission rate and sampling frequency can be figured out. Table 1 lists possible choices complying with this relationship.

The values showed in Table 1 must be divided by the number of input channels, if a polling procedure is implemented. In our application, involving four channels, the sampling frequency per channel is $F_s = 5882/4 \approx 1470$ Hz. Considering that the FSR's have a response time of about 2 ms [12], a latency that is certainly smaller than any human response to psychophysical cue changes, the obtained sampling frequency is well above twice as much the Nyquist limit of $1/0.002 = 500$ Hz.

Table 1. Relationship between sampling frequency (F_s) and transmission rate (TXrate). Values per single channel. Prescaler set to 128.

TXrate [baud]	9600	19200	38400	57600	115200
T_s [ms]	2.1	1.04	0.52	0.36	0.17
F_s [Hz]	476	961	1923	2778	5882

4   Results and Conclusions

Fig. 6 shows some plots of force signals recorded using the proposed system. These plots provide evidence of a substantial absence of noise and jitter in the data. If perhaps not accurate enough for applications where extremely high resolution is mandatory, such data is suitable for most interaction design and other applications.

In our case the force signals are sent to the host computer for further processing [16]. Still, for many other acquisition processes requiring similar performance and cost, we think that designers and others can make profitable use of the solutions and tests described in this work.

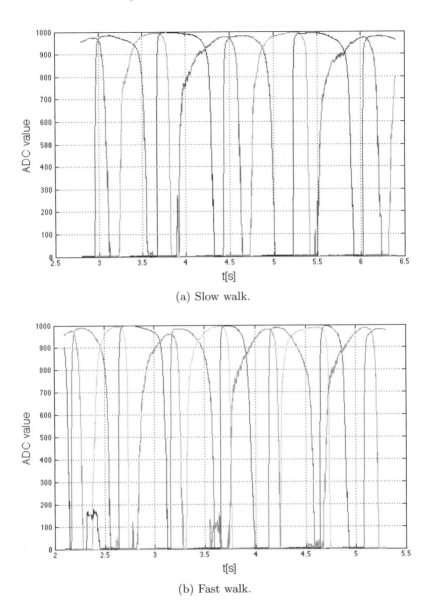

(a) Slow walk.

(b) Fast walk.

Fig. 6. Force plots. Red = left heel, green = left toe, blue = right heel, magenta = right toe.

Acknowledgments

The research leading to these results has received funding from the European Community's Seventh Framework Programme under FET-Open grant agreement 222107 NIW - Natural Interactive Walking.

References

1. Stott, J.R.R., Hutton, W.C., Stokes, I.A.F.: Forces Under the Foot. Journal of Bone and Joint Surgery 55-B, 335–345 (1973)
2. Manley, M.T., Solomon, E.: The Clinical Assessment of the Normal and Abnormal Foot During Locomotion. Journal of Prosthetics and Orthotics 3, 10–110 (1979)
3. Soames, R.W., Blake, C.D., Stott, J.R.R., Goodbody, A., Brewerton, D.A.: Measurement of pressure under the foot during function. Journal of Medical and Biological Engineering and Computing 20, 489–495 (1982)
4. Pollard, J.P., Quesne, L.P.L., Tappin, J.W.: Forces Under the Foot. Journal of Biomedical Engineering 5, 37–40 (1983)
5. Zhu, H., Maalej, N., Webster, J.G., Tompkings, W.J., Bach-Y-Rita, P., Wertsch, J.J.: An Umbilical Data-Acquisition System for Measuring Pressures Between the Foot and Shoe. IEEE Transactions on Biomedical Engineering 37, 908–911 (1990)
6. Faivre, A., Dahan, M., Parratte, B., Monnier, G.: Instrumented shoes for pathological gait assessment. Mechanics Research Communications 31, 627–632 (2004)
7. Morris, S.J.: A Shoe-Integrated Sensor System for Wireless Gait Analysis and Real-Time Therapeutic Feedback. PhD thesis, Massachusetts Institute of Technology (2004)
8. Miranda, E., Wanderley, M.: New Digital Musical Instruments: Control and Interaction Beyond the Keyboard. AR Editions (2006)
9. Papetti, S., Fontana, F., Civolani, M.: A shoe-based interface for ecological ground augmentation. In: Proc. 4th Int. Haptic and Auditory Interaction Design Workshop, Dresden, Germany, vol. 2 (2009)
10. Hollinger, A., Wanderley, M.M.: Evaluation of commercial force-sensing resistors. Unpublished report 1, Input Devices and Music Interaction Laboratory (IDMIL), Music Technology Schulich - School of Music, McGill University Montreal, QC, Canada (2006), http://www.idmil.org/publications
11. Vecchi, F., Freschi, C., Micera, S., Sabatini, A., Dario, P., Sacchetti, R.: Experimental evaluation of two commercial force sensors for applications in biomechanics and motor control. In: Proceedings of the 5th Annual Conference of the International Functional Electrical Stimulation Society, Aalborg, Denmark, p. 44 (2000)
12. Interlink: Force sensing resistor integration guide and evaluation parts catalog. Datasheet 90-45632 Rev. D, Interlink Electronics, 546 Flynn Road, Camarillo, CA 93012, USA (2009), http://www.interlinkelectronics.com/library/media/papers/pdf/fsrguide.pdf
13. Atmel: Atmega168 datasheet. Datasheet 2545RAVR07/09, Atmel Corporation, 2325 Orchard Parkway, San Jose, CA 95131, USA (2009), http://www.atmel.com/dyn/products/datasheets_v2.asp?family_id=607
14. FTDI: Data throughput, latency and handshaking. Application note AN232B-04 Rev. 1.1, Future Technology Devices International Ltd., Seaward Place, Centurion Business Park, Glasgow, G41 1HH, UK (2006), http://www.ftdichip.com/Documents/AppNotes/AN232B-04_DataLatencyFlow.pdf
15. Visell, Y., Law, A., Ip, J., Rajalingham, R., Smith, S., Cooperstock, J.R., Borin, G., Civolani, M., Fontana, F., Polotti, P., Nordahl, R., Serafin, S., Turchet, L.: Contact-based sensing methods for walking interactions. Deliverable 3.1, NIW project (2009), http://www.niwproject.eu
16. Papetti, S., Fontana, F., Civolani, M., Berrezag, A., Hayward, V.: Audio-tactile display of ground properties using interactive shoes. In: Proc. 5th Int. Haptic and Auditory Interaction Design Workshop (2010); Elsewhere in these proceedings

A Comparison of Two Wearable Tactile Interfaces with a Complementary Display in Two Orientations

Mayuree Srikulwong and Eamonn O'Neill

University of Bath, Bath, BA2 7AY, UK
{ms244,eamonn}@cs.bath.ac.uk

Abstract. Research has shown that two popular forms of wearable tactile displays, a back array and a waist belt, can aid pedestrian navigation by indicating direction. Each type has its proponents and each has been reported as successful in experimental trials, however, no direct experimental comparisons of the two approaches have been reported. We have therefore conducted a series of experiments directly comparing them on a range of measures. In this paper, we present results from a study in which we used a directional line drawing task to compare user performance with these two popular forms of wearable tactile display. We also investigated whether user performance was affected by a match between the plane of the tactile interface and the plane in which the users drew the perceived directions. Finally, we investigated the effect of adding a complementary visual display. The touch screen display on which participants drew the perceived directions presented either a blank display or a visual display of a map indicating eight directions from a central roundabout, corresponding to the eight directions indicated by the tactile stimuli. We found that participants performed significantly faster and more accurately with the belt than with the array whether they had a vertical screen or a horizontal screen. We found no difference in performance with the map display compared to the blank display.

Keywords: Evaluation/methodology, haptic i/o, user interfaces, wearable computers, pedestrian navigation.

1 Introduction

As illustrated in Table 1, researchers have proposed various forms of tactile wearable interfaces to convey directional information on different body sites. Some of these systems (e.g. [1], [2], [3]) have been tested and reported as successful in a range of environments. Of the proposed forms in Table 1, we have focused on the wearable systems that use the torso as a display site, specifically belt-type and back torso vest devices, since previous research (e.g. [4], [5]) suggests that their shape, size, and body contact areas support representation of cardinal (i.e. north, east, west and south) and ordinal (i.e. northeast, northwest, southeast, and southwest) directions and other information. We decided not to use the headband because it was reported that users had experienced discomfort wearing the system [6]. For the systems worn on wrists and feet, the size of body contact areas is too small effectively to afford the display of 8 directions. We also decided not to study the systems worn on fingers because users often require their hands to be free to perform other activities.

R. Nordahl et al. (Eds.): HAID 2010, LNCS 6306, pp. 139–148, 2010.

Table 1. Tactile wearable interfaces classified by their body contact area and form

Body contact areas	Forms	Products or Research Projects
Head	Headband	Forehead Retina System [7], Haptic Radar [8]
Shoulders	Shoulder Pad	Active Shoulder Pad [9]
Back Torso	Vest	Tactile Land Navigation [10]
Back Torso	Chair	Haptic Back Display [4]
Back Torso	Backpack	3x3 Tapping Interface Grid [1], Personal Guidance System [11]
Around the waist	Belt	ActiveBelt [5], WaistBelt [3], [12], Tactile Wayfinder [13]
Wrist	Wristband	GentleGuide [14], Personal Guide System [15]
Fingers	Wristwatch with Finger-Braille Interface	Virtual Leading Blocks [16]
Feet	Shoes	CabBoots [2]

The physical interface layout of systems worn on the torso typically follows one of two forms: (1) a back array of vibrators generating straight-line patterns (e.g. [1], [4]); and (2) a waist belt embedded with vibrators generating absolute point vibrations (e.g. [10], [3], [5]). Researchers have reported each of these interfaces as effective.

The back array represents cardinal and ordinal directions by generating stimulation patterns on an array of vibrators to create the sensation of a dotted line, known as the "cutaneous rabbit" phenomenon [17], [4]. The tactile flow patterns, also known as saltatory signals, generated by this approach represent directions of movement [1]. Most of the wearable tactile interfaces using this approach are in the form of a vest and stimulate the user's back. Tan et al. [4], and Ross and Blasch [1] built their interfaces using a 3x3 motor array. Each direction was generated as a simulated line using three motors, e.g. vibrating motors in the middle vertical row of the array from bottom to top conveyed north. The systems were tested with drawing and street-crossing tasks. The researchers reported that tactile interaction effectively presented spatial information for the drawing tasks [4] and assisted visually impaired pedestrians in street-crossing [1].

The waist belt interface represents a direction by triggering vibration of a motor at the corresponding location around the waist. The tactile representation of absolute positions directly represents directions [3]. Van Erp et al. [3], Duistermaat [10] and Tsukada et al. [5] built prototypes in the form of a waist belt with 8 embedded motors distributed around the belt. Each motor represented one of the eight cardinal and ordinal directions, with each directional signal being generated using one motor. For example, vibrating the motor located at the front in the middle of the waist conveyed north. Evaluation results suggested that tactile interfaces were practical for conveying directional information in operational environments including pedestrian navigation during daytime [5]) and in low visibility environments such as at night [10]; navigation in visually cluttered environments, e.g. in the cockpit of an aircraft [3]; and in vibrating environments, e.g. in a fast boat [3].

These two interface designs, the back array presenting a saltatory line and the waist belt presenting absolute points, have dominated research on tactile navigation displays on the torso, with each claiming success as a navigation aid. There was, however, no reported research directly comparing performance with these two approaches. Therefore, we directly compared them in a series of experiments, one of which we report here, involving directional pointing [18] and line drawing tasks.

2 Experimental Comparison

We closely followed the designs of both established interfaces, both in the form of the wearable devices and the tactile stimuli patterns used for each. Tan et al. [4] reported that different array sizes could affect performance; specifically, smaller participants performed better with an array with an inter-motor distance of 50 mm while bigger participants performed better with a bigger array (inter-motor distance of 80 mm). Geldard et al. [17] suggests that vibrators in a back array should be spaced at least at 40 mm but no greater than 100 mm to create a saltatory signal "line effect". With little other evidence, there is no established optimum value for inter-vibrator distance. Therefore, for our initial experiments we built and tested two sizes of back array, 50 mm and 80 mm. Our 50 mm back array consisted of 9 motors mounted into a fabric pad in a 3-by-3 array. The motors had an equal inter-spacing of 50 mm. Our 80 mm back array was similar in shape but had an inter-spacing distance between motors of 80 mm. Our previous experiments [18] found the 50 mm array to be significantly less effective than the 80 mm array; therefore, in this experiment we compared only the 80 mm array and the belt. Our waist belt tactile interface consisted of 8 motors mounted in a belt. Following previous research (e.g. [3], [5]), the motors had an unequal inter-spacing (from 50 mm to 130 mm) to account for participants' varying body shape and size. All the interfaces were worn over light clothing such as a T-shirt.

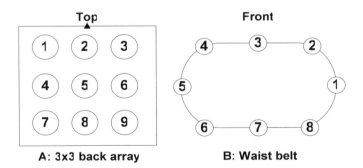

A: 3x3 back array   **B: Waist belt**

Fig. 1. Layouts of the two interfaces

The design of our tactile stimuli drew on tactile interaction design guidelines [19], the results of previous research [4] and our own pilot studies. We designed two sets of tactile stimuli: set A (Table 2) for the back array, and set B (Table 3) for the belt. Set A contained eight saltatory signals representing *east, west, south, north, southeast, southwest, northeast,* and *northwest.* Set B represented the same eight directions based on the location of the motors around the participant's waist, with *north* represented by front centre (i.e. motor number 3).

Table 2. Stimuli set A's signal pattern. Number in signal pattern represents motor number in Figure 1A.

Stimuli code	Signal pattern	Direction
A1	444455556666	East
A2	666655554444	West
A3	222255558888	South
A4	888855552222	North
A5	111155559999	Southeast
A6	333355557777	Southwest
A7	777755553333	Northeast
A8	999955551111	Northwest

Both sets of stimuli had the same constant frequency (200 Hz) and inter-stimulus duration (50 ms). The vibration pattern for stimuli set A involved actuation of 3 motors and consisted of 4 repetitions of signals at 50 ms pulse and inter-pulse on each motor, i.e. 12 pulses in total for each stimulus. The pattern for stimuli set B involved actuation of one motor and consisted of 12 repetitions of signals at 50 ms pulse and inter-pulse duration. Hence, the number of pulses and duration of signal were the same across both stimuli sets.

Table 3. Stimuli set B's signal pattern. Number in signal pattern represents motor number in Figure 1B.

Stimuli code	Signal pattern	Direction
B1	111111111111	East
B2	222222222222	Northeast
B3	333333333333	North
B4	444444444444	Northwest
B5	555555555555	West
B6	666666666666	Southwest
B7	777777777777	South
B8	888888888888	Southeast

2.1 Experimental Procedure

In this study, we investigated whether performance between the two wearable layouts would differ for a line drawing task. In addition, we investigated if the pointing task in our previous experiment [18] might have favoured the belt layout since the plane of the belt vibrators matched the plane of the wall sensors used for user responses. Hence, in this experiment we also varied the plane in which participants responded.

We used a line drawing task because it requires similar skills to those needed when using a map-based navigation system, e.g. the ability to interpret the understanding of directions into two-dimensional representations [20] and the ability to associate one's current view of the world to its location in the map [21]. The experimental conditions involved drawing arrowed lines, indicating perceived directions, on a touch screen with one of two orientations, vertical and horizontal. We hypothesized that participants would perform better when the plane of the prototype matched the plane of the screen, i.e. they would perform better with the back array when drawing directed lines on a *vertical* screen. On the other hand, they would perform better with the belt when the task involved drawing directed lines on a *horizontal* screen.

As Carter and Fourney [22] suggested that using other senses as cues may support tactile interaction, we introduced a visual display as an experimental factor with two levels. In the first level, the touch screen presented a blank display on which participants drew their directed line (Figure 2A). In the second level, the touch screen presented a visual display of a map indicating eight directions from a central roundabout, corresponding to the eight directions indicated by the tactile stimuli (Figure 2B). We predicted that the visual display of the map would aid the participant in interpreting and responding to the tactile stimuli.

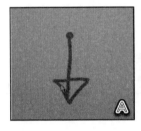

Fig. 2. A: Line drawn by a participant on the blank display. B: Line drawn by a participant on the map display.

In summary, we compared performance with the array and belt tactile interfaces and the effect on performance of (1) the plane of output display and (2) the presence or absence of a visual map display. The experimental hypotheses were as follows.

H1. Performance will be better when the plane of the tactile stimuli matches the plane of the responses, specifically:

    H1a. Participants will perform better with the back array when the task involves drawing lines on a vertical screen;

    H1b. Participants will perform better with the waist belt when the task involves drawing lines on a horizontal screen;

H2. Participants will perform better with the map display than the blank display.

There were 16 participants, 7 males and 9 females, with an average age of 29. Participants reported no abnormality with tactile perception at the time of experiment. They had no previous experience with tactile interfaces. They understood the concept of "direction" and were able to draw all cardinal and ordinal directions. Participants used both tactile interfaces. They were instructed to stand at a marked point approximately 200 mm away from the screen in the vertical display condition; and 130 mm away from the lower edge of the screen in the horizontal display condition. The height of the screen was adjusted to suit individual participants for the vertical and horizontal conditions. The order of conditions was counterbalanced.

There were 8 conditions, as shown in Table 4. Participants responded to the directions they perceived by drawing arrows with a stylus on the touch screen. Each participant responded to 8 stimuli in each condition. We compared a range of performance measures: time between the end of each stimulus and the response (response time), correctly perceived directions (accuracy), failure to identify any direction for a stimulus (breakdown), and incorrectly identified directions (error).

Participants were given a demonstration of how they would receive tactile stimuli via each prototype but were given no other training. We wanted to discover how well they could intuitively (i.e. without extensive training) interpret the meanings of different tactile patterns and to discover how usable the interfaces were without training. A key factor to successfully introducing new technology lies in its usability. Novel consumer technologies typically come with little or no training.

Table 4. Experimental conditions and their codes

Back Array				Waist Belt			
Vertical screen		Horizontal screen		Vertical screen		Horizontal screen	
Blank (C1)	Map (C2)	Blank (C3)	Map (C4)	Blank (C5)	Map (C6)	Blank (C7)	Map (C8)

2.2 Results

2.2.1 Overall Accuracy and Response Time Analysis

The mean accuracy, error, breakdowns and response times for the back array and the belt are shown in Tables 5 and 6. The data were analyzed using a three-way repeated-measures ANOVA with *tactile interface*, *screen orientation* and *visual display* (Table 4 top, second and third rows respectively) as the independent variables. There was no significant interaction effect between *tactile interface* and *screen orientation* on accuracy ($f_{1,15} = 0.54$, n.s.), errors ($f_{1,15} = 0.05$, n.s.), breakdowns ($f_{1,15} = 1$, n.s.) or response time ($f_{1,15} = 1.74$, n.s.). These results tell us that the effects of the different tactile interfaces did not vary depending on the touch screen's orientation, horizontal or vertical.

Post hoc Bonferroni pairwise comparisons showed that accuracy was significantly better with the belt than with the array in every case ($p < 0.002$); errors were significantly fewer with the belt than with the array in every case ($p < 0.002$); and response time was significantly quicker with the belt than with the array in every case ($p < 0.002$). No significant difference was found for breakdowns.

Table 5. Mean performance for vertical screen conditions. *Scores: n of 8, Time: in seconds. SDs in parentheses.*

	Back Array Vertical Screen		Waist Belt Vertical Screen	
	Blank (C1)	Map (C2)	Blank (C5)	Map (C6)
Accuracy	5.06 (1.84)	5.25 (1.65)	7.44 (0.63)	7.19 (1.11)
Error	2.81 (0.63)	2.44 (1.59)	0.50 (0.63)	0.75 (1.07)
Breakdown	0 (0.00)	0.31 (0.60)	0 (0.00)	0.06 (0.25)
Time	2.13 (0.50)	2.08 (0.83)	1.40 (0.37)	1.54 (0.67)

Table 6. Mean performance for horizontal screen conditions. *Scores: n of 8, Time: in seconds. SDs in parentheses.*

	Back Array Horizontal Screen		Waist Belt Horizontal Screen	
	Blank (C3)	Map (C4)	Blank (C7)	Map (C8)
Accuracy	5.63 (1.75)	5.63 (1.67)	7.5 (0.63)	7.63 (0.89)
Error	2.25 (1.65)	2.31 (1.66)	0.44 (0.63)	0.25 (0.58)
Breakdown	0.12 (0.34)	0.06 (0.25)	0 (0.00)	0.12 (0.50)
Time	2.08 (0.37)	2.21 (0.59)	1.28 (0.35)	1.41 (0.36)

Hypothesis H1 was rejected since participants performed significantly faster and more accurately with the belt than with the array whether they had a vertical screen or a horizontal screen.

A three-way repeated-measures ANOVA was run to compare blank displays and visual map displays on accuracy, response time, breakdowns and errors. No significant effect of display type was found on accuracy ($f_{1,15} = 0.01$, n.s.), response time ($t_{1,14} = 0.06$, n.s.), breakdowns ($t_{1,15} = 2.56$, n.s.), or errors ($t_{1,15} = 0.14$, n.s.). Thus, we rejected hypothesis H2 since display type had no effect on performance.

2.2.2 Accuracy and Response Time by Stimulus

We performed further analysis on accuracy and response times with respect to the stimuli. Using the array, participants performed worst in accuracy (C1 and C2 in Figure 3, and C3 and C4 in Figure 4) with vertical (*north* and *south*) and horizontal saltatory signals (*east* and *west*). The inaccuracy ranged widely from 45 to 180 degrees (both to the left and to the right of intended directions). Figure 5 also shows that participants responded much more slowly with the array than with the belt in all directions. They were slowest with the *north* signal. Using the belt, there was no significant difference in participants' accuracy and response times with different stimuli. Almost all incorrect answers were 45-degree errors.

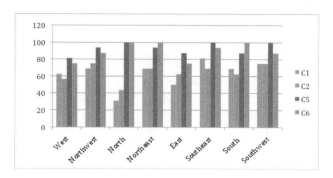

Fig. 3. Accuracy of responses (%) for all directions with the vertical screen conditions

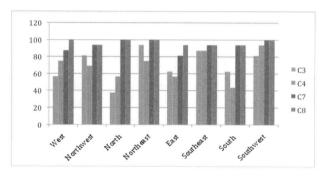

Fig. 4. Accuracy of responses (%) for all directions with the horizontal screen conditions

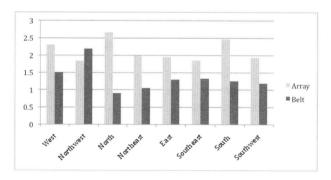

Fig. 5. Average response time (in second) for array conditions (C1 – C4) and belt conditions (C5 – C8)

3 Conclusion

Two types of wearable tactile displays, back array and waist belt, have been reported as successfully representing direction in experimental trials, however, previous research has not directly compared their performance. Our experiments reported here and in [18] show the belt to be significantly better than the array across a wide range of conditions, in this study regardless of screen orientation or visual display. The experiment reported here also suggests that the visual display of the directions (in the map condition) did not aid the perception of and response to the tactile stimuli. This offers support to the notion that a unimodal tactile system, such as the tactile navigation aids presented by Tan et al. [4] and Van Erp et al. [3], is feasible without support from other modalities such as visual displays. It does not, however, rule out the possibility that other complementary displays might provide such aid.

Overall, our results suggest that the belt is a better choice for wearable tactile direction indication than the back array, however, our experiments did not seek to tease out which particular features of these two established approaches led to the observed differences. The two approaches actually vary on at least three potentially significant features: physical layout of vibrators, stimuli patterns (tactile flow *vs* absolute point), and body contact areas. We have found no published research that attempts to systematically vary these three features. In the experiment reported here, we have shown that the belt is more effective than the array in the form in which each of these designs has most commonly been realized. We did not examine the effects of more extensive training or long-term use. Other studies will be required to investigate these effects, which might help to improve the performance of the back array.

Acknowledgements. Mayuree Srikulwong's research is supported by the University of Thai Chamber of Commerce, Thailand. Eamonn O'Neill's research is supported by a Royal Society Industry Fellowship at Vodafone Group R&D.

References

1. Ross, D.A., Blasch, B.B.: Wearable Interfaces for Orientation and Wayfinding. In: 4th International ACM Conference on Assistive Technologies (ASSETS 2000), pp. 193–200 (2000)
2. Frey, M.: CabBoots – Shoes with Integrated Guidance System. In: 1st International Conference on Tangible and Embedded Interaction (TEI 2007), pp. 245–246 (2007)
3. Van Erp, J.B.F., Van Veen, H.A.H.C., Jansen, C., Dobbins, T.: Waypoint Navigation with a Vibrotactile Waist Belt. ACM Transaction of Applied Perception 2(2), 106–117 (2005)
4. Tan, H.Z., Gray, R., Young, J.J., Traylor, R.: A Haptic Back Display for Attentional and Directional Cueing. Haptics-e: The Electronic Journal of Haptics Research 3(1) (2003)
5. Tsukada, K., Yasumura, M.: ActiveBelt: Belt-type Wearable Tactile Display for Directional Navigation. In: Davies, N., Mynatt, E.D., Siio, I. (eds.) UbiComp 2004. LNCS, vol. 3205, pp. 384–399. Springer, Heidelberg (2004)
6. Myles, K., Binseel, M.S.: The Tactile Modality: A Review of Tactile Sensitivity and Human Tactile Interfaces. U.S. Army Research Laboratory, ARL-TR-4115, Aberdeen Proving Ground, MD 21005-5425 (2007)
7. Kajimoto, H., Kanno, Y., Tachi, S.: Forehead Retina System. In: 33rd International Conference on Computer Graphics and Interactive Techniques (2006)
8. Cassinelli, A., Reynolds, C., Ishikawa, M.: Augmenting Spatial Awareness with Haptic Radar. In: 10th International Symposium on Wearable Computers (ISWC 2006), pp. 61-64 (2006)

9. Toney, A., Dunne, L., Thomas, B.H., Ashdown, S.P.: A Shoulder Pad Insert Vibrotactile Display. In: 7th IEEE International Symposium on Wearable Computers (ISWC 2003), pp. 35-44 (2003)

10. Duistermaat, M.: Tactile Land in Night Operations, TNO-Memorandum TNO-DV3 2005 M065. TNO, Soesterberg, Netherlands (2005)

11. Loomis, J.M., Golledge, R.G., Klatzky, R.L.: GPS-based Navigation Systems for the Visually Impaired. In: Barfield, W., Caudell, T. (eds.) Fundamentals of Wearable Computers and Augmented Reality, pp. 429–446. Lawrence Erlbaum, Mahwah (2001)

12. Ho, C., Tan, H.Z., Spence, C.E.: Using Spatial Vibrotactile Cues to Direct Visual Attention in Driving Scenes. Transportation Research Part F 8: Traffic Psychology and Behavior, pp. 397–412 (2005)

13. Heuten, W., Henze, N., Boll, S., Pielot, M.: Tactile Wayfinder: a Non-Visual Support System for Wayfinding. In: 5th Nordic Conference on Human-Computer Interaction: Building Bridges (NordiCHI 2008), vol. 358, pp. 172–181 (2008)

14. Bosman, S., Groenedaal, B., Findlater, J.W., Visser, T., De Graaf, M., Markopoulos, P.: GentleGuide: An Exploration of Haptic Output for Indoors Pedestrian Guidance. In: Chittaro, L. (ed.) Mobile HCI 2003. LNCS, vol. 2795, pp. 358–362. Springer, Heidelberg (2003)

15. Marston, J.R., Loomis, J.M., Klatzky, R.L., Golledge, R.G.: Nonvisual Route Following with Guidance from a Simple Haptic or Auditory Display. Journal of Visual Impairment and Blindness 101, 203–211 (2007)

16. Amemiya, T., Yamashita, J., Hirota, K., Hirose, M.: Virtual Leading Blocks for the Deaf-Blind: A Real-Time Way-Finder by Verbal-Nonverbal Hybrid Interface and High-Density RFID Tag Space. In: IEEE Virtual Reality Conference 2004 (VR 2004), pp. 165–172 (2004)

17. Geldard, F.A., Sherrick, C.E.: The Cutaneous 'Rabbit': A Perceptual Illusion. Science, 178, 4057, 178–179 (1972)

18. Srikulwong, M., O'Neill, E.: A Direct Experimental Comparison of Back Array and Waist-Belt Tactile Interfaces for Indicating Direction. In: Workshop on Multimodal Location Based Techniques for Extreme Navigation at Pervasive 2010, pp. 5–8 (2010)

19. Van Erp, J.B.F.: Guidelines for the Use of Vibro-Tactile Displays in Human Computer Interaction. In: EuroHaptics 2002, pp. 18–22 (2002)

20. Yao, X., Fickas, S.: Pedestrian Navigation Systems: a Case Study of Deep Personalization. In: 1st International Workshop on Software Engineering for Pervasive Computing Applications, Systems, and Environments (SEPCASE 2007), pp. 11–14 (2007)

21. Aretz, A.J.: The Design of Electronic Map Displays. Human Factors 33(1), 85–101 (1991)

22. Carter, J., Fourney, D.: Research Based Tactile and Haptic Interaction Guidelines. In: Guidelines on Tactile and Haptic Interaction (GOTHI 2005), pp. 84–92 (2005)

Virtual Sequencing with a Tactile Feedback Device

Victor Zappi, Marco Gaudina, Andrea Brogni, and Darwin Caldwell

Istituto Italiano di Tecnologia, Advanced Robotics Department,
Via Morego 30, 16163 Genova, Italy
{victor.zappi,marco.gaudina,andrea.brogni,darwin.caldwell}@iit.it
http://www.iit.it/en/Advanced-robotics.html

Abstract. Since the beginning of Virtual Reality many artistic applications were developed, showing how this technology could be exploited not only from a technical point of view, but also in the field of feelings and emotions. Nowadays music is one of the most interesting field of application for Virtual Reality, and many environments provide the user with means to express her/himself; our work follows this direction, aiming at developing a set of multimodal musical interfaces. In this paper we present a first simple virtual sequencer combined with a low cost tactile feedback device: some preliminary experiments were done to analyze how skilled musicians approach this unusual way of making music.

Keywords: Virtual Instrument, OSC-MIDI Controller, Tactile Feedback.

1 Introduction

In the last decade the way music is created, performed and even enjoyed is radically evolving. Among many novelties, more or less involved with a specific genre or with the ever-changing fashion of popular audience, two important innovations left a time lasting remark in music: they are new musical interfaces and visual art integration. Although classic and well known instruments (e.g. guitar, drums, violin, etc.) are still "enough" to compose and play live, it is not possible to ignore the vast number of brand new musical instruments and controllers that can be used nowadays. A typical example of a ground breaking novel instrument of 2000's is laptop [19]: by now laptop is played as a real instrument, and it is very likely to find one working during studio and live performances.

Together with this "sound evolution", the last decade was highly characterized also by a refined visual representation of music, especially on stage. However only recently this trend has been extended to live performances; modern projection technologies are now incredibly large used, permitting to experience music in a really exciting bimodal environment.

We strongly believe that these important innovations in the world of music could be combined and enhanced inside Virtual Reality (VR). Since the beginning of VR, Jaron Lanier and the team from VPL developed some interesting

R. Nordahl et al. (Eds.): HAID 2010, LNCS 6306, pp. 149–159, 2010.

musical applications and performed live [6], formerly recognizing a new powerful means of artistic expression. Twenty years have passed: nowadays a VR set up can be easily reproduced on stage, thanks to portable stereoscopic projectors [10] and quick environment sensorization [13]. With this paper we present the first of a set of studies about the possibility to use some virtual audio interfaces during live performances, thus creating an interactive 3D environment in which the performer is completely immersed. The interface is a step senquencer (from 4 to 16 steps), which supports direct hand interaction: the performer can compose dynamic loops just touching some spheres that control four different samples for each instrument. The virtual environment is projected onto a powerwall to make each performance visible also to the listeners: unlike head mounted display set up, projected VR creates a visual environment that is not limited to the perception of a single user, but instead it can be shared with a large audience.

The presented virtual interface is equipped with a simple low cost tactile device that can produce two different kinds of haptic feedbacks, each time the performer interacts with virtual objects. In the last part of this paper we describe an experiment in which five highly musical skilled people were challenged in the reconstruction of some audio drum loops, using our sequencer: data were collected to understand which of the two feedback modalities could be better exploited to support a robust interaction with objects and musical parameters, and to obtain some information about the learning curve as well.

2   Related Works

Many works present novel instruments and controllers, developed just to propose an easy way to compose music for personal entertainment [16], regardless the users' actual skill in that field [11]. In [5] Kaltenbrunner et al. introduced, instead, an innovative multiuser musical instrument, based on a tabletop tangible interface, and especially designed for professional live performances; today this wonderful device is very popular, but until now only one mainstream artist (i.e. Bjork) got one on the stage.

As showed by O'Modhrain [12] an instrument is strongly characterized by the tactile feedback it is able to provide to the user, especially concerning the accuracy level the performer wants to achieve. This is true for hardware instruments [9], as underlined in a previous research by Malloch [8]: in his study he reinforced the interaction metaphors of a digital instrument called T-Stick, adding a programmable vibro-tactile feedback on it. But the importance of a tactile feedback is even more perceived in software and virtual musical devices. Many solutions have been presented: in [2] Bertahaut et al. developed an input device for VR music creation, based on 6DOF tracking system, and using pressure sensors as passive haptics. Another interesting solution based on passive haptics was presented by Poupyrev in [15]: they presented an augmented environment (with a head mounted display system) in which users can manipulate sounds through virtual objects, linked to some fiducial marker cards. In this way sound interaction is achieved through physical objects manipulation (the cards), and visualized as part of the augmented environment.

In literature many devices can be found used to reproduce kinaesthetic and cutaneous touch feedback [3][4][1] for a virtual environment or teleoperations. Some works use vibration as tactile feedback like in [17] to analyze and improve human reactions to everyday stimuli. Also music environments are gradually improved via the implementation of specific haptic interfaces. In [18] eg. , we can found a simple vibro-tactile device, where a vibrating feedback sensation is given to improve the musician experience. The main difference of these cutaneous feedback devices, respect kinaesthetic devices, is their simplicity in construction and implementation. Furthermore, a kinaestethic exoskeleton is typically cumbersome and heavy to wear, reducing the freedom of the user.

3   Virtual Sequencing

3.1   The Sequencer

During the performance the user is immersed within a virtual environment composed by simple geometrical shapes; each shape allows her/him to change some specific parameters in order to create loops. Some of these parameters, and the related interaction metaphors, are typical of software sequencers, others reminds more physical device manipulation.

As in many software sequencers, the step quantization can be changed, in this case among three possible values (fourths, eights and sixteenths); the desired quantization can be anytime selected, acting on three exclusive cubic buttons. Doing so, the visual representation of working area changes: the core of the sequencer is a matrix of spheres, composed by four rows (each related to a specific sample), and a number of columns that varies among four, eight and sixteen, according to current quantization. Each sphere represents a note, which can be selected by the user, and triggered in syncro with main tempo. Main tempo is represented by a colored bar that cycles all columns of the matrix, as quick as defined by the currently set BPM. Each time the bar hits a column, all notes corresponding to a selected sphere are triggered, causing the related sample (linked to the row number) to play. As in hardware sequencers, the interface provides a slider to select the current BPM.

Other controllers are the play/pause and stop cubic buttons, which control the behavior of tempo bar, and the loop length slider: this slider permits the performer to dynamically change the number of active steps, giving the possibility to create odd time loops (e.g. 3/4, 7/8, etc.) or loop subsections (e.g. 4/8, 8/16, etc.).

At the moment only four samples can be loaded onto the interface at a time. Nevertheless it is possible to cycle on a vast number of sound sets. In fact as explained in section 3.3 the sequencer works as a controller, mapped onto some parameters of a commercial music engine; many devices can be created inside the engine, each containing a set of four samples: MIDI note messages are sent to all devices, but only the one that is armed is actually triggered. Thus, we added a cycling button to change the armed device, in order to dynamically change the sample set without interrupting music.

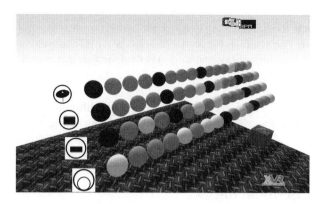

Fig. 1. A detailed view of the virtual sequencer layout

To start each kind of interaction the user has to insert her/his index finger inside the desired object. Sequencing spheres and buttons can be selected and deselected just touching them. All sliders instead are constrained to move on a single axis (X or Y), so, as long as the finger is inside, they can be dragged along the moving axis; then moving outside of the object along the Z axis determines the end of interaction. As until now we use a single passive marker to detect finger position, and just one tactile device, only single hand interaction is supported.

3.2   Layout

All spheres were given a 5 cm radius, while buttons are dimensioned 10 x 10 x10 cm3; these controllers are huge if compared to other hardware and software devices, but ensure a natural interaction and good haptic feedback control (see next session).

According to general object dimension, we defined the whole graphical layout in order to keep all controls in a comfortable position, even when all the sixty-four spheres are shown. The matrix is presented in front of the user, tilted by 45 from the XY plane (Figure 1), so that the highest row of spheres is always within the range of the performer. Other controllers are at the bottom of the matrix and on sides. A digit display is drawn on the top right corner of the application, showing the current BPM value.

All spheres are colored in light blue, except for quarter spheres. Quarter spheres are an important reference when dealing with loops: this is the reason why we chose for them a much darker tint, in order to always highlight their positions along the steps. When selected, each sphere becomes yellow, regardless of its position. When tempo is playing, the column that is currently triggered by tempo bar is all colored in pink; each time tempo bar hits a selected note, the note triggering is emphasized by a small explosion of the sphere itself.

3.3   Materials and Methods

VR projection is obtained with two Christie Mirage S+ 4000 projectors, synchronized with StereoGraphics CrystalEyes active shutter glasses. We use 4x2 m2 powerwall, and an Intersense IS-900 inertial-ultrasonic motion tracking system to sensorize the area in front of the screen; in this way the performer's head is always tracked. Finger tracking is instead achieved with a set of 12 Optitrack FLEX:100 infrared cameras; as just one passive marker is set on the finger, this is not a critical task.

The main 3D application was developed with VRMedia XVR[1] which handles graphics, scene behavior and input/output data sending. Devices and software exchange data with the main application through XVR internal modules written in C++ and Python.

The virtual sequencer is mapped onto Ableton[2] Live 8, a powerful and flexible commercial audio engine. Through a hybrid communication protocol (Figure 2), based on MIDI and OSC, the sequencer controls note triggering and floating point parameter settings of Live devices, and receives MIDI clock synchronization to support variable step quantization and BPM setting. When the user activates the sequencer, Live is set to play (via OSC), so that MIDI sync is generated: this sync signal makes the two applications run together, allowing the user to control Live devices from our external interface, in a transparent way. XVR MIDI out port is used to trigger notes of armed devices, while OSC protocol is used to control BPM, start/pause/stop controls, track arming status and, hypothetically, all the others Live parameters, like sample volume, filter cut-off, and so on.

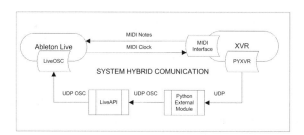

Fig. 2. XVR and Ableton Live communication schema: on both sides serialized data are formatted by external modules. OSC module produces a one way communication stream.

4   The Haptic Device

Reproducing feedback sensation is an important aspect to give the final user a better perception experience of the environment where he is operating, either

---

[1] http://www.vrmedia.it/
[2] http://www.ableton.com/

is the environment real or virtual. The aim of this work is to realize a simple and low-cost cutaneous tactile interface for the finger, the most sensitive part of the human body [7][14], to be used in a virtual environment. In the application presented the penetration depth is very important and a vibrating motor is not enough to recreate such sensation in a realistic way, and other possibilities have been evaluated. The idea is to build a device simple to use, fast to integrate and lightweight. The structure is realized with a lightweight plastic chassis, whose shape is similar to a cylinder with half a ring on the top to allow the finger to fit(Figure 3). A cavity of 6mm diameter along its vertical axis, allows the insertion of a motor and a moving circular cursor; in this way, the cursor gets in touch with the finger, simulating the contact with an object surface. The tactile cursor moves thanks to a low-cost DC motor by Precision Microdrives.

Fig. 3. The haptic device compared to a coin and the control electronic used

The planetary gearbox mounted on its shaft, creates a reduction of 255:1 with an output peak torque of 20gr*cm. To translate motion from rotation around the z-axis to a vertical translation, a worm-gear system has been used with an internally threaded plastic cursor. The cursor is fixed to move vertically using two plastic edges. This solution has been chosen for its simplicity and to avoid the usage of external gears due to vertical force need. The presented worm-gear system can generate up to 1,25 N with a speed value up to 2.9 mm/s. In this way a full and proportional deep contact can be achieved. The maximum height reachable is 3mm, but the system can be tuned to travel less space due to big finger dimension. In this way we avoid the gears of the planetary box from breaking. An external electronic board, the commercially distributed Arduino nano[3], is used to generate PWM signals and to communicate with the Virtual Environment. This board sends PWM signals to a second board that drive the motor, where an H-bridge is used to have motion in both directions.

To keep the device as simple and low-cost as possible, the motor is controlled in open loop where the only control variable is time. The simple control system is based on shifting time of the cursor and features two different operating modalities: boolean operation and stepping movement. In the boolean modality, the cursor is forced to move from the bottom position to the top one. This allows

---

[3] http://arduino.cc/

to have an on/off contact. The stepping movement allows to give a gradually insertion sensation. With this option the entire path is divided into three zones, of 1mm each.

The cursor can therefore move in accordance with the desired step, reaching the top only with the last step. These two different modalities allow the differentiation of the contact sensation. Regardless where the marker position is, with the boolean contact, the cursor will go up, instead in the stepping mode, a better penetration sensation can be achieved going up and down step by step (Figure 4).

Fig. 4. On the left is visible a user wearing the low-cost tactile device. On the right a simple schema of a finger penetrating inside a virtual object.

Using two Velcro stripes connected to the upper part of the chassis the attachment with the finger is granted. The result is a lightweight actuator that permits the user to perform actions in a virtual environment without feeling fatigue or been stressed by the device. This is very important in a long time application or doing long experiments.

5   Experiment

5.1   Reconstructing Loops

The goal of our experiment was to collect an initial set of quantitative data regarding the learning curve of the virtual instrument. We were interested in how long it takes for a performer, skilled in physical sequencing, to master the base functioning of our virtual sequencer.

Furthermore, as discussed in previous session, two haptic modalities can be exploited to provide different tactile sensations; we believe that the stepping movement could provide a better consciousness of interaction, leading to a natural and more powerful set of metaphors for virtual music creation. The whole experiment was then set up in order to understand how users approach contact interaction when multimodally stimulated, and how experience changes according to the diverse modalities.

During the experiment a simplified version of the virtual sequencer should be used to reconstruct some drum loops. Elapsed time for reconstruction were analyzed to have a quick evaluation of interaction rules. Furthermore for each note selection the step of insertion was saved, to analyze the contact approach of each haptic modality. The musical task was also meant to distract subject's attention from haptic feedback, in order to have a very natural interaction with virtual objects.

Five subjects participated: we selected them because of their skill in electronic music composition, or because of their experience in playing drums, or both. The main idea was to test whether or not our haptic system was good enough for a professional use in the future development. Using subjects with no musical experience at all would have been a problem in the evaluation, because the effect of the learning curve for the musical task would have been overlapped with the one for using the virtual sequencer itself. It is not easy to listen a composition and try to replicate with a system, and we wanted to avoid this kind of problems. Each subject was presented three sessions, composed by nine trials each; each trial corresponds to a particular drum loop. The subjects had to listen to the loop and select the correct note to play along the matrix (Figure 5). Once that a loop is correctly reconstructed the subject is presented the next one. Each trial is characterized by a step quantization (fourths, eights or sixteenths), by a BPM value (80, 120 or 160) and by one of the three available drum sets. Each session is characterized by a different haptic feedback modality (no haptic, Boolean or stepping movement), and by a set of unique drum loops; anyway session loops were generated trying to maintain the same complexity criteria, so that the perceived average difficulty of sessions does not vary. Sessions and trial were presented in shuffled order.

Fig. 5. A view of a running session of the experiment. A user is going to select a note along the matrix of spheres.

Many of the sequencer features were disabled, in order to retrieve data especially about note selection, which is the main core of the application. In this perspective all sliders were removed, as also the control buttons. Indeed some features were added to help concentrating on loop reconstruction. Sample rows were identified with an icon, useful for sample set memorization; a cue button was inserted, to re-play the sequence, when needed by the subject; the play note animation was blocked when the selected sphere does not belong to the original loop. This works as a direct visual feedback of the correct or un-correct positioning of the note along the matrix.

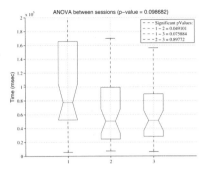

Fig. 6. The graph represents the execution time for the three different sessions

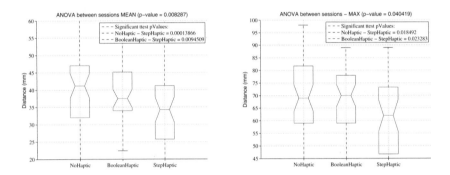

Fig. 7. The ANOVA graphs of distances from the sphere border of the three sessions, reveals a more natural interaction within the stepping session

5.2   Results

We have run an ANOVA one-way analysis of variance in the group of the three different sessions, at an overall 5% level, evaluating execution time, means of the distances and max values over all the trials. The tests were also performed on the couples of sessions.

For the time analysis data were arranged according to the order in which the three sessions were presented to each subject. The only significant (p=0.0049) variation is between the first and the second session shown.. This trend suggests that a single loop reconstruction session, regardless of the haptic methodology, is enough to obtain a noticeable improvement in performances. This is an encouraging result, but very far from an approximation of the interface learning curve. The subjects really enjoyed the application.

A significant difference between the three sessions comes out considering the distances from the border of each shape(Figure 7). The result tell us that the step session,compared to boolean and the no haptic session, takes the user to stay closer the shape border. This aspect is outlined also in the max distance value that the user reaches in the three different sessions. These results show that a haptic step contact permit a good touching sensation and gives the user a more realistic and precise contact sensation. This could probably be related to the fact that a boolean contact is not natural in a continuous contact on an object. When we touch a soft object and we penetrate it, eg water, we have a continuous contact. In the boolean case the stimulus variation is perceived only for an instant giving the user not enough information for perceiving natural sensation. In the step contact instead, contact is more similar to natural continuous contact, something like a repeated alarm.

6   Conclusion

A virtual sequencer was realized and tested with the help of five skilled musician subjects. The haptic experience recreated via a simple and low cost device was satisfying for the interviewed subjects. The results suggested to exploit the stepping methodology to support more complex and powerful metaphors, such as note velocity variation according to finger penetration. Furthermore, the same tactile feedback could be improved, refining the number of steps, and its global movement precision. The application could then be improved and transformed to support multiuser interaction and other different plattform.

References

1. Bergamasco, M.: Design of hand force feedback systems for glove-like advanced interfaces. In: Proceedings of IEEE International Workshop on Robot and Human Communication (1992)
2. Berthaut, F., Hachet, M., Desainte-Catherine, M.: Piivert: Percussion-based interaction for immersive virtual environments. In: Proceedings of the IEEE Symposium on 3D User Interfaces 2010 (2010)
3. Burdea, G.: Force and touch feedback for virtual reality. Proceedings of the IEEE (1996)
4. Burdea, G., Zhuang, J., Roskos, E., Silver, D., Langrana, N.: A portable dextrous master with force feedback. Presence: Teleoperators and Virtual Environments 1, 18–28 (1992)
5. Kaltenbrunner, M., Jordà S., Geiger, G., Alonso, M.: The reactable*: A collaborative musical instrument. In: Proceedings of 15th IEEE International Workshops on Enabling Technologies: Infrastructure for Collaborative Enterprises, WETICE 2006 (2006)
6. Lanier, J.: The sound of one hand. Whole Earth Review (1993)
7. Lofvenberg, J., Johansson, R.: Regional differences in sensitivity to vibration in the glabrous skin of the human hand. Brain Research 301, 65–72 (1984)
8. Malloch, J., Sinclair, S., Wanderley, M.M.: From controller to sound: Tools for collaborative development of digital music instruments. In: Proceedings of the International Computer Music Conference (2007)
9. Marshall, M.T., Wanderley, M.M.: Vibrotactile feedback in digital musical instruments. In: Proceedings of the 2006 International Conference on New Interfaces for Musical Expression, NIME 2006 (2006)

10. Miller, A., LaViola Jr., J.J.: Towards a handheld stereo projector system for viewing and interacting in virtual worlds. In: Proceedings of the IEEE Symposium on 3D User Interfaces 2010 (2010)
11. Newton-Dunn, H., Nakano, H., Gibson, J.: Block jam: A tangible interface for interactive music. Journal of New Music Research 32, 383–393 (2003)
12. OModhrain, M.S.: Playing by feel: Incorporating haptic feedback into computer-based musical instruments. Ph.D. thesis, University of Stanford (2000)
13. Pan, Z., Li, Y., Zhang, M., Sun, C., Guo, K., Tang, X., Zhou, S.Z.: Real-time multi-cue hand tracking algorithm based on computer vision. In: Proceedings of the IEEE Symposium on 3D User Interfaces 2010 (2010)
14. Phillips, J., Johansson, K.: Neural mechanisms of scanned and stationary touch. J. Acoust. Soc. Am. 77, 220–224 (1985)
15. Poupyrev, Berry, Kurumisawa, Nakao, Billinghurst, Airola, Kato, Yonezawa, Baldwin: Augmented groove: Collaborative jamming in augmented reality. In: SIGGRAPH Conference Abstracts and Applications (2000)
16. Reis, T., Carrio, L., Duarte, C.: Interaction design: The mobile percussionist. In: Proceedungs of the 4th International Haptic and Auditory Interaction Design Workshop, vol. I (2009)
17. Sziebig, Solvang, Kiss, Korondi: Vibro-tactile feedback for vr systems. In: Proceedings of the 2nd Conference on Human System Interactions (2009)
18. Grosshauser, T., Hermann, T.: Augmented haptics – an interactive feedback system for musicians. In: Altinsoy, M.E., Jekosch, U., Brewster, S. (eds.) HAID 2009. LNCS, vol. 5763, pp. 100–108. Springer, Heidelberg (2009)
19. Zadel, M., Scavone, G.: Laptop performance: Techniques, tools, and a new interface design. In: Proceedings of the International Computer Music Conference (2006)

The LapSlapper - Feel the Beat

Mads Stenhoj Andresen, Morten Bach, and Kristian Ross Kristensen

Audio Design, Department of Information and Media Studies, Aarhus University,
Helsingforsgade 14 8200 Aarhus N., Denmark
{mads.stenhoj,morten2bach,ross.lemur}@gmail.com
http://imv.au.dk

Abstract. The LapSlapper is an inexpensive and low-technology percussive instrument with a digital interface. In a tactile and embodied manner it allows enhanced control and promotes expressive creativity when operating with percussive elements in digital environments. By using piezo-microphones, mounted on a pair of gloves and connected with a stereo signal to a runtime-version of a Max/MSP patch, intuitive haptic properties are achieved with simple means. The LapSlapper improves the physical feeling of playing digital rhythm instruments but the concept holds furthermore the potential to promote exploration and innovation of new, digitally founded rhythmical structures and aesthetics.

Keywords: Music, instrument, MIDI, trigger, percussion, drums, glove, embodied, intuitive, mobility, tactile expression, haptic interface.

1 Introduction

The LapSlapper offers an easy and intuitive approach to work with percussive sounds through a computer. The idea for The LapSlapper came from the observation that many musicians, as well as non-musicians, play the drums on their laps or thighs. It seems like this way of creating rhythms with - and on - your body has some obvious advantages in unmediated freedom that allows complexity and great timing even for amateurs. With the LapSlapper we wanted to make it possible to capture and convert this intuitive form of percussive performance onto the digital domain in the form of MIDI-represented note values. By doing so a more tactile experience and a more bodily based, performative expressivity could be utilized than is the case for most of the existing MIDI-trigger concepts and products. In addition it would serve as a haptical tool, which could make it faster, more controllable and more fun to program rhythms and grooves in sequencer-based arrangements.

We have strived to develop a concept that is flexible and responsive enough to be used equally in the studio and on stage, mobile enough to be used in e.g. a train, and simple enough for everyone to use and still inexpensive enough to be obtainable for most people. A low-technology solution to a common problem that improves the conditions for musicians in electronic genres.[1]

---

[1] More information and demonstration video can be found at: http://thoughtsimplicit.wordpress.com/2009/06/22/the-lapslapper/

R. Nordahl et al. (Eds.): HAID 2010, LNCS 6306, pp. 160–168, 2010.

2   The Instrument

2.1   The Analogue Technology

The preliminary idea was that you should be able to play some of the traditionally most used sounds from a drum kit e.g. kick, hi-hat, snare and toms. Hereby
not said that the system should be limited to accommodate only the playing
of traditional drums nor to be build around a common drum idiomatic. The
thought was rather that if we could control these four sounds satisfactorily we
would have a good starting point for further experimentation.

After having tested several options we agreed on a construction, where a pair
of tight fitting gloves was equipped with two piezo microphones each (one on the
index and middle finger and one on the thumb) plus one optional plastic coated
piezo-microphone which could be attached under the foot. Piezo-microphones
excels by being cheap, flat and touch-sensitive enough for the purpose. In addition to that, because they send out audio signals, they raise the opportunity to
completely avoid external electronical interfaces like MAKE-boards and the like
(and thereby also unwanted latency).

Hence the LapSlapper uses nothing but a standard stereo line-in input, which
is present in almost every standard computer. The standard software setup in
the LapSlapper maps the microphone input to some of the traditionally most
used drum sounds in the following way:

Foot = kick drum
Right index/middle finger = hi-hat
Left index/middle finger = snare drum
Right thumb = snare drum
Left thumb = tom

The two instances of the snare drum is in principle the same trigger, which
just gives the opportunity to use both hands for the snare drum. This leaves us
with four triggers in total that all need an individual channel for communication
through the two channels in the stereo line-in.

PolSplit. Since each of the stereo signals two mono signals exist through a
voltage oscillating between positive and negative polarity, we saw a possibility
to limit the number of inputs by splitting this polarity to isolate the positive
and negative potential so the signal from one piezo microphone is exclusively
positive and the other exclusively negative. In this way four completely separate
channels of communication are achieved. This rectification is achieved through
the use of a relatively simple and inexpensive diode bridge. A unique concept of
doubling the amount of communication channels by isolating the potentials we
have chosen to call PolSplit.

2.2   The Digital Technology

The analogue line-output with the four microphone signals is treated and interpreted in a runtime-version of a Max/MSP 5 patch in such a way, that every

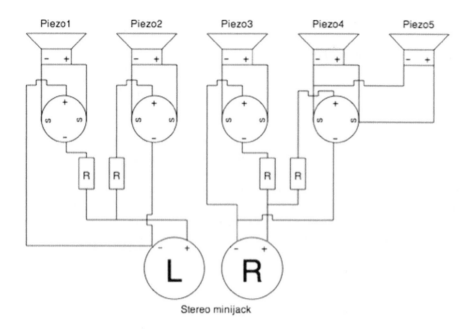

Fig. 1. Electrical diagram showing the rather simple analogue concept behind PolSplit

physical hit is converted to MIDI-values that can be used directly in most audio applications on the computer. Runtime-versions can freely be distributed and run without a licensed version of Max, which gives great freedom in the potential distribution of the LapSlapper concept by possible further development, keeping in mind that one of the main ideas was to keep the costs of the final product at a minimum.

The benefits of working with audio signals instead of other kinds of analogue data in relation to the computer are that you avoid latency increasing intermediates, which can be almost impossible to calculate and predict on different computer configurations and hardware setups. At the same time the dynamic area of each microphone is rather large and nuanced, the technique relatively uncomplicated and there is furthermore no need for an external power supply. Almost all computers especially if they are used for sound processing operates with raw sound signals in near real time, which we benefit from.

The Division of PolSplit. The first thing that happens inside the LapSlapper-application is that the compiled PolSplit signal from the stereo line-in is divided into the four individual signal ways again. This is achieved by a simple mathematical operation, where the characteristics of the square root are used to sort between the digitised values . Each of the four separated signals runs through a threshold mechanism, which takes care of filtering out unwanted analogue low-frequency noise from the signal. The threshold value parameter is accessible to and can be changed by the user instead of being locked to the analogue system.

The reason for keeping this parameter open for the user is that this, normally unwanted noise, can be used rather creatively. By tweaking the threshold values to a point near the frequency of the noise it is possible to create a quite interesting flam-effect, which, if used optimally, can lead to unique ways of electronic drumming. By such technical side-effects the LapSlapper can potentially lead to a more explorative use than the simple one-to-many mapping that its primary functionality offers.

Interpretation and Conversion of Input Signals. The heart of the interpretation part of The LapSlapper application is the Bonk-object, which works as a real time signal analyzer, developed by researchers from University of California in the late 90s. The relatively low-technology structure which is based on a bounded-Q Fast Fourier Transform-analysis of the spectral data from the audio input, is even more advantageous today, as computer processing power no longer is a problematic issue.

The Bonk-object splits each of the four audio signals in eleven locked frequency areas (hence bounded-Q) whereupon it registers changes in intensity in each area. If the change in intensity in an area exceeds the user-defined threshold value the object will send out a value equivalent of a relative representation of the velocity. This is more or less the same way you detect velocity on a musical keyboard, but the advantage of the eleven frequency areas is that it makes it possible to differentiate on the spectral type of the input signal. Hereby you can potentially register several types of hits or strikes on the same microphone input, according to what type of material you hit, as this would produce different spectral characteristics. This option is not implemented In the first prototype of The LapSlapper but further development could unfold this possibility. It is definitely an aspect which could expand and improve the mapping possibilities - and thereby release a many-to-many mapping potential - and the resulting promotion of expressivity in future versions.

The relative representation of the velocity measured by the bonk-object is converted to a value between 0 and 127, so it can be applied as velocity parameter in the MIDI-standard. Since the force applied to the LapSlapper by different users, this conversion can be calibrated for each microphone input so the dynamic magnitude corresponds to the users efforts.

Layered Velocity Mapping. A registered hit releases an internal represented MIDI-event including, besides the given velocity, information about which note value it represents. These note values are user assignable directly in the application, so every hotspot on the gloves corresponds to a certain note value. As default though, the gloves will be initiated with a common drum setup. In this prototype it is possible to assign two different note values to each input and let a user defined velocity threshold determine which of the two is activated. This gives opportunity to control for instance both a closed and a open hi-hat with one hotspot, dependent on how hard you hit, which gives an immediate increment of the given leeway.

Routing of MIDI-Signals. In the last part of the signaling pathway it is possible to define what the registered MIDI-values should be used for. If you just want to test the gloves right away you can choose the internal sampler that will play drum sounds embedded in the application. If you own some interesting VST-plugins The LapSlapper can work as a VST-host, hereby making it possible to use it as a standalone-application in e.g. a live setup or a practice situation. Last, but not least, it is possible to route the MIDI-signal to other applications e.g. a Digital Audio Workstation making the full potential of The LapSlapper as a recording instrument unfold.

3   Pros and Cons

3.1   Existing Solutions

When a musician or a composer wishes to record his music on a computer, there are several ways to do this. Often particularly in smaller studio setups a MIDI-keyboard is used to record drum parts, which are then assigned to sounds from VST-plugins, samplers or the like. There are obvious advantages to this; you do not need a skilled drummer or expensive studio time to record the drums. Nor are you dependent on the physical setup when you record. Alternatively you can replace the MIDI-keyboard with the computer mouse and manually insert each single note by clicking around in a rhythm matrix in ones sequencer. This is rather laborious work; especially if you want to nuance your beats. On the up-side it doesnt require any real time rhythmical competences, though. There are certain drawbacks when recording drums through such methods. Besides the fact, that you would probably never reach a 100 percent realistic and living sound, even though if this was your aim, the locked position in which the user sits or stands (and the relatively small part of the human body being involved during interaction) will insert a unnecessary level of abstraction on the musicians actual rhythmic idea and the actual playing of it. The keyboard is just not sufficient as a medium for the physical outburst of energy and gesticulation it demands to control rhythm in a living and an expressive way. At the same time it gives a minimum of tactile feedback which can make it hard to be tight both rhythmically and dynamically. This results in a rhythm track that will necessarily need some sort of aftercare to sound right. Most likely it will need some changes in parameters such as velocity and timing, and also some variation (avoidance of copy/paste) to reach a desirable result. To avoid some of this time consuming aftercare you could choose to use a MIDI-drum kit and in a simple way get all of the natural occurring variations in the drumming recorded. At the same time you would also be limited to using only four sounds at the same time (after all, humans only have one pair of arms and one pair of legs)! But in this example youre almost back to status quo when it comes to disadvantages, given the facts that it takes up almost as much space as a standard drum kit, it calls for a skilled drummer and finally it is relatively expensive.

In addition to this, and besides the fact that our aim with The LapSlapper is not only to make it easier and more bodily founded when working with digital percussive elements, it is also meant to promote new modes of expression and id-iomatic properties that are not like the way you traditionally play the drums. The control of the digital rhythm is linked closer to the body with the LapSlapper, but the actual way you choose to play on your thighs (or whatever you want to hit with your hands) together with how you choose to map the input to different sounds, is up to the individual user. Hereby it is possible to investigate potential new aesthetic expressions which will be further elaborated in the discussion section.

3.2 Similar Systems

In the search of inspiration to the LapSlapper we found some systems with similarities. All have a tendency towards trying to be more than just a MIDI-interface. For example, the Bento-Box, a musical instrument designed to en-tertain the musician in transit in e.g. buses or trains. It is best described as a mixture of an accordion and an electric keyboard. The size of the accordion makes it easy to carry, but the rather loud sound level makes it non-usable in public, since it will clearly disturb people. The electrical keyboard can be played without disturbing other people with sound, but the size is a hindrance that makes it an undesirable choice. The Bento-Box tries to make a mixture of these two and the result is a little handheld electronic instrument, which can be played without disturbing people in the vicinity. This instrument has two advantages; the compact size and the low acoustic output. Both are features we chose to strive for during development as one of the original ideas was to create a tool for drummers who wanted to record drum tracks while riding e.g. a train.

The product most similar to The LapSlapper is probably the BD-1 Body Pad Drum rigger, made by Pulse Percussions. The idea behind this interface is, that the musician places the drum pad on his leg, arm or wherever he wants and hits it with his hands. It needs to be connected to a module that can translate a trigger signal, which makes it a simple trigger and nothing more. The LapSlapper is built on the same idea; the fact that many musicians play their thighs. We have put the sensors on the hands instead of on the thighs, which results in a much wider expression potential and a better tactile feeling. Furthermore the rendition part of The LapSlapper is software based, which gives a complete solution without the obligation to invest in expensive extra equipment. Judging from user comments the BD-1 Body Pad Drum was not that big a success, as your fingers would start to hurt after a short time of using it, since it is like banging your fingers against a sheet of wood. Furthermore the sensors they used were of fluctuating quality, so even with two identical Body Pads, you still couldnt be sure to have to identically reacting triggers. This is not judged to be an issue with the LapSlapper, as the sensitivity of the piezo-microphones is remarkably great and allows for even very light drumming without loss of dynamic versatility.

3.3 LapSlapper Advantages

We have tried to combine the advantages from the different systems during development of the LapSlapper and have therefore created a prototype of a interface which takes the best of several worlds:

1. Versatile potential with the digital freedom applied a bodily control
2. You dont have to learn how to play the drums on a keyboard. By using a technique many musicians already have practiced, playing rhythms on their thighs, we have removed (or at least smoothened) a learning curve that can be both steep and time consuming.
3. It doesnt take up much time to record a drum track to a song given the fact that it can be done in real time, as if you were using a MIDI-drum kit and hereafter correcting eventual mistakes by moving the individual notes.
4. Mobile and very little space consuming solution.

Beside these advantages there are other advantages as well, which none of the other solutions apparently contain:

1. No need for a MIDI-input or a latency increasing USB-solution.
2. Inexpensive. The working prototype was constructed for less than 10 EUR. Besides working as a drum-kit substitute it is also usable when it comes to other percussive instruments, which gives it a larger expressive scope.
3. The LapSlapper adds a visual dimension to live acts, where neither MIDI-drums nor keyboards have the same performance and communication potentials.
4. Embodied digitality and not digitalized analogity.

3.4   LapSlapper Limitations

Our first prototype of The LapSlapper holds a number of limitations that have complicated development of it, as a working instrument. Mechanically there is a problem with the piezo microphones used in our prototype. Over time these become moist through the gloves and thereby unstable. A solution to this problem could be to enclose the microphones in a non-conductive material, which also could protect the microphones against the relatively rough treatment they receive, which again will be necessary if the product is supposed to be more durable and constant. In addition to this, the wires tend to disturb the experience, when using the gloves, but this can be solved by using a standard radio based sender/receiver, which is already known from wireless microphones. In this case you are literally no longer bound to your computer to the same extent as you are without the LapSlapper.

4   Future Development

The LapSlapper can easily be developed further. At the moment the PolSplit circuit is set on a large print board, the case built of LEGO, and the piezo microphones are stuck on with Gaffa tape. By replacing these temporary constructions with more sturdy solutions like customized print boards and an aluminium case, we will be able to minimize the physical size, maximize the durability and thus make it even easier to use the LapSlapper on stage, in the studio or even while using the bus or the train.

It would seem fruitful to expand the mapping-complexity by utilizing the signals of the existing microphones, as already mentioned in the section about the digital technology (3.2). The Max/MSP patch already has all the means necessary to be able to differentiate for instance high and low frequency input, which would expand the potential for expression even further.

5 Discussion

The potential for expression is a central point to the concept of the LapSlapper. It is possible to use the instrument as a simple replacement for an acoustic drum kit, but it is not our goal to try to remediate the acoustic experience you get by playing a drum kit, into a digital context. The ideology behind the LapSlapper is an attempt to give digitally founded sounds bodily control and tactile, performance oriented expressivity. Hence, it is not an attempt to force digital control on simulated acoustic drums. It is our hope that the instrument will promote an exploratory approach to the instrument itself which may hopefully expand the potential expressions in digitally founded percussive elements.

With different mapping configurations and the possibility of working with the analogue sources of errors (noise-gate threshold) and the digital filters (through the inclusion of open bonk-object settings) in a creative way, the potential of the exploration of new performative and aesthetical expressions will be helped along in the best way possible.

6 Conclusion

With the LapSlapper project we have demonstrated that a simple idea and a simple realization of the same can lead to surprisingly good results. With very few means a prototype of a percussive MIDI-interface has been made, which gives the user a sublime tactile experience and a satisfying auditory, rhythmical response in real time that exceeds the haptic potential of many expensive and professional counterparts.

References

1. Brown, J.C., Puckette, M.S.: An efficient algorithm for the calculation of a constant Q transform. Journal of Acoustical Society (5), 2698–2701 (November 1992)
2. Chuchacz, K., OModhrain, S., Woods, R.: Physical models and musical controllers designing a novel electronic percussion instrument. In: Proceedings of the 2007 Conference on New Instruments for Musical Expression (NIME 2007), New York, NY, USA (2007)
3. DAlessandro, N., Dutoit, T.: HandSketch Bimanual controller. In: Proceedings of the 2007 Conference on New Instruments for Musical Expression (NIME 2007), New York, NY, USA (2007)
4. Hatanaka, M.: Ergonomic Design of a Portable Musical Instrument. In: Proceedings of the 2003 Conference on New Instruments for Musical Expression (NIME 2003), Montreal, Canada (2003)

5. Hunt, A., Wanderley, M.M., Paradis, M.: The importance of parameter mapping in electronic instrument design. In: Proceedings of the 2002 Conference on New Instruments for Musical Expression (NIME 2002), Dublin, Ireland (2002)
6. Lugo, R., Jack, D.: Beat Boxing: Expressive Control For Electronic Music Performance And Musical Applications. In: Proceedings of the 2053 Conference on New Instruments for Musical Expression (NIME 2003), Vancouver, BC, Canada (2005)
7. Paine, G., Stevenson, I., Pearce, A.: The Thummer Mapping Project. In: Proceedings of the 2007 Conference on New Instruments for Musical Expression (NIME 2007), New York, NY, USA (2007)
8. Puckette, M.S., Apel, T., Zicarelli, D.D.: Real-time audio analysis tools for Pd and MSP. In: Proceedings from ICMC (1998)
9. Wessel, D., Avizienis, R., Freed, A., Wright, M.: A Force Sensitive Multi-touch Array Supporting Multiple 2-D Musical Control Structures. In: Proceedings of the 2007 Conference on New Instruments for Musical Expression (NIME 2007), New York, NY, USA (2007)
10. Young, D., Fujinaga, I.: AoBachi: a New Interface For Japanese Drumming. In: Proceedings of the 2004 Conference on New Instruments for Musical Expression (NIME 2004), Hamamatsu, Japan (2004)
11. Zaborowski, P.S.: ThumbTec: A New Handheld Input Device. In: Proceedings of the 2004 Conference on New Instruments for Musical Expression (NIME 2004), Hamamatsu, Japan (2004)

Product Design Review Application Based on a Vision-Sound-Haptic Interface

Francesco Ferrise*, Monica Bordegoni, and Joseba Lizaranzu

Politecnico di Milano
Dipartimento di Meccanica
20156, Milano, Italy
{francesco.ferrise,monica.bordegoni}@polimi.it,
joseba.lizaranzu@mail.polimi.it

Abstract. Most of the activities concerning the design review of new products based on Virtual Reality are conducted from a visual point of view, thus limiting the realism of the reviewing activities. Adding the sense of touch and the sense of hearing to traditional virtual prototypes, may help in making the interaction with the prototype more natural, realistic and similar to the interaction with real prototypes. Consequently, this would also contribute in making design review phases more effective, accurate and reliable. In this paper we describe an application for product design review where haptic, sound and vision channels have been used to simulate the interaction with a household appliance.

Keywords: Multimodal Interaction, Interaction Design, Virtual Prototyping, Product Design Review.

1 Introduction

Virtual Prototypes (VP) have partially substituted real prototypes in several activities of the design process. Design review of products is one of them, where aesthetic, functional and ergonomics aspects of products are tested and assessed. Many companies have spent considerable effort in equipping their labs with Virtual Reality technologies. In most cases they have concentrated on visualization systems, because of the major availability on the market and of the quality of the systems from a technological point of view.

The quality and the quantity of the information about a product that can be represented through current state-of-the-art visualization technologies is indeed very high, but the kinds of interaction that can be performed with virtual prototypes is still limited. We have made the hypothesis that adding touch and hearing to the traditional visual interaction modality would increase the quantity of information that can be transferred from VP to humans. This may finally enlarge and make more effective the review activities that can be performed on VPs.

In order to use virtual prototypes instead of physical mock-ups with a high level of confidence, it is important to understand the limits of the technologies

---

* Corresponding author.

R. Nordahl et al. (Eds.): HAID 2010, LNCS 6306, pp. 169–178, 2010.

we use and to determine what quality of simulation we can really obtain with the VP, and subsequently how close to reality the interaction may be. Then, once we have determined the limits we begin to exploit the potentialities of the VPs in terms of modifiability of parameters such as dimensions, weights and so on. Our research work presented in this paper aims at addressing these issues.

The paper presents an application for design review of products that is based on a user interface integrating visualization with the sense of touch and the sense of hearing. The design review activity consists of the evaluation of the moving components of household appliances, like knobs, buttons, doors and so on. This activity is usually performed for ergonomics purposes, or for evaluating the perceived quality of the product.

2   Multimodal Interaction in Products Design Review

Design review is an important activity of the design process [12] where some decisions are taken on the evolution and future development of the product. The use of virtual prototypes instead of physical prototypes can influence the time required for the overall product design activity, and also the cost of the entire process, being the modification of the digital information included in the VPs faster and less expensive than the modification of a physical prototype, that may also require that a new prototype is built.

In order to effectively perform this activity in virtual environments, it is necessary to have a virtual model that has the same characteristics of, and behaves like the corresponding physical one for what concerns the aspects we are interested to simulate and validate. Several research activities have tried to push the design review activities toward the use of VPs, like for example in [9] where Santos et al. explore the possibility of using an immersive visualization system for creating a collaborative design review environment. These review activities are done on static prototypes that cannot be modified. This example, like several other research activities [10,13], shows which kind of review tasks can be done when visualization is the unique available information channel.

In [2] Bordegoni et al. explore the possibility to use a multimodal approach based on the combination of vision, sound and touch in creating a design review activity on continuously evolving shapes. In this application, industrial designers, that are manually skilled, have the possibility to interact with the evolving shape of an object using their hands, and to continuously evaluate and modify the model.

Sometimes, the design review activity involves multiple users that can be geographically dislocated and may require different perceptual representation of the same digital information. In this case a multimodal approach helps in exploiting the potentialities offered by VPs in terms of easiness of modification, and of sharing and transferring of information [1].

From the analysis of literature on design review it results that a multimodal approach in the interaction with VPs is beneficial in order to get an evaluation model that really allows us to test and validate effectively and accurately the various characteristics of future products.

3   Multimodal Interaction Model

In this section we present the multimodal interaction model that we have used to define the design review application developed. The model is based on the results of the research activity reported in [4], and describes the flow of information from the VP to the user.

Figure 3 shows the sequence of actions performed on the information extracted form a VP and transferred to the user. In the diagram, the VP is a sum of time-dependent geometrical and physical information that is continuously extracted and translated into different sensorial inputs for each of the considered sense (i.e. vision, touch and hearing).

There are different modalities that we can use for sending a piece of information to the user. These modalities do not necessarily replicate faithfully what happens in the human interaction with the real world. For example, geometrical information can be communicated through the visualization channel by continuously sending two updated images, one for each eye, in order to get a stereoscopic visualization of the object. But we can also translate the geometrical information into haptic cues, so that the user can haptically feel the shape by means of an active hand exploration [7]. Physical properties of rigid bodies like weight and inertia can be in someway represented as in the real life, through a combination of visual and touch cues, or by using the visual channel to create a tactile cue by means of the so called pseudo-haptic feedback [8]. If we use different sensory channels to send cues regarding the same information, they are then merged together into a unique perception, that can be the expected information or an illusion [11].

Perceptual illusions do not necessarily have to be considered bad results. Instead, they can be used as a means to communicate in someway information when we face limitations in the devices and technology that we have at disposal [3]. So, for example, we can simulate the presence of a bump or a hole by adding a sound, or we can simulate the click of a rotating knob by using a sound (as it happens in the Apple Ipods). These phenomena are usually known as cross-modal illusions. But there are also illusions for each single sense that can be helpful in solving various problems [6]. For example it happens when playing with the dynamic friction of a surface: we are able to communicate a small curvature also with a haptic device that has a limited working volume [5].

So, if our goal is not necessarily replicating exactly the physical phenomena, but instead is about communicating effectively some specific pieces of information extracted from the VP to the user, we can use a multimodal approach that can simplify our work.

4   Design Review Application

The application for the design review of a product (a washing machine by Whirlpool company in our study case) consists of the virtual representation of the product with the possibility of interacting with its moving components.

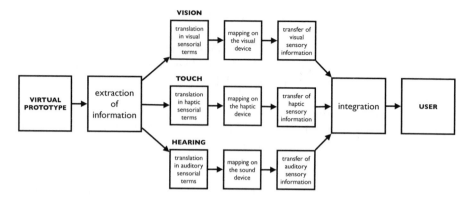

Fig. 1. Representation of the sequence of actions transforming the information from the virtual prototype to the user

As a first objective, we intended to replicate as much as possible the experience that the user makes when interacting with the real washing machine. Then, we intended to exploit the potentialities offered by virtual prototyping techniques compared with the use of real mock-ups of products. We have exploited the capability of easily modifying the information included in the virtual prototype (shape, color, materials, physical behaviour of components, etc.). We have also proved that the manipulation of some pieces of information may become a means to design, or re-design the interaction with the product on the basis of its virtual prototype.

4.1   Description of the Application Set-up

This section describes the various application components. The hardware set-up is based on commercial VR devices and is illustrated in Figure 2.

It consists of:

- a rear-projected wall display Cyviz for stereoscopic visualization of the product, which is based on two projectors and linear polarizers mounted first on the projectors and then also worn by the user as lightweight glasses;
- a six DOF haptic device by Haption that returns both forces and torques, used for simulating the haptic interaction with the washing machine components;
- a wireless headset system for sound rendering, which has been preferred to simple acoustic speakers in order to avoid user's distraction due to external noises;
- an optical tracking system by ARTracking used to calculate the user's point of view position and orientation in real-time, which is useful for allowing the user to visually explore the VP.

Fig. 2. Set-up of the design review application and its hardware components: rear-projected wall display, optical tracking system, stereo glasses, headsets, haptic device

Fig. 3. Example of the visual interaction environment

For what concerns the software implementation, we have used SolidWorks CAD tool for modeling the product and its components, and VirTools environment dedicated to the development of VR application.

4.2   The Visual Environment

From the visual point of view we have decided to represent only fundamental information, trying not to overload this channel. Therefore, the washing machine is rendered with a quality that we cannot consider as highly realistic, but that is good enough. In fact, our major aim concerns the evaluation and testing of the product interaction and not of its visual and aesthetic features.

Figure 3 illustrates the information of the visual environment that the user perceives. The visual environment contains information about the VP and a hand that changes its shape according to the component of the washing machine the user is interacting with. In order to improve the visibility of some small details like the text on the knob, or the text included in the display, we have given the user the possibility to represent a zoom-in of the washing machine control panel, which is displayed on the top part of the wall display, as illustrated in Figure 2.

4.3 The Haptic Environment

In the development of the haptic environment we have concentrated on the rendering of the proper information to convey to the user rather than on the simulation of the physical phenomenon that is behind it. For example, Figure 4 shows how we have handled two major behaviors related to the drawer. Practically, the rendered force that is related to the translational limits of the drawer is obtained from the computation of the collision of the door with two blocks that are present in the scene only from the haptic point of view, and not visualized. Figure 4b illustrates how we have implemented the "click-effect" of the drawer while opening and closing. Similar approaches have been used to simulate the forces and the click-like effects of the door, the knob, and the buttons of the washing machine.

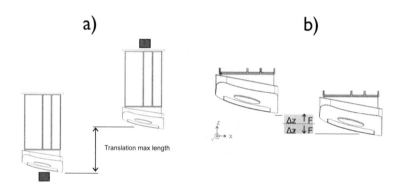

Fig. 4. Haptic behavior of the drawer a) constraints used to define the translation limits b) the forces added to simulate the opening and closure effects

In order to improve the overall haptic usability of the application, we have introduced two additional haptic features, which are:

- the use of a haptic snap when the user is close to the targets but not yet in contact with them. This is useful because the user does not need to be exactly on the surface to handle the component, but instead sufficiently close to it;
- a different proportion of the real working volume of the haptic device and the volume of its avatar in the virtual environment. This is important to solve the problem of the limits of the working volume of the haptic devices, and can be solved here simply changing the scale of the real-to-virtual working volumes.

4.4   The Sound Environment

In order to introduce the sound in the virtual prototype of the washing machine, a set of sounds have been recorded from a real washing machine. From these, we have selected some sounds as the click-like sound of the door, of the drawer, knob and buttons and we have processed them. Figure 5 shows the processing of the sound related to the drawer. We have modified the sounds by playing with several effects with the aim of simulating different clicks. Once added to the visuo-haptic prototype, we have noticed that sounds alter the human perceived force of the clicks, in the sense that the perceived effect seems controlled by the sound instead of by the force-feedback. This effect can be considered as an illusion, and as it commonly happens with several kinds of illusions, this effect disappears after some trials. But anyway, we have realized that in applications like ours, which is usually oriented to users who have to perform tests for short periods in time and who are not required to play continuously with the VP, the use of illusions may become an important tool for designing the interaction.

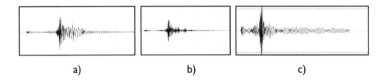

a)   b)   c)

Fig. 5. Different sounds used to represent the closing effects of the door a) sound as recorded from the real washing machine b) use of the equalizer to represent tiny forces c) use of compressor and reverbs to simulate an hermetic effect

5   Users' Test

We have performed a set of preliminary tests with users in order to evaluate some aspects of the application, mainly related to the novel use of haptic and sound in virtual prototyping of products. Ten users (8 male and 2 female, of age 20-35) have been selected to perform two different tests on the VP of the washing machine:

- the first test consists in the evaluation of the quality of the simulation comparing the VP with the real appliance. Testers were asked first to use some components (button, knob, door, drawer) of the real washing machine and then with the ones of the virtual washing machine, and to compare the following aspects in terms of realism: 1) haptic response of buttons; 2) knob click-effect; 3) knob torque; 4) door weight; 5) door click-effect when closing; 6) drawer weight; 7) drawer click when closing.
- the second test aims at demonstrating how the use of different sounds can alter the perception of a particular information. The participants were asked to select three different behaviors of the click-effect of the drawer and indicate

the one that they preferred to have in a real washing machine. The rendered click-effects are: a) sound of real washing machine; b) tiny-force sound c) hermetic sound.

The users were asked to wear the stereo glasses, the headset and to use the 6-DOF haptic device to interact with the washing machine components. Each user was trained for 10 minutes before starting the tests for getting acquainted with the haptic device and with the application. After the tests, the users were asked to fill in a questionnaire, by using scores from 1(bad) to 6(good) to evaluate the various aspects.

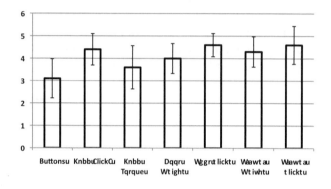

Fig. 6. Evaluation of degree of realism of the components of the virtual washing machine compared with the real washing machine

Figure 6 reports the results of the first test. The effect that appears to be less realistic is the one related to the buttons, while those connected to the door and the drawer have reported high scores. Regarding the knob, the click-effect is perceived as being similar to the real ones, while it does not happen for the torque. This is partially due to the kind of haptic device, that exerts a continuous torque that is difficult to hide. Figure 7 reports the results of the second test. It seems that users prefer a click-effect that is not the real one but instead the hermetic one. A paired samples t-test between Sounds "a" and "c" ($\alpha=0.05$, $P=0.57$) shows that there is no statistically significant difference between the means. Nevertheless it demonstrates how the integration of sound in virtual prototypes can be used for re-designing the interactive behavior of a product.

6   Discussion and Conclusion

In the paper we have discussed about the combined use of vision, haptic and sound as a way to improve the effectiveness of virtual prototyping. While visuo-haptic interfaces have been used in virtual prototyping application, the combination of the three senses has seldom been studied. In particular, we have

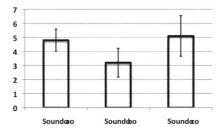

Fig. 7. Results of the test about the preferred click-effects of the drawer

used sounds as a way to increase the realism of the application. We have presented an application we have developed for the design review of an existing washing machine. The virtual prototypes of the washing machine simulates the haptic behavior of some moving components, and also the sounds they make. Then, we have performed some tests for evaluating the potentiality of this virtual prototype.

First, we were interested in testing how the haptic interaction with the moving parts is close to reality, and thus with which level of confidence we may use the virtual prototype for the ergonomics evaluation of a product. So, we have tried to replicate the experience that the user makes when using some moving parts of the washing machine. The tests have demonstrated that some haptic effects are realistic, some others are less realistic and maybe not good enough for substituting a virtual test with one performed on a real product. We think that this is due to the kind of the haptic device that we have used, that is not suitable for simulating all objects behaviors. Probably, dedicated devices, or the modification of the shape of the end effectors of this device would solve the problem.

Then, we wanted to check the potentialities and configurability of virtual prototyping for the validation of various configurations of a product, that can be easily and quickly achieved through the modification of some parameters. So we have performed a simple experiment where the user can interact with the washing machine drawer and hear different click-effects associated with the closure of the drawer. He may decide which one he prefers, and this is included in the specification of the product design. Therefore, such application can also be used not only for testing, but also for designing the interaction with a product.

We have also noticed that in the design of the interaction with a virtual prototype it is not always important to replicate the phenomena as they are in the real life, but instead it is important to concentrate on the perception of the product that we are able to convey to the user. Various interesting studies can be made combining the senses, and using illusions for simulating at best the phenomena. In our future work, we aim at studying how sound can alter the perceived force, and how long this phenomenon may persist. This would be useful in order to overcome the limits of rendered forces of current available haptic systems.

References

1. Bordegoni, M., Ferrise, F., Ambrogio, M., Caruso, F., Bruno, F.: Data exchange and multi-layered architecture for a collaborative design process in virtual environments. International Journal on Interactive Design and Manufacturing 4(2), 137–148 (2010)
2. Bordegoni, M., Ferrise, F., Shelley, S., Alonso, M., Hermes, D.: Sound and tangible interface for shape evaluation and modification. In: Proceeding of HAVE 2008 - IEEE International Workshop on Haptic Audio Visual Environments and their Applications, Ottawa, Canada (2008)
3. Cugini, U., Bordegoni, M.: The role of illusions in multimodal interaction. In: Proceedings of IDMME - Virtual Concept 2008, Beijing, China (2008)
4. Ferrise, F.: Multimodal Interaction in the Aesthetic Product Design. Ph.D. thesis, Politecnico di Milano, Dipartimento di Meccanica, via La Masa 1, Milano (2009)
5. Gosline, A., Turgay, E., Brouwer, I.: Haptic illusions: What you feel isn't always what you get (2002)
6. Hayward, V.: A brief taxonomy of tactile illusions and demonstrations that can be done in a hardware store. Brain Research Bulletin 75(6), 742–752 (2008)
7. Jones, L.A., Lederman, S.J.: Human Hand Function, 1st edn. Oxford University Press, USA (2006)
8. Lécuyer, A., Burkhardt, J.M., Etienne, L.: Feeling bumps and holes without a haptic interface: the perception of pseudo-haptic textures. In: CHI 2004: Proceedings of the SIGCHI conference on Human factors in computing systems, pp. 239–246. ACM, New York (2004)
9. Santos, P., Stork, A., Gierlinger, T., Pagani, A., Paloc, C., Barandarian, I., Conti, G., Amicis, R.D., Witzel, M., Machui, O., Jiménez, J., Araujo, B., Jorge, J., Bodammer, G.: Improve: An innovative application for collaborative mobile mixed reality design review. International Journal on Interactive Design and Manufacturing 1(2), 115–126 (2007)
10. Schmalstieg, D., Fuhrmann, A., Hesina, G., Szalavári, Z.: Encarnação, L.M., Gervautz, M., Purgathofer, W.: The studierstube augmented reality project. Tech. Rep. TR-186-2-00-22, Institute of Computer Graphics and Algorithms, Vienna University of Technology, Favoritenstrasse 9-11/186, A-1040 Vienna, Austria (2000)
11. Stein, B.E., Meredith, M.A.: The Merging of the Senses. The MIT Press, Cambridge (1993)
12. Ulrich, K., Eppinger, S.: Product Design and Development, 4th edn. McGraw-Hill, New York (2008)
13. Verlinden, J., Horváth, I., Nam, T.J.: Recording augmented reality experiences to capture design reviews. International Journal on Interactive Design and Manufacturing 3(3), 189–200 (2009)

The Phantom versus the Falcon: Force Feedback Magnitude Effects on User's Performance during Target Acquisition

Lode Vanacken, Joan De Boeck, and Karin Coninx

Hasselt University - tUL - IBBT , Expertise Centre for Digital Media (EDM)
Wetenschapspark 2, B-3590 Diepenbeek, Belgium
{lode.vanacken,joan.deboeck,karin.coninx}@uhasselt.be

Abstract. Applying force feedback applications in a therapy environment allows the patient to practice in a more independent manner, with
less intervention of the therapist. Currently however, high-end devices
such as the Phantom or the HapticMaster are far too expensive to provide a device per patient. Recently Novint launched a low-cost haptic
device for the gaming market: the Falcon. In this paper we report on an
experiment that we conducted in order to compare the Falcon and the
Phantom, based on a Fitts' law targeting task. We deduced physical parameters such as inertia and damping, which were found to be different
for the devices. Although from a velocity analysis these differences can
be clearly seen, it turns out that the influence of different forces does not
show significant differences when taking completion time and error rate
into account. From a subjective experiment, we can learn that users allow the Falcon to produce slightly higher forces than the Phantom before
forces are judged as too strong.

1 Introduction

Haptic interfaces are applied in an increasing number of domains, going from
training to entertainment. In a recent pilot study, we used a Phantom Premium
1.0 haptic device (sold by Sensable Technologies) as a force feedback input device
in a rehabilitation program for the upper limbs of Multiple Sclerosis (MS) patients [2] (figure 1). Three simple game-like applications were developed, which
were included in the patient's therapy during a period of four weeks. The generated force feedback was meant to support, assist or resist patients according
to their individual capabilities. Based on the pilot study, this research is continued in a research project with a workplan for basic and applied research in a
multidisciplinary consortium.

The benefit of bringing force feedback to a therapy environment is that training sessions can be finely tailored to the patient's need, with a minimal intervention of the therapist. The ultimate goal in this approach is a setup that can be
placed at the patient's home, where the follow-up is mainly done remotely [4].
Although the Phantom haptic device we used in the pilot study contributed to

R. Nordahl et al. (Eds.): HAID 2010, LNCS 6306, pp. 179–188, 2010.
© Springer-Verlag Berlin Heidelberg 2010

(a)   (b)

Fig. 1. (a) One of the games of the rehabilitation project: patients have to keep the car in the middle of the road while the force feedback can be used guide them. (b) Setup of the experiments: Phantom and Falcon with the ISO 9241-9 tapping circle.

promising results, it is very expensive. Providing an individual MS patient with his/her Phantom at home is very unlikely for the next few years.

Recently a new haptic device, the Falcon (by Novint inc), has been launched. The device focusses on a broad consumer market especially for gaming purposes, but has also been sparsely used in some rehabilitation projects [1]. Although it can be expected that this device will have less optimal device characteristics compared to the more expensive Phantom, its current pricing is by far better keeping a home setup in mind. Moreover, a comparison of the devices can also contain interesting information for other application types or interaction techniques.

Due to the different characteristics, a force may be felt differently on different devices, at its turn having implications on the performance and/or the satisfaction of the user or patient. Few studies currently exist that compared haptic devices for certain tasks [9,5]. Usually, focus is only on the performance of the user with regard to task completion time, but it is also important to take perception into account as well. Both Yu et al. [9] and Harders et al. [5] found small but non-significant differences with regard to completion time and subjective preference. These experiments only compared the devices using a user's task, whereas we also perform an analysis of their mechanical parameters.

In order to investigate whether or not we have to take the Falcon into account as a possible alternative in our rehabilitation setup, we report on an experiment in which we compare the devices (Phantom Premium 1.0 and a Novint Falcon). In section 2 we deduce the main parameters, mass and damping for the devices. Afterwards section 3 and 4 compare the devices in two target acquisition experiments, respectively targeted towards objective and subjective measures.

2   Phantom versus Falcon

The Phantom Premium 1.0 haptic device is a high-end device with prices starting from 24,250 dollar (price from early 2010). On the other hand, the Falcon haptic

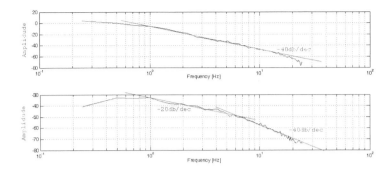

Fig. 2. Transfer functions according to the X-axis for the Phantom premium 1.0 (upper plot) and the Falcon (lower plot)

device is a very low cost haptic device (180 dollar, early 2010) focusing on the consumer market. Both devices are impedance controlled devices, measuring the user's movement at the input and producing a force at the output.

The Phantom premium 1.0 has a workspace of about $25 \times 18 \times 12$ cm ($W \times H \times D$). The Falcon's workspace is somewhat smaller with $10 \times 10 \times 10$ cm. They produce comparable force magnitudes. Besides these general specifications, found on the data sheets, we would like to know parameters such as the damping (mainly caused by friction) and inertia (apparent mass at the device's handle), because the result of the applied forces can be different when a device has a higher inertia or a higher friction.

To achieve this, we a parametric identification using the transfer function had been applied as described by Pintelon et al. [8]. For the devices, white noise in the form of random forces was applied at the input (motors). While the device was in open loop (not held by a user) we measured the position of the end-effector (output).

The transfer functions (ouput/input) in the frequency domain for the devices are given in Figure 2. The phase diagrams have been omitted as we don't use them during the identification process.

Given that the general transfer function is given by $\frac{1}{ms^2+bs}$ we know

$$Y_{(db)} = |20 \log(\frac{1}{ms^2 + bs})| \qquad (1)$$

where m can be identified as the mass, b as the damping, and s as the Laplace transform parameter. Two poles can be found, resulting in a transfer function that has a slope of -20 db/dec starting from the pole at 0 Hz, and a slope of -40 db/dec after the second pole (see Figure 2).

Elaborating the formula towards f ($s = j\omega = 2\pi jf$), and solving for m and b gives us:

$$m = |\frac{-1}{(2\pi f)^2 \cdot 10^{\frac{-Y_{db}}{20}}}| \quad and \quad b = |\frac{-j}{(2\pi f) \cdot 10^{\frac{-Y_{db}}{20}}} - (2\pi j \cdot m \cdot f)| \qquad (2)$$

For calculating m, f is a frequency high enough to ignore the influence of the damping and Y is the amplitude read on the graph (in db). For calculating b, f is a frequency, small enough to minimise the influence of m and Y is again the amplitude read on the graph in db.

The results of the identification can be found in figure 3(a). The values indicated with an asterisk (*) could not be identified with sufficient accuracy. For the devices, the transfer functions for the y-axis were too noisy to make a decent estimation. For the Phantom, it appears that the damping (mainly caused by the friction) is small compared to the influence of the inertia. Therefore, it is very difficult to make good estimations for this parameter. It may attract the attention that the mass of the phantom for the z-axis is significantly higher, but this may not be surprising because movements around y and z cause the motors to move. With the Falcon, the friction appears to be the main factor. As a result, the mass can only be identified using a higher frequency (in order to be able to ignore the friction), resulting in a less accurate result.

The most important conclusion for the purpose of this paper, is the fact that the Falcon appears to have a higher damping. We may expect that this will have an influence on the device's behaviour. As the inertia differs not so much (at least not for the z-axis), its influence will be less pronounced.

3   Objective Comparison

One of the main purposes of our rehabilitation program is increasing the patient's 'motor control'. Consequently, 'target acquisition' is an important aspect of this training. Fitts' law tasks therefore appear to be suitable for our comparison experiment. Recently, we performed a Fitts' law test (in a different context) in order to investigate how different forces with different duration, amplitude and shape could influence the user's performance [3]. We believe the different force shapes and durations in this former experiment are suitable to compare haptic devices.

From the previous experiment, we could learn that the performance deterioration was a result of a stabilising action of the user, reducing the oscillation caused by the force bump by 'suspending' the targeting movement. As mass and damping have a direct influence on the oscillation, it may sound obvious that other device parameters, may lead to different behaviour. Hence, a similar experiment has been set up comparing the Phantom and the Falcon devices.

3.1   Apparatus, Procedure and Participants

Apparatus. A Phantom premium 1.0 with stylus and gimbal encoders and a Falcon haptic display was used. The visual output was provided by a 19-inch monitor. For the devices, a control display unitary gain was used.For validition purposes, before starting the experiment, extra care had been taken in calibrating the input devices. Using a 'forcemeter', we measured the influence of the gravity on the grips of the devices (for gravity compensation), as well as the gain factor

	Phantom	Falcon
m_x	0.06	0.17
b_x	0.51	8.20
m_y	*	*
b_y	*	*
m_z	0.41	0.23
b_z	*	9,28

(a)

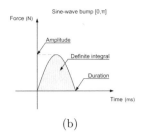

(b)

Fig. 3. (a) The identified parameters (mass(m) and damping(b)) of the Phantom and the Falcon. (b) Illustration of the force evolution of a sinusoidal haptic bump over time.

between the force requested in the software (CHAI3D API) and the final result at the device. The forces for the Phantom were quite correct, for the Falcon a multiplication factor of 3 had to be used, to achieve the same output.

Procedure. A simple multidirectional point-select task, as described in ISO 9241-9, was used for this experiment. Ten target circles are placed in a circle on the screen (see Figure 1(b)). The diameter of the circle is determined at 6 cm and the size of each target is 0.7 cm (we use physical measures rather than pixels, since pixel sizes vary from display to display). This task has a Fitts' index of difficulty of 3.26 bits. The value is chosen to be comparable to the task difficulty of a typical icon selection task.

During the test, the ten target circles were highlighted one after the other and users were requested to select the highlighted target 'as most efficiently' (rapidly and accurately) as possible, by pointing and clicking. Highlighting is altered between opposite sides of the circle so that it requires the user to make equally distributed movements among all directions with a maximum distance between the targets.

Other measures (2D force feedback plane, visual feedback, ...) were made to ensure experimental validity, these are elaborately discussed in [3] and omitted here due to space constraints.

Finally, force feedback appearing in the form of a force bump with given shape, duration and amplitude was activated when half-way in the path to the next target. Half-way the path is calculated using a simple Euclidian distance. Note that this activation strategy serves as a distractor without any purpose of being beneficial, but similar forces can be used for instance to indicate a transition between two regions.

Participants. Seventeen healthy male and one female unpaid volunteers, ranging in age from 20 to 28 with an average of 22.7, served as participants in this experiment. They were recruited among computer science students and had not taken part in any of our previous experiments. All participants were right-handed and used their dominant hand during the experiment. We preferred healthy subjects in this fundamental phase of the research in order to avoid the strong individual differences between different MS patients.

Force Integral	$\sin_{[0,\pi]}$ (75 ms)	sqr (40 ms)	$\sin_{[0,\pi]}$ (110 ms)	$\sin_{[0,2\pi]}$ (75 ms)
0.0	0.0N	0.0N	0.0N	0.0N
9.55	0.2N	0.24N	0.14N	0.2N
19.10	0.4N	0.48N	0.27N	0.4N
28.65	0.6N	0.72N	0.41N	0.6N
38.20	0.8N	0.96N	0.55N	0.8N
47.75	1.0N	1.19N	0.68N	1.0N
57.30	1.2N	1.43N	0.82N	1.2N
66.85	1.4N	1.67N	0.95N	1.4N
76.39	1.6N	1.91N	1.09N	1.6N
85.94	1.8N	2.15N	1.23N	1.8N
95.49	2.0N	2.39N	1.36N	2.0N

(a)

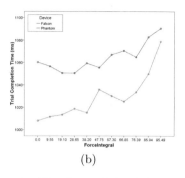

(b)

Fig. 4. (a) Force amplitudes calculated using the *FI* value and the definite integral. (b) Force integral values by input device (*FI* × *ID*).

3.2 Independent Variables and Design

As we are primary comparing the haptic devices, the first independent variable is the input device (*ID*). All the other remaining independent variables are those with regard to the selection experiment, similar as in [3]. The applied force bump is activated lateral to the movement direction.

The amplitude of the force bump over time (*T*) follows a mathematical pattern such as a sine or a step function, which we define as the force shape (*S*). For the shape $S = \sin_{[0,\pi]}$, *T*=75ms eleven amplitudes are considered. The amplitudes are converted to the integral of the force profile (see figure 3(b)) which we will refer to as the Force Integral (*FI*). For the three other shapes the same FI is taken. An overview of the shapes and their amplitudes is given in figure 4(a).

A mixed design was applied: a repeated measures within-participant design for all independent variables was used except for input device *ID*, which is a between-participant factor. We preferred a between-participant design over a within-participant as carry-over between these devices will be large for participants. The independent variables were: force integral *FI* (0.0, 9.55, 19.10, ...); and shape *S* ($\sin_{[0,\pi]}$, *T*=75ms; sqr, *T*=40ms; $\sin_{[0,\pi]}$, *T*=110ms; and $\sin_{[0,2\pi]}$, *T*=75ms). A fully crossed design resulted in 44 combinations of *FI* and *S*.

Each participant was randomly assigned to a device and performed the experiment in one session lasting about 25 minutes. This way nine participants were assigned to each device. The session consisted of five blocks with each block containing the 44 combinations (11 *FI*s and 4 *S*s) repeated three times in a random order. For a total of 132 trials per block, this resulted in 660 trials per participant. Between each block, users were obliged to take a 15 seconds' break to minimise fatigue during the test. Before the experiment, participants were given all 44 conditions in random order to familiarise them with the task.

For each selected target, the logged parameters (at 200Hz) include completion time, the actual position of the cursor, velocity, the exerted force bump and the number of clicks before a successful selection.

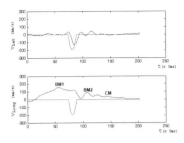 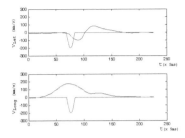

Fig. 5. Velocity profiles of the Phantom (left) and Falcon (right) during a selection trial ($FI = 95.49$). The top graph is the lateral velocity, the bottom graph represents the longitudinal.

3.3   Results

Trial Completion Time. First, we will investigate the learning effects. Repeated measures analysis of variance of the faultless trials, showed a main effect for *Block* ($F_{4,64} = 18.991$, p $<$ .0001), post hoc comparisons showed that the learning effect continued throughout all the blocks: participants were still improving their performance, even in the last block. With regard to the input device *ID* no interaction effect could be seen with *Block* ($F_{4,64} = .155$, p $=$ .960), from which we can conclude that the devices had a similar learning curve. As the learning effect did not influence the device and was present in all blocks, we will continue our repeated measures analysis of variance including all blocks.

Input device *ID* ($F_{1,16} = .256$, p $=$ .620) did not show a main effect. Therefore we can conclude that we found no significant difference between the devices. However, we saw that the overall trial completion time for the Phantom was 1029ms and the Falcon 1064ms. Even in if this result would become significant in a longitudinal study, such a small difference can be argued to be of less practical use. The interactions $S \times ID$ ($F_{3,48} = .811$, p $=$ .494) and $FI \times ID$ ($F_{3,48} = 1.07$, p $=$ .385) were not significant and showed a very similar trend. The Falcon consequently performs slightly slower. Figure 4(b) illustrates how each device behaves according to the respective force integral values. Not only is the Falcon consequently slower but it appears that for the highest *FI* conditions the Falcon has a less strong trial completion time deterioration compared to the Phantom.

Similarly as in our previous work, shape S ($F_{3,48} = .952$, p $=$ .423) did not show a significant main effect and force integral *FI* ($F_{10,160} = 8.0$, p $<$ .0001) did show a significant main effect. Post hoc comparisons for *FI* showed that above a certain force integral value ($FI = 85.94$) the trial completion time deteriorated significantly (p $<$ .01). This value, 85.94, is somewhat higher than in our previous experiments [3].

Finally, with regard to error rates during the experiment (wrong clicks) no significant difference between the Phantom (3.3%) and the Falcon (2.0%) was found.

Velocity Analysis. Although we found no statistical significant differences between the devices, we are interested in the velocity behaviour during a selection task. Figure 5 depicts typical velocity profiles respectively from the Phantom and the Falcon. The uppermost graph contains the evolution of the lateral velocity over time, the bottommost graph the longitudinal velocity in the highest amplitude condition ($FI = 95.49$).

With regard to the Phantom, from the uppermost graph in figure 5, we can learn that the force bump causes an oscillation lateral to the movement direction. For the bottommost graph we can see that the longitudinal velocity, does not completely behave according to the optimised initial impulse model of Meyer et al. [7]. The ballistic movement phase (BM1) is interrupted after the force bump, possibly to tackle the oscillation caused by the force feedback. A second but shorter ballistic movement (BM2) is initiated afterwards. Finally, the controlled movement (CM) brings the cursor in an accurate way to the target. It can be assumed that the majority of the performance penalty is caused by the interruption of the ballistic movement. In our previous work [3] more graphs are available motivating this statement.

When considering the velocity behaviour of the Falcon, we see a similar effect, but the effect of the higher damping is clearly visible, as well. After the force bump, a more strongly damped oscillation occurs. Here again, the ballistic movement is interrupted, but in general in a less pronounced way. Keeping these figures in mind may help us to explain the behaviour in figure 4(b). At the no force condition ($FI = 0$) the Falcon appears to be (non-significantly) slower than the Phantom, which may not be surprisingly, because of the higher damping causing a lower longitudinal velocity (Average max. long. vel. for the Phantom: $\bar{v}_{max} = 60.12$ mm/s; For the Falcon: $\bar{v}_{max} = 42.03$ mm/s). Alternatively, the high forces cause less oscillation, and hence require a less severe interruption of the ballistic movement phase, which at its turn explains the lower performance deterioration in the higher force conditions ($FI = 85.94$ and $FI = 95.49$).

4   Subjective Comparison

To further compare the difference between the haptic devices, we conducted a second experiment sounding out for the users' subjective experience with respect to the different devices. For this experiment, we used the same apparatus and applied the same experimental procedure as in the previous experiment. The force bump had a lateral force direction with $S=\sin_{[0,\pi]}$, $T=75$ms which was also present in the other experiment. The participants from the previous objective device experiment immediately participated in this experiment. Hence, a between-participant design was used.

4.1   Stimuli and Design

For this experiment, we applied an adaptive staircase method [6]. In our case we will ask the users if they consider the current force as too strong. In the conducted experiment, we simultaneously interleaved two staircases: a 'one-up two-down' design starting from 2.0N and a 'two-up one-down' design starting from 0.6N. This design ensures that the user approaches the threshold from two different sides. For the first four reversals the step size was set to 0.3N, thereafter a smaller step size for a resolution of 0.1N has been taken for the next six reversals. Hence, the experiment ended after a total of ten reversals.

The user had to perform five selections after which we asked the question 'Do the forces complicate the execution of the selection task in any way?' The user had to answer 'yes' or 'no' using the keyboard with the non-dominant hand and depending on the answer and staircase, the force strength was changed accordingly. Each participant performed the experiment in one session lasting about 15 minutes depending on the time necessary to complete the 10 reversals. We logged the current strength value, step size and amount of reversals so far.

4.2   Results

For each device, for each participant, the mean force strength value for both staircases was calculated by averaging the force strengths of the last 6 resolution reversals. Averaging these values for the Phantom, we found that the one-up two-down staircase (started at 2.0N) had an average of 1.45N (sd = 0.48) and the two-up one down staircase (coming from 0.6N) an average of 1.05N (sd = 0.35), which results in an overall average of 1.25N (sd = 0.41) (FI = 59.68). For the Falcon we found that the one-up two-down staircase (started at 2.0N) had an average of 1.64N (sd = 0.71) and the two-up one down staircase (coming from 0.6N) an average of 1.17N (sd = 0.60), which results in an overall average of 1.41N (sd = 0.66) (FI = 67.32).

The Falcon thus resulted in a higher value for the mean force strength than the Phantom, respectively 1.41N and 1.25N. The higher damping for the Falcon might influence the perception and hence cause this result. Moreover, Falcon participants had to answer the question 27% more often. This could imply that forces are less distinguishable with the Falcon. In order to justify this finding, a force discrimination experiment comparing the devices would be necessary.

5   Discussion and Conclusion

In order to investigate in what respect the Falcon haptic device may serve as a low-cost alternative for the Phantom, we compared these haptic devices. We discussed the differences between the devices and deduced their most important mechanical characteristics. This calculation learned us that the Falcon has a higher damping than the Phantom. The devices were then compared in a target acquisition task using an objective and subjective experiment. In the objective experiment we found no significant difference for the trial completion time between the devices. Note that this is no other conclusion than in previously conducted haptic device comparison experiments, comparing the Phantom to other haptic devices [9,5]. We did notice that the velocity profile due to the force feedback behaves differently because of the higher damping of the Falcon. The subjective experiment showed that the Falcon allows for higher force amplitudes than the Phantom, probably due to higher damping which decreases the 'correct' discrimination of the applied forces.

We can conclude that the higher damping of the Falcon with regard to the Phantom plays a role in the perception and behaviour of the user during a target acquisition task, but in practice, the differences in performance are small and non-significant. This may strengthen our idea of further investigating the use of the Falcon in the context of our rehabilitation project. In a next step, we can apply and compare the Falcon in a practical setup with patients, and investigate for what exercises it is most suitable or not. This may possibly reveal other issues as well, such as the limited workspace, shifting of the device, or differences between the grip (knob or stylus) of the devices. A force discrimination experiment between the two devices (including also patients) may be useful, as well.

Acknowledgments

Part of the research at EDM is funded by the ERDF and the Flemish government. This research was funded through the INTERREG-IV program (project 4-BMG-II-1-84 and IVA-VLANED-1.14, Euregio Benelux).

References

1. Chortis, A., Standen, P.J., Walker, M.: Virtual reality system for upper extremity rehabilitation of chronic stroke patients living in the community. In: International Conference Series on Disability, Virtual Reality and Associated Technologies (2008)
2. De Boeck, J., Alders, G., Gijbels, D., De Weyer, T., Raymaekers, C., Coninx, K., Feys, P.: The learning effect of force feedback enabled robotic rehabilitation of the upper limbs in persons with MS - a pilot study. In: ENACTIVE 2008, pp. 117–122 (2008)
3. De Boeck, J., Vanacken, L., Coninx, K.: Target aquisition with force feedback: The effect of different forces on the user's performance. In: Altinsoy, M.E., Jekosch, U., Brewster, S. (eds.) HAID 2009. LNCS, vol. 5763, pp. 11–20. Springer, Heidelberg (2009)
4. Deutsch, J.E., Latonio, J., Burdea, G.C., Boian, R.: Post-stroke rehabilitation with the rutgers ankle system: A case study. Presence 10(4), 416–430 (2001)
5. Harders, M., Barlit, A., Akahane, K., Sato, M., Szekely, G.: Comparing 6DOF Haptic Interfaces for Application in 3D Assembly Task. In: Eurohaptics 2006, pp. 523–526 (2006)
6. Leek, M.: Adaptive procedures in psychophysical research. Perception & Psychophysics 63(8), 1279–1292 (2001)
7. Meyer, D., Abrams, R., Kornblum, S., Wright, C., Smith, J.: Optimality in human motor performance: Ideal control of rapid aiming movements, pp. 340–370 (1988)
8. Pintelon, R., Guillaume, P., Rolain, Y., Schoukens, J., Vanhamme, H.: Parametric idenitifcation of transfer-functions in the frequency-domain - a survey. IEEE Transactions on Automatic Control 39, 2245–2260 (1994)
9. Yu, W., Brewster, S.: Comparing two haptic interfaces for multimodal graph rendering. In: HAPTICS 2002, pp. 3–9 (2002)

Building a Framework for Communication of Emotional State through Interaction with Haptic Devices

Eric W. Cooper, Victor V. Kryssanov, and Hitoshi Ogawa

College of Information Science and Engineering, Ritsumeikan University
Nojihigashi 1-1-1, Shiga 525-8577, Japan
{cooper,kvvictor,ogawa}@is.ritsumei.ac.jp

Abstract. Brief and high speed semantic communication, such as through texting and e-mail, leaves users without the ability to fully comprehend emotional content and vulnerable to emotional misunderstanding. The need to communicate emotional states, or to elicit sympathetic response in the receiver is evident in emotive icons and other relatively new applications of existing modes of communication. Haptic interfaces offer users a non-verbal way to communicate remotely, opening the door to a richer vocabulary and greater accessibility in emotive and affective communication. The studies described here investigate a possible framework for communication through haptic interface devices using existing models of emotional state. The semantic studies offer a look at users' naïve understanding of the emotive content of haptic sensations. Further experiments with haptic devices show that while communication through these modes can be implemented, the range of possible responses depends as much on the type of interaction used as on the users' understanding of emotive content.

Keywords: haptic communication, emotional communication, affective engineering.

1 Introduction

Humans communicate emotions through a variety of channels but one of the earliest to develop, and perhaps most powerful, is the sense of touch. The relationship of the sense of touch to communication of emotional state is observed in language, for example the English word "feeling". A large number of adjectives and verbs are used in various languages to indicate a haptic or tactile sensation as well as an emotional state or response. Despite these implied connections, and some attempts to communicate personally through haptic devices, they have yet to be employed as tools for the indirect communication and elicitation of emotional states [1, 2, 3]. For a state-of-the-art survey of haptic communication studies, please refer to Haans and IJsselsteijn [4].

Increases in the speed and frequency of communication in non-verbal modalities, such as text messaging, have made users susceptible to misunderstanding or insufficient communication of emotional content. The importance of this issue is most evident in the emergence of emoticons, originally socially and culturally defined combinations of punctuation meant to convey a facial expression. Emoticons have proven to be such a valuable communication tool that their more elaborate graphic counterparts are now

R. Nordahl et al. (Eds.): HAID 2010, LNCS 6306, pp. 189–196, 2010.

almost universally employed [5]. The emoticon may make a recipient much more attentive to a message that would have otherwise been ignored. A "smiley" emoticon can reverse the tone of a message that would have otherwise been interpreted as a sign of curt displeasure. Emoticons allow essential social interactions to move ahead without major misunderstandings, giving users some emotional communication rather than none but their spontaneous evolution shows that there is clearly a need to communicate emotional states and other affective concepts as directly as possible [1, 5]. Haptic modes of communication offer one way of exchanging these essential signals with the added advantage that it is likely there are strong innate or socially acquired responses available, which do not require the user to learn how to interpret the signals [3].

The aim of the research described herein is to explore the feasibility of using widely available 3D force feedback displays as tools for the indirect communication (or, potentially, elicitation) of emotional states from user to user, or from system to user. For practical purposes, feasibility requires some latent understanding of common associations between haptic sensations and emotional states. In order to establish the plausibility of such understanding, a survey of semantic associations was carried out and is presented in Section 2. The establishment of a mode of tactile communication is by no means straightforward. For example, force feedback haptic displays are not normally used in a passive mode but require the user to interact in some way. The experiment described in Section 3 investigates how such a system might work on a basic interactive task level, and what kinds of affective responses can be expected. Another objective was to compare the results to semantic survey results to detect similarities and differences between the naïve understandings of emotive associations versus the associations invoked when a task-based stimulus is present, as discussed in Section 4. The study's conclusions and implications are formulated in Section 5.

2 Surveys of Users' Semantic Understanding

Communication of emotive states by haptic devices requires a background understanding of the spontaneous associations between haptic sensations and affective responses. If such associations occur naturally then the practical usability of these devices is far more likely. Without the associations, however, users would have to either build their own vocabularies or rely on some "standard" interpretations predefined or borrowed for the given communication context [4]. It is therefore essential to establish the nature of tactile-emotive associations, their relative conformity, and relationship to useful models of emotional state.

As a preliminary investigation, an online survey was conducted in which survey participants identified associations between eight categories of emotional state and basic tactile definitions. The goal of the experiment was to lay a foundation for a model relating haptic sensations to affective responses in the context of ordinary computer users in the Japanese society and language [6].

230 Japanese subjects participated in the online survey, 51% male and 49% female, mostly in their 20's. The task of the survey was to read one of eight adjectives intended to characterize a haptic sensation and then to interpret it in terms of eight categories of emotional state by associating that adjective with zero or more emotional categories.

The categories used were based on the Russell circumplex model of emotional state, divided into eight sectors [7]. This model is defined on a plane with the vertical axis indicating an emotional state ranging from excitement to calmness, and the horizontal axis indicating pleasant or comfortable, opposed by unpleasant or uncomfortable emotional states. Representative adjectives were selected for each state, based on Desmet's interpretation of the model [8], as shown in Table 1. (The survey was conducted in Japanese and adjectives used were general translations, not exact or expected to achieve the same response in their English translations and/or with non-Japanese speakers.)

Table 1. Categories of emotion, after Desmet [8], with abbreviations used in the figures and typical representative words used to elicit responses in the experiments

Circumplex category		Representative words for elicitation
Neutrally excited	NE	Surprised, concentrated, eager, astonished, amazed, aroused, longing, avaricious, curious
Pleasantly excited	PE	Loving, jubilant, excited, desiring, inspired, enthusiastic
Pleasantly average	PA	Entertained, admiring, joyful, fascinated, yearning, pleased, proud, surprised, happy, appreciating, amused, cheerful, sociable, attracted
Pleasantly calm	PC	Fulfilled, intimate, satisfied, cozy, comfortable, relaxed
Neutrally calm	NC	Composed, awaiting, deferent, passive
Unpleasantly calm	UC	Gloomy, melancholic, isolated, sad, disillusioned, bored
Unpleasantly average	UA	Contemptuous, disturbed, flabbergasted, jealous, aversive, irked, moody, grouchy, ashamed, cynical, embarrassed, disappointed, dissatisfied, disapproving, confused
Unpleasantly excited	UE	Disgusted, frightened, annoyed, hostile, indignant, alarmed, irritated, frustrated, bewildered, nervous

As can be seen from Fig. 1, the results showed relatively strong associations for all of the haptic semantic labels tested. A simplified model based on four sectors of the Russell circumplex was then developed for preliminary investigation of the feasibility of using such a model for communication with interactive haptic devices [6].

3 Experimental Investigation of the Naïve Associations

The semantic surveys suggested that users have shared associations between concepts of haptic sensations and emotional states. The next set of experiments was conducted to determine ways of eliciting responses to haptic stimuli and to get a broad snapshot of associations that may occur, especially whether they would resemble the patterns observed in the semantic tests. One objective is to examine ways of collecting such data. Another is to compare and contrast the collected data with the semantic associations. Finally, these experiments are to explore the feasibility of modeling the interaction in a way that the resulting models are applicable to real-world uses.

The validation experiment presented in this section adapted the semantic definitions used in the preliminary investigations described above to reveal their relationship with haptic stimuli provided by a 3D haptic force feedback device (also see [10]).

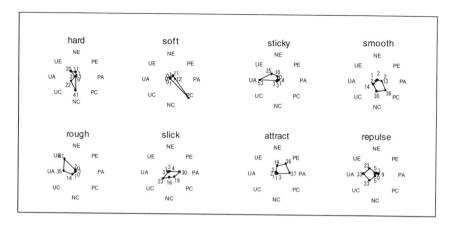

Fig. 1. Results of a survey of naïve associations between words commonly used to describe haptic sensations and emotional states

The experiment was designed to allow the subject to interact with a 3D haptic stimulus setting but without unduly influencing the emotive response with 3D representations or other potentially priming factors. After considering various interaction scenarios, the authors arrived at the task of tracing a thick black line on a planar surface that appears flush with the computer monitor surface (see Fig. 2). The 3D haptic interface pointer (HIP) is shown (without shadow) on the GUI "in front" of the flat figure. The subject first touches the circle as if drawing with a pen, which is thought to be a natural movement, since the PHANToM interactive device used is pen-like in shape and is held with a similar grasping position. This action gives the user a sense of the friction and feel of the "surface" of the stimuli. The next task is to use the device to "touch" the middle of the circle by homing the HIP to the center of the figure and gently "poking". This action provides the subject with sensations in the soft-hard and attraction-repulsion dimensions of haptic perceptions.

After performing these tasks to personal satisfaction for a single stimulus, the subject fills out the responses on a questionnaire. Because this survey was based on the previous semantic surveys, described in Section 2, the (Japanese) keywords used have not yet been vetted with formal tools, such as factor analysis, to find the best combination. Instead, the goal was to keep them close to the original studies, to allow a comparison of the results.

First, the subject characterizes the haptic sensation on a differential scale. The opponent adjective pairs are based on the preliminary model: hard-soft, smooth-rough, sticky-slick, and attracting-repelling. The responses are by semantic differential (SD) method, with five possible selections for each of the four pairs: the central one being labeled "neither", the two on either side of the center "somewhat," and those nearest the adjective terms "very". Finally, the subject selects the emotional states "invoked," if any, by the haptic stimulus. As in the previous experiments, emotional states are identified as eight groups of emotional terms based on the Russell circumplex model.

Fig. 2. The experimental setup interface designed to provide a specific task that would require, or at least encourage, the user to experience tactile sensations with the haptic device

Table 2. PHANToM settings for the haptic stimulus used in the experiments

Set	Stiffness	Static Friction	Dynamic Friction
A	0.99	0.99	0.99
B	0.99	0.5	0.5
C	0.99	0.01	0.01
D	0.5	0.99	0.99
E	0.5	0.5	0.5
F	0.5	0.01	0.01
G	0.01	0.99	0.99
H	0.01	0.5	0.5
I	0.01	0.01	0.01

The appropriate haptic parameter space for the communication of emotive signals by haptic stimuli has not yet been determined. For these validation experiments, the haptic stimulus was kept as simple as possible, examining only the "stiffness" and "friction" parameters. These parameters were set at three different levels, each, for a total of nine different stimulus sets, as shown in Table 2. These settings are for SmartCollision Studio commercial software [9] and the interactive haptic device used was a standard force display PHANToM from SensAble Technologies. The order of the stimulus sets was randomized for each subject. The relevant responses were "soft-hard" and, to a lesser extent, "smooth-rough". The (objective) stimulus space did not include many samples that would be expected to have strong "sticky-slick" or "repelling-attracting" interpretations. These (subjective) responses were, however, included in the questionnaire for consistency with the original survey and as controls for the experimental protocol.

4   Results and Discussion

A total of ten university students, all Japanese, participated as subjects in the experiments, five women and five men. The results showed significant responses to most of the stimulus sets tested. As in the preliminary experiments, the direction of the emotional state response was established by combining each of the three categories on one or the other side of the two main axes of the Russell model [10].

Despite the sometimes ambiguous interpretation of this broad but limited set of haptic stimuli, the correlations between individual semantic responses support the relationships obtained in the previous semantic experiments. The correlation for hard-soft response was positively associated with the direction of relaxation at a correlation coefficient of 0.56. Conversely, the axis had a positive correlation with "hard", in the direction of "angry", with a correlation coefficient of 0.54. The smooth-rough response had strong associations with many emotional states. The positive correlation with the negative axis, having "very rough" interpreted most unfavorably, showed a correlation coefficient of 0.63, consistent with the previously developed model. A surprising result was the strong association of "smooth" with excitement, at a correlation of 0.83, meriting further investigation as a possible key factor in communication of state of arousal. The "sticky-slick" interpretation had a positive correlation with low arousal, consistent with the model, but did not show any other associations, as expected with this limited stimulus sample set. Repelling and attracting, included as control responses, also showed no strong correlation with any emotional state.

Next, we compared the results of the semantic association to the associations made when induced by a stimulus. Fig. 3 shows the average of each emotional state response weighted by the positive response of the given haptic adjective. (Negative responses to a given adjective were not counted as they were included in the opposite of the SD pair.) The results show significant associations for the haptic sensations, somewhat compatible with the results of the semantic associations, with significant differences only for "slick" and "smooth". However, each affective response shows deviation from the semantic association in that the results are shifted up to the active area of the model. As indicated in Fig. 4, the shift toward the "excited" or "aroused" side of emotional model was also accompanied by a nearly complete lack of responses in the "pleasantly calm" sector.

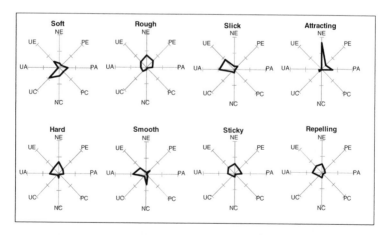

Fig. 3. Results of a survey of stimulus-induced associations between haptic sensations and emotional states in an emotional circumplex

These results thus show significant similarities with the semantic model but also suggest that certain areas of the haptic space may be ambiguous. The results strongly support the general concept that, with proper expansion and application of the interpretation of haptic stimuli, communication of emotional state is feasible with ambiguity kept reasonably low enough for many practical purposes.

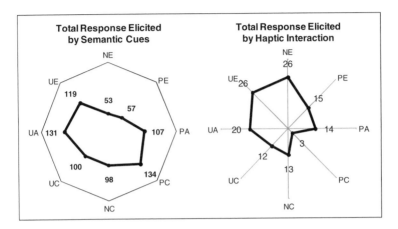

Fig. 4. Total results of the semantic survey compared to the total results of the haptically-induced survey suggest active the interface shifts responses toward the excited (elevated) states

5   Conclusions

This paper discussed investigations of the feasibility of communication of emotive states through haptic interfaces, especially active haptic force feedback devices. The results of experimentation with the physical stimuli of performing tasks with a haptic device showed that the whole emotional state space was not equally used. In particular, subjects rarely associated a haptic sensation with adjectives describing the "pleasant calm" segment of the emotion model. This indicates the need to further develop the interface, perhaps by creating more passive (from the user's point of view) methods and allow a rich interaction vocabulary, including this category of affective response.

On the other hand, these results demonstrate that communication of emotional state through haptic stimuli is feasible with proper modeling of those stimuli that impart an unambiguous signal to recipients. The settings for the validation experiments cut a broad profile through a multi-dimensional parameter space for haptic stimuli. Also, actual stimuli would have to make use of the 3D virtual space in which the interactive device is moved. Therefore, there is a great deal of future work in elucidating these relationships to determine unambiguous, easily interpretable haptic signals which, the results suggest, will also convey "standard," or at least predictable, responses for a relatively homogeneous socio-cultural group.

These latest experiments show that, with such detailed analysis and restructuring, one way to develop relevant models is to collect large sets of empirical data, based only on actual responses to haptic sensations. The results of our preliminary studies also hint that, as with other modes of emotive communication, ambiguity can be reduced through habitual use. Users will build on the foundations investigated in such experiments, as well as models developed from the general concepts, to learn to communicate emotive responses with haptic devices, and unambiguously convey the social cues that are so very essential to personal communication.

References

1. Paterson, M.: The Senses of Touch: Haptics, Affects and Technologies. Berg Publishers (2007)
2. Bailenson, J.N., Yee, N., Brave, S., Merget, D., Koslow, D.: Virtual Interpersonal Touch: Expressing and Recognizing Emotions Through Haptic Devices. Human-Computer Interaction 22(3), 325–353 (2007)
3. Oakley, I., Brewster, S., Gray, P.: Can You Feel the Force? An Investigation of Haptic Collaboration in Shared Editors. In: Proceedings of EuroHaptics, Birmingham, pp. 54–59 (2001)
4. Haans, A., IJsselsteijn, W.: Mediated social touch: a review of current research and future directions. Virtual Reality 9(2-3), 149–159 (2006)
5. Walther, J.B., D'Addario, K.P.: The Impacts of Emoticons on Message Interpretation in Computer-Mediated Communication. Social Science Computer Review 19, 324–347 (2001)
6. Kryssanov, V., Cooper, E., Ogawa, H., Kurose, I.: A Computational Model to Relay Emotions with Tactile Stimuli. In: Proceedings of ACII 2009, Amsterdam, pp. 288–293 (2009)
7. Russell, J.A.: A circumplex model of affect. Journal of Personality & Social Psychology 39, 1161–1178 (1980)
8. Desmet, P.M.A.: Designing Emotions. Doctoral Dissertation. Delft. TU Delft, the Netherlands (2002)
9. Tamura, Y., Matsumoto, S., Ueki, H., Mizuguchi, N.: Construction of design support system with interference detection in the immersive projection display. IEICE Transactions on Information and Systems (Japanese Edition) J90-D(10), 2927–2931 (2007)
10. Cooper, E., Kumokawa, S., Kryssanov, V., Ogawa, H.: Computer Mediated Feelings: A Model for Tactile Representation of Emotional States. In: Proceedings of Human Interface Symposium, Tokyo, pp. 715–718 (2009)

A Trajectory-Based Approach for Device Independent Gesture Recognition in Multimodal User Interfaces

Mathias Wilhelm, Dirk Roscher, Marco Blumendorf, and Sahin Albayrak

DAI-Labor, TU Berlin
Ernst-Reuter-Platz 7
10587 Berlin, Germany
Firstname.Lastname@dai-labor.de

Abstract. With the rise of technology in all areas of life new interaction techniques are required. With gestures and voice being the most natural ways to interact, it is a goal to also support this in human-computer interaction. In this paper, we introduce our approach to multimodal interaction in smart home environments and illustrate how device independent gesture recognition can be of great support in this area. We describe a trajectory-based approach that is applied to support device independent dynamic hand gesture recognition from vision systems, accelerometers or pen devices. The recorded data from the different devices is transformed to a common basis (2D-space) and the feature extraction and recognition is done on this basis. In a comprehensive case study we show the feasibility of the recognition and the integration with a multimodal and adaptive home operating system.

Keywords: gesture recognition, device independence, trajectory matching, generalized Procrustes analysis, multimodality.

1 Introduction

As the computer moves away from a production tool towards a ubiquitous life support facility, interaction with computers is undergoing a radical change. Applications are being deployed in dynamic and changing environments and instead of requiring the user to adapt to the user interface, applications should be build to support various interaction technologies. Multimodal interaction, integrating voice and gestures as a natural way of interaction is a good example in this area. It can be realized via various devices and technologies like local or telephony-based recognition systems, dynamic or prerecorded speech output, vision-based, accelerometer-based or pen-based gesture input, and any combination of these. This makes the actual hardware exchangeable and provides flexibility for the user but raises the need for the application developer to abstract from the actually available configuration. To support this flexibility in the area of dynamic hand gestures, the gestures have to be recognized in many different ways (e.g. via a camera, a smart phone or graphic tablet). The different recognition ways can be classified based on the device recording the gesture into vision-based, accelerometer-based and pen-based. Each class of devices has different properties (like intrusiveness or handling) which influence its usability for different applications

R. Nordahl et al. (Eds.): HAID 2010, LNCS 6306, pp. 197–206, 2010.

but also for specific situations. To optimally use gesture interaction, it is therefore required to utilize the different recognition ways for the same application. This however, requires adaptations of the applications as well as training and configuration for each device.

Currently, different gesture recognition methods for each way have been studied and applied, but most of these methods underlie two constraints: (1) they are only applicable for a small gesture device set or even only for one special device and (2) they also cannot be extended to further device types as their recognition algorithm works on the specific data recorded by this device (set). Consequently, it is currently not possible to utilize devices from different classes. One has to combine different approaches and each utilized approach has to be trained again.

Our approach presented in this paper allows recognizing gestures independent of the used gesture device, whereas the device can be from any of the three classes. We transform the recorded data to a common basis (trajectories in 2D space) and apply the Procrustes analysis [4] to recognize the performed gesture on this common basis. We already presented first results of our preliminary work that showed its feasibility [17]. However, these results also pointed out some necessary improvements and open issues. The main points were the improvement of the trajectory extraction from acceleration values and the feature extraction respectively the classification process itself. In this paper, we present a largely extended version of our approach with regard to the points and describe comprehensive experiments.

The remainder of the paper is organized as follows: Section 2 presents related work in the domain of device independent gesture recognition and points out the need of this work. Section 3 describes the overall algorithm of our approach and describes the underlying stages in more detail. In section 4, we present comprehensive experimental results and a case study with a multimodal and adaptive Home Operating System (HomeOS). We close with a conclusion and outlook of further work in section 5.

2 Related Work

There are existing approaches that tackle the problem of device independence for a limited device set or for all devices belonging to one of the classes mentioned above. Devices with accelerometers are mostly trained for one device. It is possible to apply another device with different accelerometers, but in general this requires retraining of the entire system (it is very rare that different accelerometers deliver data that is similar enough). To overcome this issue, Keir et al. [5] presented an accelerometer independent software development kit, called 3motion^{TM}, which uses a non-parametric curve matching method for recognizing gestures.

Most approaches for the recognition with pen devices are by nature independent of the used pen device (apart from scale effects). Nevertheless, most frameworks for pen devices have a lack of extensibility and flexibility, even for device independence as they do not consider the possibility to utilize different devices. iGesture, presented by Signer et al. in [12], is a highly generalized gesture recognition framework for pen devices that addresses this features. It allows an easy integration of devices and additional gesture recognition algorithms. The authors already pre-implemented several algorithms including Rubine [12], E-Rubine [12], SiGrid [12] and SiGeR [12], whereas the last three are algorithms extended and/or developed by Signer.

A general approach for data glove independent gesture recognition was presented by Parvini et al. [11]. Their approach addresses user independence, glove independence, noisy sensor data and also does not require a training phase (as known from approaches using machine learning). To achieve these key points, they utilized the concept of "range of motion", a bio-mechanical approach.

Eisenstein et al. [3] introduced a multilayer neuronal network structure to solve the issue of data glove independence for pure accelerometer-based gloves. They were able to show the general feasibility of their approach in experiments with six different data gloves, but the overall recognition rate was very low (in particular for data gloves with a small number of sensors). Another disadvantage of their approach is the lack of support for data gloves with finger flexion sensors to measure the finger posture. As our approach also abstract from device specifics, we also cannot utilize them for the recognition. But our goal is the utilization of arbitrary gesture devices and the abstraction is needed to reach this goal.

In [10], Olivrin describes a linguistically driven approach for an input method editor for sign languages that should be device independent for all types of existing multimodalities, scalable and flexible. However, he only pointed out the importance and some requirements of device independence, but he did not propose how it should be realized in practice. With respect to flexibility and extensibility, Lyons et al. [8] introduced the Gesture Activity Recognition Toolkit (GART) that provides devices interfaces for cameras, accelerometers and pen devices and for the following machine recognition toolkits: hidden Markov model toolkit (HTK)[1] and Weka[2]. GART aims to abstract the gesture recognition process without requiring being an expert in machine learning. However, every device interface is handled separately in respect of data preparation, feature extraction and recognition.

None of these approaches overcome the challenge of a device independent gesture recognition approach with different device groups. It can be seen that most approaches achieve device independence only for a specific set of devices or device class.

3   Gesture Recognition with Arbitrary Devices

This section describes our method to support gesture recognition with arbitrary gesture devices. The method proposed consists of the three basic stages, shown in Figure 1. The first stage accepts gestures, in form of a sequence of sensor values, from an arbitrary gesture device (from one of the three classes). Based on the device class a different algorithm is used to transform the received sensors values to the corresponding gesture trajectory in the 2D spatial space. This representation of the gesture allows a device independent interpretation. From a quality point of view this also means it is not possible to associate a gesture trajectory to the gesture device that produced it. The extraction is the most critical part as the representation of the same gesture done with different devices has to be very similar to achieve an acceptable recognition rate. The second stage generates a representation that is independent from scale, rotation and

---

[1] http://htk.eng.cam.ac.uk/
[2] http://www.cs.waikato.ac.nz/~ml/

translation from the obtained trajectory and passes them to the recognizer stage, where the gesture is classified. The recognizer has to be trained in a previous step by an arbitrary gesture device in the same manner. Each of the three steps is explained in detail in the following.

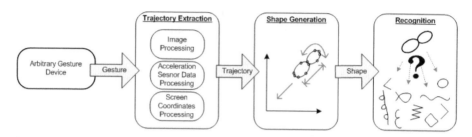

Fig. 1. Overview of the method with its different stages

3.1 Trajectory Extraction

The basic operation of this stage is the extraction of a proper trajectory from the sensor values obtained from a gesture device. For pen devices this is a very easy step because the device already provides a trajectory in the spatial space. Depending on the pen device, it could be necessary to sample down the obtained trajectory to reduce the number of data points. This smoothes the trajectory and decreases the computational complexity. The extraction of the performed gesture trajectory from acceleration data and images is quite complex and is described in more detail in the following.

3.1.1 Acceleration Data

Obtaining the gesture trajectory performed in space from acceleration values is a difficult task. Before extracting the trajectory from the measured accelerometer values, the values have to be prepared and cleaned up. The measured accelerometer values also contain the gravity beneath the needed motion acceleration. The gravity effect has to be heavily reduced before further handling. Considering that gravity is a constant effect with low frequency, we applied a linear high pass filter to reduce the gravity effect. Furthermore, the acceleration values also contain a number of further errors (such as measurement noise). Thus, we applied a Kalman filter [15] to reduce the level of noise in the signal. However, these two filters are not able to eliminate the gravity and noise effect completely, in particular when gesture device was tilted or pitched too much while the gesture was performed. If the gesture device also provides a 3-axis gyroscope and/or a 3-axis magnetometer, these can be used to eliminate the gravity effect more precisely [13]. Finally, we apply a double integration on the prepared acceleration signal to obtain the performed gesture trajectory. To make this 3D trajectory better comparable to the 2D trajectory obtained from pen devices, we project this trajectory into a 2D plane using orthogonal projection [9].

3.1.2 Vision Data

To extract a gesture trajectory from an image sequence, different methods can be used such as CAMShift-based method [2] or particle filter based method [1]. We prefer the application of an active hand contour tracking with a particle filter, because it performs well under clutter and rapid motion as well as for articulated and camouflaged objects. However, particle filters have a high computational cost and are consequently not suitable for small devices such as netbooks or smart and mobile phones. In this case, we use a motion field based method [14].

3.2 Shape of Trajectory

The gesture trajectories obtained from the previous extraction stage are a device independent representation in the 2D Cartesian coordinate system. However, they differ highly in scale, rotation and location. Additionally, we are confronted with high variability and deformations of the trajectory, in particular for trajectories obtained from accelerometers. These facts make it difficult to select an appropriative feature selection and comparison method. We need an affine invariant representation of the trajectories, which is at least independent of scale, rotation and translation. The concept of shape for trajectories is an example of such an invariant representation [6]. Shape for trajectories is a representation of a trajectory that is free of scale, rotation and location information. It is described by so called landmarks, which are a finite number of points along the contour of the trajectory. Suitable landmarks are trajectory points that have a mathematical characteristic, e.g. extreme points. The shape is generated by a so called shape description method, which generates a parameterized curve of the trajectory. The shape contains all essential information, depending on the shape description method. In this manner, we apply the (generalized) Procrustes analysis [4] to generate an affine invariant shape for trajectories. The Procrustes analysis algorithm involves the affine invariant transformations and the matching procedure of two shapes as explained in the next subsection.

3.3 Recognition

To match two shapes, the Procrustes analysis algorithm tries to align an unknown shape with a reference shape by the means of affine transformations and measures the distance between the both aligned shapes with a Riemannian distance measurement, a least square type [7]. This kind of distance measurement requires that all shapes must have the same number of landmarks. The shape alignment and comparison by distance measurement are applied on all stored reference trajectories. The reference shape that has the smallest Riemannian distance to the unknown shape, seems to represent the performed gesture. If the smallest shape distance exceeds a predefined threshold, we reject the unknown gesture under the assumption it was a not trained. The reference trajectories are generated by the means of the generalized Procrustes analysis [4] as follow:

1. For every gesture we collect between 2 and 20 reference trajectories with any gesture device.
2. For each reference set:
    2.1. Initialization step: We assign one shape from the reference set to the mean shape.
    2.2. Alignment step: We align each remaining reference shape to the mean shape by the mean of affine transformations.

2.3. Mean shape estimation step: We update the mean shape by estimating it from the aligned shapes using the arithmetic mean.

2.4. Convergence check: We measure the distance between the recently estimated mean shape and the previous mean shape. If the distance exceeds a threshold, then we return to step 2.2.

Besides the advantages of the Procrustes analysis, such as robustness, very good comparability of gestures and easy extensibility in respect to new gestures, there are also two difficulties. The benefit of affine invariance, obtained from the application of the shapes, effects undistinguishable gestures. For instance, the two different gestures 'c' and 'C' and the two gestures '/' and '\' are undistinguishable because of scale and rotation invariance, respectively. However, it is possible to cover these gestures by additionally conditions, such as storing direction or orientation information for these affected gestures.

4 Experiments

To evaluate the described method and show its feasibility we conducted two experiments with eight persons in total (four per experiment). Each experiment utilizes the same set of gesture devices (one pen-based, two accelerometer-based and one vision-based device) but the initial training process is done with devices from different recognition classes (one pen-based and one accelerometer-based). For the pen-based device we utilize a standard computer mouse. The start of a gesture is signalized by pressing down the middle mouse button and the end by releasing the button. One of the accelerometer-based devices is a SHAKE-module[3] (a small pluggable sensor module) and the only button on the device is utilized for starting and ending a gesture. The other is a Nintendo Wii controller, where the B-button is used for signalizing the gesture start and end points. A Logitech "Clicksmart 510" webcam is used as a vision-based device. Start and end point of the gestures are signalized by the Nintendo Wii controller, again holding down the B-button to start the gesture and releasing it for signalizing the end of the gesture.

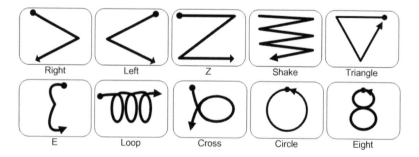

Fig. 2. Overview of the gesture set used for the experiments

---

[3] http://code.google.com/p/shake-drivers/

For both experiments we used the same set of gestures (see Figure 2). The gestures ranges from simple gestures like the left and right arrows, over more advanced gestures like the "Shake"-gesture to complicated gestures with "overlapping" curves like the "Loop"-gesture. Before the experiments every gesture was trained ten times and the number of landmarks to describe the shape was set to eight. For the landmark selection we computed the first derivative of the trajectory and assign the eight strongest extremum points that exceed a threshold. If the trajectory has less than eight extremum points, e.g. the "Circle"- and the "Right"-gesture, then we space out evenly the remaining points about the trajectory. The rejection threshold of 1.0 for the first experiment and 1.25 for the second one were determined in previous experiments. In the first experiments the computer mouse was used for the training process, in the second one the SHAKE-device was used.

The eight test persons did not know the system before and had no special gesture experiences. Every person got an instruction and demonstration of the system and then had several minutes to test the system with the different devices on their own. Afterwards the actual experiment started and every person tested every gesture 25 times. This results in 100 tests samples for every gesture in each experiment. After every performed gesture the users were presented the calculated shape. The overall results of the experiments are presented in Figure 3 (computer mouse as training device) and Figure 4 (SHAKE-device as training device).

The results show the overall feasibility of the approach but also the necessity of some improvements especially for certain device gesture combinations. The overall recognition rate for the first experiment is 82% and for the second experiment 70 %. The overall rates are not impressive but certain device gesture combinations pulled down the results and the recognition rates also improves over time.

In the first experiments the computer mouse was by far the best device. This is also quite obvious as the computer mouse was also the training device. By the way, also the camera approach performed well because its resulting trajectories resemble the trajectories of the computer mouse. Problems occurred especially with accelerometer-based devices as a result of lack of the used trajectory extraction algorithm. The applied algorithm cannot handle proper changes in the velocity and in device orientation during the gesture performance. For example, these artefacts can lead to too short or too long endings of the "Cross"-gesture, which affect a resulting shape that is very similar to a circle or an arrow. Another example is an imprecise "Eight"-gesture where an open ending results in a cross shape. These insights are backed up by the first experiment: One can see that the "Cross"- and "Eight"-gesture have the lowest recognition results in average of all gestures. In both experiments the Nintendo Wii controller falls a little bit of as it seems to be not as precise as the one from the SHAKE-device.

The feedback of the performed gesture trajectory results in constantly better recognition rates from the beginning to the end of the tests. It was helpful to prevent the recognition problems described in the paragraph before as the users know what to do to achieve better recognition results. The test persons also stated after the experiments, that the feedback was very comfortable and helped them in the execution of the gestures.

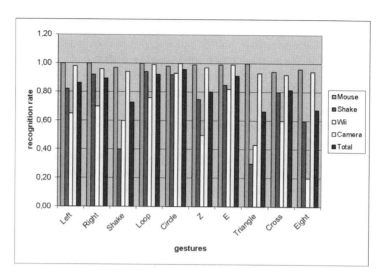

Fig. 3. Recognition rates of the first experiment for all gestures and all devices. The computer mouse was used as training device.

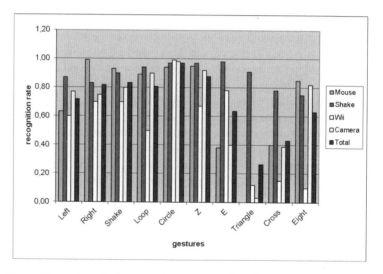

Fig. 4. Recognition rates of the second experiment for all gestures and all devices. The SHAKE-device was used as training device.

In general the cause of a false classification can mainly be traced back by the fact, that the extraction of the trajectory from the recorded values sometimes seems to reach its limit. Additionally, certain gestures like the "Triangle"-gesture are hard to draw exactly, especially in the spatial space. This effect was reduced over time because of the feedback and users getting more experienced.

The resulting system has been integrated into a smart home operating system to support dynamic multimodal interaction with changing devices as described in [16]. The system allows controlling the user interface of a home operating system via various gesture devices that can be dynamically exchanged during the interaction. The graphical user interface of the application illustrates the possible interactions via appearances that change according to the currently available modalities and their characteristics (Figure 5).

Fig. 5. Illustration of a multimodal oven control with voice, touch and gesture support

5   Conclusion and Future Work

We described a method for a trajectory-based approach for device independent gesture recognition. The method allows training the gesture recognition system with an arbitrary device from one of the three gesture recognition classes (vision-based, pen-based, and accelerometer-based) and afterwards utilize any device from the three classes for recognizing gestures. This allows a rapid testing and evaluation of different gesture devices without the need to train the every gesture again for every other gesture device. The training process of the overall system is also very fast as in most of the cases one reference example is enough. Furthermore, we evaluated the approach with two experiments and showed its feasibility.

In the future we want to integrate the described method into a larger framework to create a development environment for the rapid development of gesture interaction with many different devices. Furthermore, we are investigating the improvement of the transformation of the accelerometer values to the trajectory. We have to admit that the algorithm currently used does not have large optimization possibilities or algorithmic improvements. We are also investigating further improvements to overcome the false classification for certain gesture device combinations. Other optimization possibilities are the utilization of device specific features and the enhancements of the extracted shapes with alignments to overcome the issue of invariant shapes.

References

1. Blake, A., Isard, M.: Active Contours: The Application of Techniques from Graphics, Vision, Control Theory and Statistics to Visual Tracking of Shapes in Motion. Springer, New York (1998)

2. Bradski, G.R.: Computer Vision Face Tracking for Use in a Perceptual User Interface (1998)

3. Eisenstein, J., Ghandeharizadeh, S., Golubchik, L., Shahabi, C., Yan, D., Zimmermann, R.: Device Independence and Extensibility in Gesture Recognition. In: Proceedings of the IEEE Virtual Reality 2003 (2003)

4. Dryden, I.L., Mardia, K.V.: Statistical Shape Analysis. Wiley, Chichester (1998)

5. Keir, P., Payne, J., Anderson, P., Elgoyhen, J., Horner, M., Naef, M.: Gesture Recognition with Non-referenced Tracking. In: Proceedings of the 3D User Interfaces, pp. 151–158 (2006)

6. Kendall, D.G.: A Survey of the Statistical Theory of Shape. Statistical Science 4, 87–99 (1989)

7. Kendall, D.G.: Shape Manifolds, Procrustean Metrics and Complex Projective Spaces. Bulletin of the London Mathematical Society, 81–121 (1984)

8. Lyons, K., Brashear, H., Westeyn, T., Kim, J.S., Starner, T.: GART: The Gesture and Activity Recognition Toolkit. In: Jacko, J.A. (ed.) HCI 2007. LNCS, vol. 4552, pp. 718–727. Springer, Heidelberg (2007)

9. Maynard, P.: Drawing Distinctions: The Varieties of Graphic Expression. Cornell University Press (2005)

10. Olivrin, G.J.: Gesture Modelling for Linguistic Purposes, pp. 145–150 (2009)

11. Parvini, F., Shahabi, C.: An Algorithmic Approach for Static and Dynamic Gesture Recognition Utilising Mechanical and Biomechanical Characteristics. Int. J. Bioinformatics Res. Appl. 3, 4–23 (2007)

12. Signer, B., Kurmann, U., Norrie, M.C.: igesture: A General Gesture Recognition Framework. In: Proceedings of the Ninth International Conference on Document Analysis and Recognition, vol. 2, pp. 954–958 (2007)

13. Titterton, D.H., Weston, J.L.: Strapdown Inertial Navigation Technology, 2nd edn. Institution of Engineering and Technology (2004)

14. Wang, J., Zhai, S., Canny, J.: Camera Phone based Motion Sensing: Interaction Techniques, Applications and Performance Study. In: Proceedings of the 19th Annual ACM Symposium on User Interface Software and Technology, pp. 101–110 (2006)

15. Welch, G., Bishop, G.: An Introduction to the Kalman Filter. Technical report (2006)

16. Weingarten, F., Blumendorf, M., Albayrak, S.: Conveying Multimodal Interaction Possibilities through the use of Appearances. In: Creative Inventions and Innovations for Everyday HCI, Edinburgh (2010)

17. Wilhelm, M., Blumendorf, M., Roscher, D., Albayrak, D.: A Novel Approach for Device Independent Gesture Recognition. In: Haptic Audio Interaction Design (2009)

Author Index

Printing: Mercedes-Druck, Berlin
Binding: Stein+Lehmann, Berlin